Sandra Lee is an Australian journalist and author whose work has appeared in the *New York Post* and *USA Today Weekend* and *People* magazines. She is currently the back page columnist at *The Sunday Telegraph*. Previously, she was an assistant editor, foreign correspondent and columnist for *The Daily Telegraph*, as well as editor-at-large at *marie claire* magazine. She is also the author of *Beyond Bad: The Life and Crimes of Katherine Knight, Australia's Hannibal*. Sandra lives in Sydney.

Guzin Najim's

the
PROMISE

The true story of a mother's courageous
flight to freedom in Australia

SANDRA LEE

BANTAM
SYDNEY AUCKLAND TORONTO NEW YORK LONDON

GUZIN NAJIM'S THE PROMISE
A BANTAM BOOK

First published in Australia and New Zealand in 2003 by Bantam
This edition published in 2004

National Library of Australia
Cataloguing-in-Publication Entry

    Lee, Sandra (Sandra E.).
    Guzin Najim's the promise: the true story of a mother's courageous flight to freedom in Australia.

    ISBN 1 86325 419 6.

    1. Najim, Guzin. 2. Mothers – Iraq – Biography.
    3. Iraq – Politics and government – 1979–.
    I. Title. II. Title: Promise: an Iraqi mother's desperate flight to freedom.

    956.7044092

Transworld Publishers,
a division of Random House Australia Pty Ltd
20 Alfred Street, Milsons Point, NSW 2061
http://www.randomhouse.com.au

Random House New Zealand Limited
18 Poland Road, Glenfield, Auckland

Transworld Publishers,
a division of The Random House Group Ltd
61–63 Uxbridge Road, London W5 5SA

Random House Inc
1745 Broadway, New York, New York 10036

Typeset by Midland Typesetters, Maryborough, Victoria
Printed and bound by Griffin Press, Netley, South Australia

10 9 8 7 6 5 4 3 2 1

This book is dedicated to all the victims of
Saddam Hussein's regime – to those who perished
and those who survived.

Prologue

By the morning of 8 December 1995, a winter chill had settled on Baghdad. The city, known as the cradle of civilisation, is nestled on the lush and fertile plain between two ancient rivers, the Euphrates to the west and the Tigris snaking closer to the east. Weeks earlier, frigid winds had begun rolling down from the mountains hundreds of kilometres to the north, moving steadily over the deserts and flatlands of Iraq, whipping up sandstorms and changing the landscape as they went. It was cold, but Iraqis knew what to expect at that time of year.

For Ra'ad Mohammed Said and his wife, Guzin Shawket Najim, it was just another December day. Nothing unusual was planned, and nothing unusual was expected. After twenty-one years of marriage, they had a comfortable life which, early on, had found its own balance, like quicksilver. The couple met in 1973 while at university in Baghdad. Ra'ad fell in love with Guzin instantly, but she took her time, slowly warming to his gentle and sincere advances.

As it turned out, they were perfectly matched. Their intellects blended seamlessly and they were on the same rung of the social ladder. They came from well-to-do families, each with its own connections to the upper echelons of society. In Iraq, which is a complex weave of feudal tribes and modern high society, issues of personal pedigree are of vital importance.

Ra'ad and Guzin married in 1974 and within five years they had two children, Lina and Mohammed. From all accounts, it was a truly loving marriage. Ra'ad began a steady ascent as a diplomat in the foreign ministry and, over the next two decades, would be posted to five countries as a diplomatic representative for Iraq.

That Friday morning in 1995, Ra'ad drove his 20-year-old daughter to university, as he always did, before heading in to his office in downtown Baghdad. Mid-morning, Lina rang her mother to say her classes had been cancelled and Guzin subsequently telephoned her husband to arrange a time for him to collect Lina and take her home. Young women do not wander the streets of Baghdad alone.

But when Guzin rang, Ra'ad's secretary said her husband was gone. He had been taken from the office by two government officials driving a black car and she had no idea when he would be back. The men had given her no details. However, the secretary told Guzin not to worry. The men were from the prime minister's office and official meetings were fairly routine for diplomats. In the Republic of Iraq, though, the prime minister was also the president: Saddam Hussein.

A few hours later, a black car ominously drove up to the family home on Princess Street in the salubrious Baghdad suburb of Al Mansour. Guzin watched through the window as two officials dragged her limp husband from the back seat of the car, slumped him over their broad shoulders and carried him inside.

When the officials dropped Ra'ad into a chair in the lobby of the house, he almost collapsed. They said nothing, just turned and left. The whites of Ra'ad's eyes were a bloodshot crimson. His face was bright red and he was burning with fever. Guzin held his hand and it, too, was hot. Ra'ad could barely speak and his wife feared he was about to fall into a coma. She shouted at him, wanting to know what was wrong.

He didn't look as if he had been injured. There were no obvious cuts or broken bones, but Ra'ad was terrified. Tears began to roll down his cheeks. Guzin could feel the fear rising in her throat.

As Guzin held her husband's hand, he tried to speak, gasping for air, struggling in pain.

'Promise me, take my children and leave my country,' Ra'ad told his wife. 'Get out of Iraq. Don't ever come back.'

Chapter One

Some people are born lucky and Guzin Najim is one of them. She was fortunate to be the first grandchild in her extended family, which consisted of seventeen aunts and uncles, and was even more fortunate to have parents who didn't mind that she was a girl. In some Iraqi families her sex would have been regarded dimly as a black trick of nature, a deeply disappointing inconvenience that diminished her starring role in the blessed beginning of a new chapter in her family's history. The newborn's young mother, Majida Al Tell, didn't quite see it like that, nor, when he came to visit her in hospital, did the infant's father, a dashingly handsome bear of a man who was instantly besotted with the open-mouthed, pink-faced bundle swathed in a soft white muslin wrap. As she announced her arrival with a scream that came from somewhere deep inside her belly, Shawket Najim looked at his child in wonderment, held her protectively to his chest, felt her tiny, beating heart and unexpectedly discovered a bond of primal dimensions.

With one look at his exhausted wife, who had struggled through a painful labour, he decided right then and there to call the baby Angela, a Greek name meaning 'heavenly messenger'. Shawket believed in fate and felt that the name Angela was just the thing for a baby who had arrived in the world a ghostly shade of blue from lack of oxygen. Angela had gasped desperately for her first precarious breaths. With such determination, her father thought to himself, his firstborn simply had to be meant for bigger things. How could it be otherwise?

As beginnings go, it was auspicious, and Majida Al Tell's entry into motherhood was feted by her family and friends who filled the hospital room with heavily perfumed flowers and brought gifts for the baby. Shawket Najim, from whom the baby would take her surname in accordance with Iraqi tradition, puffed away on cigars as he strode through the hospital corridors in full uniform, the height of military elegance, proudly plotting a daring future for the daughter who looked so familiar to him. Three days later, Shawket began recording his thoughts and hopes for her in a hard-covered journal, its lined pages bound with canvas.

'In the name of God, I open this copy book for my daughter, Angela, who was born at eleven o'clock, before noon, on Thursday 18 April 1956 in Kirkuk', he wrote, full of awe and ceremony:

My daughter, Angela, I am speaking to you while you are sleeping in your bed. You know nothing about life, but I hope you will grow up with dignity and character and be kind to others. Now, my dignity is in your hands. I hope that God will give me strength to let me

5

give you all the things that will make you happy in your life. I have to fight for this for you. You are my eyes, and you will be the happiness in my life or the sadness, and I will take care of you and teach you to have a good education and be intelligent, and also healthy.

His emotions were raw and robust, lacking the self-consciousness one might expect from a man used to presenting a controlled face to the world. They flowed through the ink of his fountain pen onto the off-white pages that would become loose with the passage of time.

Days later Shawket, who was then a middle-ranking officer in the royal Iraqi army based in Kirkuk, the oil-rich city in the Kurdish area of northern Iraq, returned to the hospital to collect his wife and baby and take them home. The army had provided him with a new house befitting his rank in the city at the foot of the rugged Zagros Mountains, from where the Kurds had repeatedly fought for autonomy from Iraq. The Kurdish men stood out in their colourful traditional dress of *sharwal* – baggy wool pants – accented with a threatening dagger or a pipe and bag of tobacco hanging from their cummerbunds, and tasselled turbans on their jet black hair. Those who fought against Iraq identified themselves by wearing two bandoleers draped across their shoulders, front to back, crisscrossing above the heart. The women were equally distinctive in their long bright dresses, beads, silver jewellery and shawls. Kirkuk was hundreds of miles from Baghdad, but with the arrival of the baby it was more than home. The baby Angela brought with her the sweetness of childhood, the innocent smells of baby powder and a curiosity for the untold promises of the future.

Shawket was an arch observer and noted his baby's progress with growing pride, recording the ever-changing length of her body, how she liked to throw her arms and legs in the air when she was being changed, free of the encumbering cloth nappies, and how she would wake up after exactly three hours demanding with a raucous little cry to be fed at her mother's breast. When she was twenty-seven days old, Shawket, tickled pink at the infant's precocity, wrote: 'She tries to teach us a lesson. She cries very strongly and loudly so that we pick her up and hold her. We didn't – we let her cry for one hour. She is already very clever.'

Fatherhood came naturally to Shawket. He had longed to be a father ever since he met and unexpectedly fell in love with Majida during a visit with his aunt in Jordan. Rugged and tanned from the outdoors, Shawket was newly returned from fighting with the Iraqi army as part of the Arab League in the 1948 War for Palestine. Majida was about to turn seventeen and was already engaged to a cousin, a respectable eye doctor, while Shawket was similarly engaged to one of his cousins. The engagement of cousins is not an unusual practice in many Arab societies, where family connections are of utmost importance, and yet Shawket knew from the very first moment he saw Majida that he was going to have a fight to win her. She was beautiful, with pouty, kissable lips and a proud Grecian nose. She wore her thick dark hair down to her shoulders in a soft wave fashionable for the times. There was no doubting her beauty and, just as Shawket was struck by it, Majida felt the same when she saw him. The attraction was instant and mutual.

Shawket walked into his aunt's house with the regal bearing of a man who is sure of himself – and has been all his life. He wasn't cocky, just quietly confident, a quality some women find irresistible. His father, Najim Abdullah el-Salihi, was a well-known member of the Baghdad community and owned huge swathes of land in the Iraqi countryside which he governed with aplomb. Shawket was his only son and had grown up proud of his heritage. And he was also blessed in the looks department. He was of average height and devastatingly handsome. His black eyes were framed by full eyebrows and he wore a moustache which he never shaved.

By the time he met Majida, he had the added self-assurance that comes with having graduated as an officer from the prestigious Baghdad military academy. Shawket Najim had enrolled in the academy in 1942, student number 2041. The college was located in east al Karrada, a plum neighbourhood in grand old Baghdad, which was founded by the Abbasid caliph al-Mansur in 762 AD on the western banks of the Tigris. Modern Baghdad came into existence after the defeat of the Turks in World War I and was established with all due pomp and circumstance by Britain's Winston Churchill in 1922. Shawket's first commission on passing out of the academy was with the Queen Alia regiment, and by 1949 he was stationed in the tinderbox region of Kirkuk.

Majida was born in the ancient land of Jordan in 1932. One of seventeen children, she boasted a lineage even more impressive than Shawket's. Her father, Ali Neyazi Al Tell, had graduated as dux of Istanbul University with a mathematics degree. He became a regional politician in Jordan, building a sweeping family property in the fertile agricultural region of Irbid, which was built on early Bronze Age settlements in the far northwest of the country, close to the borders of Syria and Israel. The lush area with its rich biblical history stands in stark contrast to the surrounding deserts, which are often hit by the hot, dry, dusty *khamsin* winds in summer, and are chilled by the colder temperatures from the mountains to the north and east in winter.

The Al Tell land was a massive affair and had views that extended far into the distance. Rows of bushes surrounded yards where horses, donkeys and other farm animals were kept. Orange, lemon and lime trees provided a vibrant riot of colour and almond and olive trees thrived in the climate. Architecturally designed houses peppered the spread, which was also serviced by two schools, one of which, surprisingly, was the Al Wardya Christian School. It also had a Catholic church which was built on land generously donated as a gift to the Catholic community by Ali Neyazi Al Tell.

From this majestic plot he governed his surrounding fiefdom. The Al Tells were a powerful and influential family, making their money from the land. Majida's cousin Wasfi Al Tell would eventually become Jordan's prime minister and was widely regarded as one of the most loved politicians of the Hashemite Kingdom during his time in office. Ali Neyazi Al Tell built a close friendship with King Abdullah, the first king of Jordan, who ruled for thirty years, starting as Emir Abdullah in 1921 when the country was founded as the Emirate of Transjordan. Abdullah was the brother of King Faisal I, who ruled Iraq from 1921 to his death in 1933. Three years after Jordan gained independence from Britain in 1946 and became known as the Hashemite Kingdom of Jordan, Abdullah proclaimed himself king of the culturally and geographically diverse nation. His people were the tent-dwelling nomadic

Bedouins who herded camel, sheep and goat across the desert and lived according to traditions thousands of years old, small villagers who prayed in their local mosque and sent their children to the local schools, and modern urbanites in humming cities like the capital Amman, Irbid and Az-Zarqa.

Abdullah I frequently visited the Al Tell family in Irbid with his royal court accompanying him. Sometimes he would come on official business to discuss with Ali Neyazi Al Tell the state of the kingdom, its culture and heritage, or the fractious politics of the region with its inherent religious conflicts and the newly formed League of Arab States. At other times, his visits would be purely social, marking the respect and depth of friendship between the families. The imposing Al Tell property was fit for a king and a royal visit conferred a special cachet on the family, which was already in good standing in the eyes of the community. Tragically, the glory days were shattered when the king was assassinated by a lone gunman while saying his traditional Friday prayers at the al-Aqsa mosque in Jerusalem in 1951. Wasfi Al Tell would also be assassinated twenty years later in Egypt in front of the Sheraton Hotel, one more victim of the internecine politics of the Middle East.

Politics and education were highly rated in the Al Tell family and another of Majida's cousins, Said Al Tell, became the minister of education and then deputy prime minister of Jordan. Majida herself studied English literature at Beirut University in neighbouring Lebanon before going home, which was where, as fate would have it, she met her future husband.

Majida and Shawket knew of each other's families and when they met, it struck them that they were meant to be together. But it was not going to be easy. Shawket had to prove himself to her extended family. Despite each being engaged to a cousin, they embarked on a courtship. Years later in his journal to his daughter, Shawket wrote that he had to fight for her mother's hand in marriage and, declaring a profound affection that exposed him as a natural born romantic, said: 'I will love her till the last minute of my life'.

Eventually, Majida summoned the courage to confront her father, telling him she was not in love with her cousin, the eye doctor, but instead was head over heels in love with Shawket Najim. She pointed out that he was rising steadily through the ranks of the Iraqi army and therefore had good prospects as a husband and father. Furthermore, his political convictions were similar to the Al Tell family's, and he was a resolute supporter of the royal family. With so much going for him, a headstrong and determined Majida insisted on returning the engagement ring given to her by her cousin and, in so doing, was officially free to return Shawket's waiting affections. Her father could not deny her the one thing she truly wanted, and the couple married in Baghdad in the winter of 1954 and followed the ceremony with a honeymoon to Beirut. To cement the union, Majida became an Iraqi national on 24 May 1955.

Soon after, Angela arrived, but it wasn't long before her name caused problems for family and friends who had trouble wrapping their tongues around it because it was unusually un-Arabic. So Shawket changed it and Angela became Guzin, a sweet-sounding Turkish name that honoured a relative on his mother's side, and everyone was happy. For the next two years until her sister Buthaina was born, Guzin had the undivided attention of her parents. Her father assiduously noted every new achievement and triumph for his baby, the journal pages bursting with 'firsts'. Nothing was spared, not even the most trivial developmental change.

'You are now 37 days old and you are 4.55 kilos and 52 cm long', he wrote. Two months later: 'From your first month to three months old, you have already begun to show your cleverness. You are smart – you don't want to be in [nappies].' On her first birthday, a wistful Shawket wrote of his absence from his daughter as a result of his military service: 'Today is your first birthday and we are very happy on this occasion. Your mother is playing with you all the time because I am always busy. I am writing now and you are playing. We are trying very hard to build a good future for you.' And on 9 December 1957: 'I hope that when I am an old man you will take care of me and I will live with you without being a burden on your life'.

Shawket boasted of Guzin's first tentative steps which, he noted, were well ahead of her developmental stage, as well as her ability to put on her own shoes and socks. Her first illness, chicken pox, hit on 9 May 1957 and was dutifully recorded – another milestone. Her first words were spoken in Kurdish, not Arabic, perhaps unsurprisingly since Guzin's nanny at the time was Kurdish and lovingly cooed to the baby in her native tongue. With much amusement, Guzin's father recorded her infantile curiosity which blossomed into vanity when she discovered with fascination another baby who looked just like her in the mirror. At two Guzin watched her mother doing her makeup and cried when she wasn't allowed to smear red lipstick over her lips like mummy, and by three she was such a princess that she insisted on changing her dress three times a day, for breakfast, lunch and dinner. She demanded elegance as she toddled around in pretty frocks with Peter Pan collars and puffy sleeves, always with a bow in her hair and her beloved doll in her hand.

Her keen fashion sense was a result of her mother's elegance. Clothes of the finest cottons and wools were bought in Beirut or Italy, and handcrafted leather and wool slippers came from Istanbul. Majida insisted that Guzin never appear for breakfast unless she was properly attired, wearing a special house-robe and her little blue and pink slippers with off-white wool inside. And she rarely came to the table without her doll, which had a porcelain face topped with a broad-brimmed straw hat and was dressed in a knee-length dress with contrasting ribbon that was almost a direct replica of one of Guzin's outfits. The doll was half her size and Guzin considered it an absolute outrage to be separated from her.

Reading the pages of her father's journal nearly fifty years later in Sydney, half a world away from where it all began, Guzin laughs with delight at her behaviour, before her face dissolves into floods of tears at the poignancy of the rare document she holds in her hand. It is a testimony of a father's love, pure and undiluted with the passage of years.

'Guzin, today is your second birthday and you are a very sensitive little girl. If we look at you or are angry with you, you start to cry. But you are strong-willed and you don't obey anybody unless they are kind to you,' her father wrote.

Guzin was doubly blessed because she was also adored by her grandfather Ali Neyazi Al Tell, who showered his first grandchild with affection and attention and encouraged what would be a lifelong feistiness and independence. There was nothing her parents and grandfather wouldn't do for her.

Early on it became clear to Shawket that his firstborn was strong willed and wily but, more than that, she was determined, knowing how to get what she wanted from her parents: characteristics they fostered in a way that is much more typical for boys in Arab society. Each day at precisely 2 pm, Shawket, as a ranking officer, sent a soldier from the barracks to take Guzin lunch, which always included a fried egg. Sometimes, Guzin remembers now, he had been instructed by her father to bring her back to the regiment, where Shawket would sit the tiny girl in front of him on his cavalry steed and pose for photographs, a proud father in full uniform showing off his family's future. At other times, he would prop her up at the table in the mess hall where the officers were having lunch and they would talk to her as if she were a grown-up. She learned from an early age that she had something to say and she was encouraged always to say it. Once, Shawket instructed the army carpenter at Kirkuk to build Guzin an exquisite wooden doll's house because she loved her doll so much. It was a perfect imitation of the most elegant mansions in Baghdad and came fully outfitted with handmade miniature furniture in brightly painted colours.

'My parents tried to give me everything so that I would have self-confidence from early in childhood,' Guzin says now. 'It's not normal, because I am a girl. It's unusual in our society but it was because my father had no son and he believes there is no difference between boys and girls. My father was very progressive, as was my mother.'

Shawket and Majida adopted a broad-minded approach to raising their daughter. They taught her to be strong and confident. Shawket decided that Guzin, as the firstborn, deserved the respect worthy of a first child, boy or girl.

He taught her politics and entrusted her with his beliefs, fostering an abiding and patriotic sense of community and citizenship. In December 1957, before Guzin was even two years old, he wrote that he had been troubled by an order from his superiors to stop a public demonstration against the government. 'The army must not deal with politics and when the army begins to deal with politics, it is the end of it. The army must be kept away from politics. These are my people and I am a military man – I can't hurt my people,' Shawket Najim wrote, revealing himself as a man of conscience and character.

Her mother, Majida, spoke directly to her daughter on the same page, lovingly addressing the bond between father and daughter. 'You would ask me every minute, "Where is my father?" I told you he went to Baghdad for the army and he will bring you some bananas and toys, and you told me, "I don't want anything. I want my father". When I told you to eat you said, "No, I will wait for my baba". You said you loved him very much.'

Guzin and her father were like two peas in a pod. There was no denying that she was her father's daughter. She may have inherited her exotic looks from her mother, with her beautiful almond-shaped eyes and high rosy cheeks that resembled tiny ripe apple plums, but she inherited her personality from her father, which gave him no small measure of delight. Indeed, a brave soul could have rightly accused Shawket of indulging his first child, but his rank and the social standing that came with it prevented anyone saying so. Majida was similarly enchanted with their daughter. Shawket gave in to Guzin's every whim simply because he couldn't bear to see her cry or be unhappy. But just as she was indulged, she was aware of her parents' authority and she obeyed them. She was inculcated with the traditions of her Muslim faith and Arab society, which meant respecting her elders and accepting their wisdom. It was, in every sense, a picture perfect tableau of a very privileged upbringing.

Chapter Two

Two things happened in 1958 that would change Shawket Najim's life forever. On 18 August, Majida Al Tell gave birth to their second child, a daughter they named Buthaina. The child was greeted with mixed emotions. Buthaina was very much wanted but she was to be the last child for Shawket and Majida. Unlike many young Iraqi couples who opt for large families with four, five or six children, they decided to give the two they had the best chance at a well-rounded life in which they would want for nothing. Shawket and Majida had high hopes for their daughters, and didn't want a large, rambunctious brood squabbling for attention and fighting for recognition. And so it was that when Buthaina arrived, their family was complete.

Five weeks earlier, on 14 July, a group of Shawket's peers in the national army staged a pre-dawn coup at Qasr al-Rihab, the royal palace in Baghdad, which would later be renamed Qasr al-Nihayah, or The Palace of The End.

King Faisal II, the ruling monarch and the grandson of the first king of Iraq, was ousted by the group, who called themselves the Free Officers, in an orgy of violence that would be remembered for its unbridled savagery. The barbarism spared no one. In the space of several minutes that hot July morning men, women and children of the royal household – nobility along with commoners – were slaughtered in a hail of machinegun bullets in the palace courtyard as they tried to flee the artillery fire which strafed the building. All but one of the extended royal family of Iraq was annihilated – and she was saved because she had the horrific fortune to fall among a pile of corpses which shielded her from the attack.

King Faisal II had ascended to the throne at the age of four in 1939 after his father, King Ghazi, was killed in a car crash. He had been educated in Britain all his life while a proxy regent ruled the nation. He returned when he was barely in his twenties to take his rightful position as the monarch of modern Baghdad, but his homecoming was not well received by all Iraqis. A groundswell of Iraqi nationalism had been rumbling across the young and fragile country. It was led largely by the Shiah Muslim majority, who felt dispossessed and alienated by Iraqi politics and society which was ruled by the pro-British monarchy and dominated at government level by the elitist Sunni minority. Faisal II was seen as a puppet of Britain by the rapidly growing number of nationalists, particularly those in high positions in the military who wanted Iraq for Iraqis. The 14 July coup was led by General Abdul Karim Qassem who, along with many of his comrades, was fuelled by fervent Iraqi nationalism and a raging desire to cut Iraq's apron strings to Britain. Among the revolutionaries were those who subscribed to a wider view and supported a larger pan-Arab state. While the officer ranks, which were dominated by Sunni Muslims, differed on the particular details of Iraqi nationalism, they were all fired by the singular, overriding motivation of anti-imperialism.

At 6.30 am, the coup was publicly deemed a success on Baghdad radio. The 27-year-old king's body had been removed from the palace secretly, wrapped in a carpet. With him went the vestiges of the previous thirty-seven years of a monarchy which had been installed by Britain on the fall of the Ottoman Empire at the end of World War I. Abdul Salam Arif, one of Qassem's conspirators who led the coup with him, jubilantly announced to the Iraqi population that the nation was now a republic. 'Citizens of Baghdad, the monarchy is dead! The republic is here!' Arif declared, according to a *Time Magazine* report in 1958. In a speech that was part *cri de coeur* and part call to arms, Arif detailed the framework within which the brand new republic would function in language that was pure revolutionary rhetoric. Iraq, he said, had been liberated from the corrupt crew of imperialism and Qassem was its new – and first – president. Rioting followed for days in the streets of Baghdad.

The palace revolution and the birth of Buthaina Najim five weeks later were totally unrelated events, but they would become irrevocably interwoven for Shawket Najim. By sheer dint of his rank, Shawket, then a colonel, was a peer of the elite band of brothers from which the revolutionaries had sprung. But he was not involved in the coup. Shawket was based on the border of Jordan and Iraq in a region known as H3, hundreds of kilometres to the west of the capital. He protected his young family from news of the butchery in Baghdad and the days of fatal rioting in the city streets that followed. As he had written to Guzin in his journal less than a year earlier, he didn't have much heart for combining politics with military service. He believed first and foremost that the role of the military was to protect its people, its government and its borders, three of the main reasons the Iraqi army had been created in the early 1920s. Indeed, when King Faisal I launched the new army, he declared it 'the spinal column of the young nation.' Similarly, Shawket did not believe the military should be launching coups against the legally installed ruling monarchy.

Despite his views, Shawket had a personal interest in the events as they unfolded. Abdul Salam Arif, the man whose voice was heard declaring victory for nationalism on scratchy wirelesses throughout Baghdad on the morning of 14 July 1958, had been Shawket's mentor and teacher at the military academy. They had remained close friends in the years since the student graduated with the master's best wishes. The murder of the king, the viciousness of the coup and the rioting that followed, however, planted a seed of doubt in Shawket's mind. In his journal to Guzin soon after the monarch was buried, he wrote of his country: 'Iraq will pay until the last day of Earth because they killed the King. Those who did this will not live a good life.'

In the months to come, his concerns proved prescient. The revolutionaries and many of their fellow officers were consumed with internal wars over political and national alliances. The debates focused on the concept of pan-Arabism, which held that all Arab states unite to form a greater Arab nation that would match the leading powers in the west, versus a distinctly Iraqi nationalism – or Iraqi first. And so they started to disintegrate. Qassem's new nationalist government found an increasingly willing ally in the Iraqi Communist Party. 'With the leftists and the Communists occupying top positions in the ministries of economics, education, agriculture, and justice, the country marched toward the left despite the large numbers of anti-Communist pan-Arabs within the officer corps of the Army', wrote Sandra Mackey in *The Reckoning: Iraq and the Legacy of Saddam Hussein.*

It wasn't long before Qassem had several pan-Arab supporters on trial for treason, including his former conspirator in the coup, Abdul Salam Arif. Qassem suspected Arif of harbouring leadership aspirations of his own and his pan-Arabism was in direct conflict with Qassem's Iraqi-first beliefs. Arif and several fellow Free Officers were initially handed the death sentence, but Qassem later commuted these to life imprisonment.

The following March, in 1959, Qassem was the target of an unsuccessful coup by a splinter group among the officers corps who opposed the increasing influence of the Communist Party on the new government and particularly on Qassem, who, they claimed, had betrayed them. The coup was a complete failure from start to finish and the president survived.

In retaliation, Qassem launched a second round of bloodshed that rivalled the palace revolution's for its barbarism. He targeted the men of the rebellion who had tried to oust him from office, many of whom had supported him in overthrowing the monarchy the previous July. Qassem gave no quarter. 'In addition to disposing of all the officers who had staged the rebellion in Mosul, the communists killed many Arab nationalists who had supported them', wrote Con Coughlin in his book *Saddam: The Secret Life*. 'Some of the Free Officers who had helped to overthrow the monarch were tried as traitors. In Mosul itself a communist-inspired mob indulged in a week-long orgy of rape, looting, and summary trials, which culminated in the accused being machine-gunned to death in front of cheering mobs.' According to Sandra Mackey in *The Reckoning*, 'group preyed on group, employing every device of elimination from gunfire to dragging victims behind cars until they died. Each group was motivated by the fear that if it did not prevail, it would be destroyed at the hands of its adversaries.'

In the complex web of Iraqi politics, where a common goal was never articulated and community stood against community and religion against ethnicity, uprisings and coups were typical – and always had been. Politics was like a jigsaw puzzle in which the pieces never properly fitted. It was in this climate, then, with its distinct lack of any political cohesiveness or a clear direction for the country's future, that the relatively new Ba'ath Party saw an opportunity. Then a small group of about three hundred members, including one Saddam Hussein, the Ba'ath made the most of the yawning gap in the body politic of Iraq and slowly started to fill it. Meanwhile, a cult of personality enveloped Qassem and, for the next few years, his rule became more and more autocratic.

It was against this backdrop of fomenting political unrest and internal divisions in his officer ranks that Colonel Shawket Najim decided to retire his commission in the Iraqi army. He detested the Communists and leftists and on 9 September 1959 his military days were over. President

Qassem accepted his voluntary retirement and decommissioned him from the officer corps.

◆ ◆ ◆

The politics of twentieth century Iraq were single-handedly shaped by Britain in the aftermath of World War I. When Emir Faisal was crowned the first King of Iraq in 1921, he inherited 6000 years of culture and traditions, with the blessings of the British, who ruled from behind the scenes. A lean man with a long, thin face that was dominated by the contours of his cheekbones, Faisal also inherited tribal and religious rivalries that had bled into the foundations of the desert landscape, colouring it forever. Modern Iraq is made up of Christians and non-Christians, Arabs and non-Arabs. The people are Shiah and Sunni – Muslims both – Christian, Persian, Kurd and Jew. Each is the custodian of its own cultural and religious heritage, its own ethnicity, faith and language. While Shiah was the majority religion and its followers were spread far across the plains in tribes and villages, it was the urban Sunni minority who made up the elite.

Geographically, Iraq is a changing canvas. The soaring and treacherous mountain ranges to the north and east which separate it from Turkey and Iran had never been able to hold back the conquering Persians and Mongols or the migration of the Kurds. On the western plains, the landscape stretches to meet the harsh Syrian deserts, uninhabitable to anyone but the nomads who have traversed the plains since antiquity. South of the capital of Baghdad, Marsh Arabs lay a direct claim to the vibrant ancestry of the Sumerians, who first rocked the cradle of civilisation in the lush plains between the Tigris and the Euphrates.

Iraq's ethnic and religious diversity is matched only by the sweep of cultural and socioeconomic differences which pit class against class. For every rich man, woman and child, it has dozens more who are poor. Dirt poor. Illiterate peasants battle the unforgiving climate and pray to their gods for rich harvests while nomadic desert dwellers fear evil spirits known as *jinn*, which they believe exist only to terrorise them. Neither ever believed they could achieve the relative riches of the merchants in the crowded market bazaars of Baghdad, the intelligentsia in the schools and halls of academia, the bourgeoisie in the corridors of power, or the traders and craftsmen in the port city of Basra. The tribal sheik with his traditions and history was no match for the *effendi* – the new man of property and education who emerged in the early years of modern Iraq when mandatory education gave every boy and girl the chance to go to school. The rich ethnicities and differences travelled with time, surviving as they always had from antiquity, and are still in place even now. With such insurmountable internal differences, Iraq was never able to enjoy a specific national identity. Instead, it has been marked by instability and uncertainty, revolts and military coups, and murderous counter-coups. It was never harmonious, as history tells it, and it was always thus.

The ancient peoples of Mesopotamia spanned four millennia before the birth of Christ and lived within fluid borders in city-states that rose and sank almost without physical trace. The mud-brick architecture of the times has vanished, as have the impressive ziggurats – majestic stepped pyramids constructed entirely of sun-baked clay bricks and sometimes mounted with a temple – from which kings, priests, gods and goddesses ruled. But their legacy has survived the unpredictable forces of nature and the bloodthirsty invasions and brutal carnage of rival peoples who, one after the other, laid waste to successive enemies in some of the most violent massacres ever imaginable. Conquest gave way to defeat. As one city fell, another would ascend to rule the land, then fall again as the cycle was repeated. Military expansion ensured the continual building and rebuilding of empires and the evolving social systems thrived on clearly defined hierarchies and hegemonies. Merchants travelled freely, trading their wares and paying taxes as they went. Languages and religions emerged and submerged, ethnicities blended as empires were built before collapsing with time, and corruption became part of the realpolitik.

The antiquities and priceless relics found buried in the earth in the last millennium are a beautiful reminder and haunting echo of that past. Artisans, sculptors and craftsmen erected steles, great slabs of stone on which they chiselled dedications and laws, and built masonry reliefs depicting the warfare and weaponry of the times: bows and arrows and battering rams. Horses in armour ridden at full gallop by armed warriors were etched into stone, or depicted two abreast pulling chariots with fearsome spokes protruding from their wheels. Pictures of goddesses being worshipped by minions on riverbanks were delicately engraved into alabaster urns. Clay tablets created in the fourth millennium BC, about the size of the palm of a man's hand, record the trade of livestock.

The Sumerians were the first Mesopotamians, settling in the south around 4000 BC, close to what was then and is now

Basra. Abraham, the father of the Jews and Arabs and the founder of Judaism, came from ancient Sumer. Both the Akkadians, who conquered the Sumerians and extended the empire north, and the Babylonians would, at different times, make their home closer to the geographic heart of modern Baghdad between the flood-prone Tigris and Euphrates. The Assyrians later established their roots on the Tigris to the north.

The Sumerians are credited with building the political infrastructure of the city-state. They invented the wheel, and a system of mathematics based on the number sixty which included the very first-known concept of zero. Their kings and priests ruled from towering ziggurats. They used an inchoate language and invented writing using soft clay tablets and wedge-shaped instruments cut from marsh reeds, known as cuneiform. Poetry and storytelling were the creative offspring of the Sumerians. Long before the ancient Greeks had Homer and 'The Iliad' and 'The Odyssey', the Mesopotamians wrote the famous 'Epic of Gilgamesh', an ambitious tale about the Sumerian king Gilgamesh's unsuccessful quest for immortality.

The Akkadians assumed control of the region from the Sumerians, led by a gardener named Sargon who would eventually become king. He developed an intricate irrigation system which harnessed the waters of the two rivers surrounding the empire and made strategic use of a military. Both were venerable achievements and intended to guarantee the survival of the people in the land. Yet as the Sumerians fell to the Akkadians, so too did the Akkadians fall to Babylon. Known in the Bible as the den of iniquity, Babylon was located 50 kilometres directly south of where Baghdad stands today and would eventually be protected inside a double-walled fortress. Located on the east bank of the Euphrates River inside the fortress was one of the seven wonders of the ancient world, the Hanging Garden of Babylon. Tumbling down a terraced ziggurat, the gardens resembled a lush mountain towering over the surrounds and offering magnificent views of the valley. The Babylonians also built the fabled Tower of Babel, hoping it would reach heaven and lead them to nirvana.

Babylon's most famous king, Hammurabi, wrote the first set of laws which became known as the Code of Hammurabi and would eventually prove to be the foundation underpinning modern western law. The code grew from Hammurabi's belief in a just and equitable society for all, based on the concept of an eye for an eye and a tooth for a tooth. It meted out barbaric penalties to those who fell foul of it and enshrined the practice of honour killings, an abhorrent system of justice which is still being used in many Middle Eastern countries today, particularly against women. Hammurabi established taxes and tariffs to govern the economies of the city-states, and wrote intricate sections on civil, criminal and family law.

Around 900 BC Babylon succumbed to the warmongering Assyrians who, for the next three centuries, ruled with an effective system of terror and fear, building monuments and grand edifices which they decorated with detailed artwork bearing testimony to a succession of brutal kings and their conquests. Despite their skill at warfare, they were not barbarians intellectually, and instead of eradicating the history before them, they nurtured the legacy of the Sumerians, Akkadians and Babylonians. The Babylonians rose up again to reclaim their empire, only to hand it to Cyrus of Persia, who led his army from over the Zagros Mountains in the east. The Persian rule lasted two centuries before Alexander the Great from Macedonia conquered the empire around 331 BC.

Eventually the metropolis disappeared, leaving nothing but a historical mosaic of ancient peoples and the legacies that created civilisation in the land that is now Iraq. In the first and second millennia AD, the land would host the Abbasids, the Arabs, the Mongols, the Turks, the British and finally, halfway through last century, the Iraqis. The ancient history of turmoil and bloodshed in the quest for empire set the only stage possible for modern Iraq.

◆ ◆ ◆

In the uncertainty of President Qassem's Iraq of 1960, the officer corps of the army had split into two distinct camps with opposite ideologies about nationalist identity. The politicisation of Shawket Najim's army turned his stomach and slowly ate away at him. He detested the Communists who ruled at the top of the regime, and he wanted to be as far away from it as possible. Shawket Najim decided he had seen enough. He was a dedicated father and he wanted to protect his daughters. Guzin was four years old and her sister Buthaina was three months away from her second birthday. Shawket did not want them exposed to the bloodshed in Baghdad and what he saw as the degeneration of his country and his army. With his politics far removed from those of the government, Shawket sent himself and his family into exile in Jordan, secretly slipping out of the country under the guise of an annual summer holiday. It was a huge risk, but in Jordan, under the ongoing rule of the Hashemite Kingdom, he knew his family would be safe.

In the days leading up to their departure on 28 May 1960, Shawket and Majida hosted a series of discreet get-togethers in which friends and family bid them bon voyage. The night before they were due to leave, Majida's brother, Tariq Al Tell, joined the family's table for a traditional Iraqi dinner. Tariq had lived with his sister and brother-in-law during the past year while he was studying at Baghdad University. After they had finished their meal, followed by the requisite Iraqi tea, Shawket handed Tariq his journal and asked him to write a note to his eldest and first niece, Guzin.

Tariq was overwhelmed by the impending departure of his sister and the two little girls to whom he had grown so close in the past year, and admitted in faltering penmanship that he didn't quite know what to say: 'Dear Guzin, tomorrow you will escape to Lebanon, you are leaving by plane. I don't know what to write to you but I will write what I see'. It was easier for Tariq to talk about his adorable niece rather than address the huge upheaval that was about to separate his close-knit family. 'You are very smart, very active, you like to play and you like to go outside the house. Guzin, you have very good taste that I haven't seen in a child your age. I think you must have taken these things from your mother and your father – this is what I see in your house.'

The 28th of May was a Saturday. Guzin was too little to recognise the anxiety in her parents' unusual behaviour as they spent the morning packing their bags and fussing over the girls. Her mother told Guzin they were going on an annual summer holiday to Beirut in Lebanon, which was then a peaceful, picturesque city on the Mediterranean. It made perfect sense. Summers in Iraq are unbearably hot and the furnace-like temperatures push those who can afford it away from sunburnt Baghdad for two to three months at a time. Shawket had always taken his family away for a long summer break, and to the outside world this year would be the same. If anyone wanted to know, it was business as usual – just another summer holiday. Guzin was excited about the holiday but even more excited about seeing her beloved grandfather, Ali Neyazi Al Tell, at the end of the trip. With typical childish enthusiasm, she couldn't wait to get going.

Shawket Najim was dressed in a smart business suit as he led his family through Baghdad airport. The manager of the airport spotted him and walked over, surreptitiously handing him a package full of money. He was an old friend who, weeks before, received the money from Shawket for safekeeping. After the usual courtesies and some small talk that would offend no one if they happened to be overheard, the manager told Shawket and a nervous Majida that it was time to go and led them to the waiting aircraft. As they flew out of Baghdad, they breathed a sigh of relief. Everything had gone so smoothly. Three hours later they were in Beirut, and two weeks after that they were settled safely on the family property of Ali Neyazi Al Tell in Irbid, Jordan.

'I will never forget those three years in Jordan,' Guzin recalls forty-three years later. 'They were the happiest years of my life.' Her father, however, became a marked man, wanted by the Communists and military leaders of the regime he had deserted. 'They wanted to kill him,' Guzin says.

Chapter Three

Guzin and Buthaina were cosseted from the calamities of the world around them. They were too young to understand the tumultuous political situation in their country or the emotional strength it took their parents to leave Iraq, let alone the risk. And besides, they had more important things on their minds. The 200,000 square metre homestead of Ali Neyazi Al Tell in Irbid was every child's idea of paradise and they were only too keen to explore it. Encouraged in their spirited playfulness and indulged by the extended family, which included several of Ali's children from his three marriages, the girls ran around the property at full speed dressed casually in shorts and t-shirts.

Guzin, particularly, developed a fierce independence. She learned to ride horses but only after she got a feel for being in the saddle from learning on the smaller, slower donkeys that worked on the farm. She rode her tricycle and climbed the fruit-laden trees in the orchards – much to the chagrin of the farmers, who complained to no avail to her grandfather. 'I was the oldest grandchild, the first grandchild, and the most spoiled one. My grandfather loved me very much. Also because he is a very intelligent man, he always encouraged me to be self-confident. He gave me everything,' Guzin recalls. 'The farmers on the property always became angry with me because I would climb their trees. They said to my grandfather, "Come and see what Guzin does", and he just laughed and didn't say anything. But for his sons, it was forbidden. I was his favourite.'

Shaking her head at the recollections, Guzin chuckles and says she paid a price for being her grandfather's favourite. Occasionally the boys, who were technically her uncles though only a few years older than her, would extract their jealousy-fuelled revenge. When Guzin was out of her grandfather's sight they would tease her and pull her ears until she was white with rage, stamping her feet and proclaiming with childish indignation that she would get even with them one day. But they also made good use of their precocious niece, knowing that because she was the favoured grandchild she had their father well and truly wrapped around her little finger. If they wanted to go to the cinema or to a café in town, they sent Guzin as their emissary, coaching her to cadge money from their father. With her cherubic little face and her forefinger touching her bottom lip, she was the epitome of coyness and she never failed to get what they wanted. For her efforts, the boys frequently took her with them, showing her how grown-ups behaved, smoking cigarettes and drinking coffee.

Shawket Najim built a house for his family on the property while Majida raised the girls, and they enjoyed an idyllic life free from any concerns about troubles in Iraq.

Ali bought his granddaughters a German shepherd pup and he gave Guzin a cat. He would sit with her at the end of the day in the large salon reading books and teaching her how to spell, telling her all about his family history, revealing the fascinating stories of his cultured past. Guzin was enthralled. She loved spending time with her grandfather and developed a growing thirst for knowledge, which he inspired. She was a clever and fast student.

As soon as she was old enough Guzin was enrolled in the Saffya School in Irbid. In her first year she was awarded dux of the class. Ever sure of herself, she protested to her grandfather that she did not receive a prize for her academic efforts, insisting that he do something about it. As always, Ali indulged his granddaughter and, using his contacts and status, called the minister for education in Irbid. Ali informed him that Guzin was an exceptional student and deserved an award to commemorate her grades. 'They gave me a doll,' she says, laughing. It was the start of a long and stellar academic career. Even though they were all Sunni Muslims, Buthaina was enrolled with her uncles at the Christian school, Al Wardya, which was run by a Jordanian priest whom they all called Father George. Guzin remembers that Buthaina often ran away from class, sneaking out the back door of the school and scampering straight back home to the familial embrace of the farm.

On Sundays the girls would dress up in their favourite frocks and, each taking one of their grandfather's hands, would join in Father George's liturgical masses. Guzin, a Muslim, cheekily followed the Catholic children's lead and genuflected on entering the church while making the sign of the cross, all under the amused gaze of her grandfather.

Sometimes she mustered up the required solemnity and joined the procession to take Holy Communion. But by the time she returned to the pew next to her beloved Ali, she would be grinning from ear to ear at having taken part in this strange religious ritual which was a mystery to her. After the service, Buthaina and Guzin would stand around and listen while Ali Neyazi Al Tell chatted with his good friend Father George and the nuns who ran the school.

Every summer Shawket packed the family up into his dark blue Mercedes sedan and they travelled by road to Europe, stopping along the way in places like Istanbul, Syria and Bonne. At other times Shawket took his family for kebab barbecues high in the mountains. During the cooler months in Jordan, they travelled south to the stunning port town of Aqaba, Jordan's only outlet to the Red Sea. The five-year-old Guzin learnt to swim in the crystal blue waters in the Gulf of Aqaba, earning herself the nickname Froggy. She loved Aqaba and its place in Arab history, which had been rapturously taught to her by her grandfather, richly embroidered with details and romance.

In 1917 Aqaba had played host to the then Emir Faisal as he fought against the Ottoman Empire with the help of the British Lawrence of Arabia, who led a guerilla outfit that worked behind Turkish lines, blowing up railways and earning the nickname Amir Dynamite from the Bedouins. Wrapped in flowing white robes and passionately zealous about an Arabia for Arabs, Lawrence led the uprising into Aqaba in the summer of 1917 after a two-month march, and seized the coastal town from the Turks, cementing his place in Aqaba history.

Guzin's most precious childhood memories come from those days in Jordan at Irbid, when she was taught to be strong and independent, and just like her uncles. There was no place for weakness in the Najim family, and even though she was a girl, she was as good as any boy, if not better. 'My father always said to me, "Guzin, you can do anything. It's always possible, there is no impossible". I am very strong because I am like my father, even when I was four years old.' Guzin remembers that one household servant used to address her mother as 'mama', 'And I said to him, "Why are you calling her mama? Don't call her mama, that's my mama".'

In many countries in the Middle East, women live under a strict set of guidelines which are ingrained in the patriarchal culture or enshrined by law. Depending on the country, women's freedoms are granted on a sliding scale. Even if they are allowed to vote, work, drive, get an education, wear western dress and be seen in mixed company, thousands of years of traditions and social mores prevail on them to maintain their place as second to their men. Many Middle Eastern countries have strict dress codes which conceal women from head to toe in a burqa, chador or abaya, a bell-shaped tent which falls to the floor, varying only slightly from region to region. Others wear head coverings to prevent their hair and neck from being seen by non-related males.

A barbaric law also permits the practice of honour killing in several Middle Eastern countries. Some, like Jordan and Iran, hide it under the name of Islamic Sharia law, while others don't even bother with the religious justification. The practice gives men the right to murder a female family member if they believe she has brought shame and dishonour on the family name. Sometimes the shame and dishonour are figments of an overly active imagination or the result of a rumour or, worse, the result of a crime against the woman. Newspaper reports frequently recount the atrocities against rape and incest victims who have been killed by an emotionally stunted male relative hell-bent on cleansing the family name. Thousands of women of varying religions – Christian, non-Christian and Muslim – have been killed by this ancient tradition which predates Islam. They have had their throats slashed by a father, brother, uncle or husband, or had their skulls caved in with rocks, or been stabbed to death or shot with a gun. Humiliated and murdered for their sins, real or imagined, some women and girls are further degraded in death when their families deny their existence by burying them in unmarked graves, eliminating them from all memory, past and future.

In Saudi Arabia, women are prohibited from driving and from mixing with men who are not close relatives or husbands. Women need their father's or husband's permission to get a job, go to college or university, or have surgery. Religious police known as the Mutawa'een can arrest women on the merest suspicion of breaking the law and imprison them for days without trial. Restaurants have segregated entries and seating for men and women. A Saudi Supreme Court judge told the *Al Riyadh* newspaper in 2002 that 'a woman has a shelf life' that lasts only as long as she can have children.

Over the western border in neighbouring Kuwait, women only won the right to vote in the last year of the twentieth century and single foreign women are not allowed to visit the country unless they are on business, or visiting a blood relative or husband. To the east in Jordan, many women are not permitted to work or leave the house without their father's, brother's or husband's permission, and Muslims are forbidden from marrying non-Muslims. In Iran and the United Arab Emirates, women are stoned to death for adultery.

While women in Iraq experience perhaps some of the greatest freedoms of all women in Arab nations, they are not entirely free. In the Iraq of Saddam Hussein, for instance, women aged under forty-five were only allowed to travel outside the country in the presence of an escort, a father or husband, or a close male family friend who has permission from the household's male authority figure. Culturally, women rarely mixed with men who were not relatives and sex outside of marriage was forbidden. In 1990, the brutal dictator enacted Article 111 in the Iraqi Penal Code, legalising honour killings. Effectively, Article 111 made it impossible to prosecute and punish men who killed a female relative in order to restore a family's honour. In the decade that followed, there were 4000 known cases of women killed. As well, units from the paramilitary organisation Firqat Fedayeen Saddam, which was run by Saddam's eldest son Uday, beheaded more than 200 women, supposedly for prostitution. According to an Amnesty International report, Saddam's butchers would dump the severed head on the victim's family's doorstep or force them to display the head on fences around the house for several days as a cruel trophy of terror and a public reminder of their shame.

Even without such practices, the prejudices against and the oppression of women is stitched into the ornate fabric of Middle Eastern culture and is not necessarily confined to religion or ethnicity. Guzin Najim was lucky. With the guidance of her father and grandfather, she grew up embracing many aspects of her heritage and religion with its adherence to modesty and reliance on custom. Yet the repressive dictates of Arab culture and the Muslim faith had no place in the family household. With the patronage of Shawket and Ali, Guzin openly defied the cultural demands that could have relegated her to an underclass of womanhood, where her sex marked her as a second-class citizen. She thought that was normal, but as she grew up she realised just how lucky she had been.

Chapter four

The revolutionary government of Iraq's new president Abdul Karim Qassem staggered through the early years of the 1960s. As head of the military junta which ousted the monarchy in 1958, Qassem was meant to steer Iraq into a position of power in a unified pan-Arab nation. Instead, he was a vainglorious man who succumbed to a cult of personality. The former army general refused to discard his uniform, and pompously hung a giant portrait of himself at the front of the ministry of defence in Baghdad, from where he ran the country. Powerful spotlights ensured it could be seen day and night. Qassem's vanities, which would be mirrored and then multiplied more than a decade later by Saddam Hussein, were excessive and deserving of mockery but they were not his gravest sin. Qassem's biggest failing was that he rejected the larger pan-Arab vision in which all Arab states would form a unified Arab nation to equal that of the reviled western powers. Instead his regime relied on Iraqi communists and turned to China and Russia, which was emerging as a world superpower, for support.

In the hazardous political spectrum of Iraqi politics, Qassem's political and military enemies were rallying. Members of the elite officers corps who had never given up on pan-Arabism joined forces with the nascent Ba'ath Party who had their own view of what a unified Arab nation would be like. So it was no surprise when, five years after Qassem came to power, the officers and Ba'athists opposed to him staged another bloody coup. Qassem and his cohorts were captured on 9 February 1963 and put on trial in a makeshift courtroom at the national television station in the heart of Baghdad, overlooking the Tigris. Within an hour they were found guilty of betraying the revolution of 1958 which also turfed Britain out of the country. Minutes later, they were summarily executed. Given the location of the executions, the assassins panned the television cameras over the bullet-riddled bodies, broadcasting the gruesome scene to cheering Iraqis. As a final insult, they dragged Qassem's head up and pushed it in front of a camera.

Before the day was out, yet another shaky alliance was forged to lead the country. Ironically, Qassem's co-conspirator in the 1958 coup, General Abdul Salam Arif, was appointed president of Iraq, but the real power lay with the Ba'ath Party. It appointed the prime minister, Ahmed Hasan al-Bakr, and took up most of the places in the government. Lurking in the background, meticulously laying the foundation for his later success, was Saddam Hussein. Already feared for his viciousness and thuggery, Saddam was assiduously building his empire with al-Bakr, and it was based almost entirely on tribalism. Al-Bakr was a fellow Tikriti.

The Ba'athists immediately developed a well-earned reputation for brutality. The party's national guard quickly grew from a few thousand men into a 34,000-strong para-military force which terrorised Baghdad. The guards went on vicious and murderous witch-hunts for communists and leftists. Armed with machine guns, they took prisoners and seized property at will. They revelled in their unchecked savagery and instilled a sense of abject fear into the Iraqi people. With the Ba'ath leader's authority, the national guard commandeered cinemas, clubs and private homes, turning them into torture chambers and execution centres – a precursor of what would be refined later under Saddam Hussein's long reign of terror. Prisoners who were taken to the dreaded Qasr al-Nihayah – the aptly named Palace of the End where the royal family was massacred in 1958 – suffered abominably. They were forced to sit on pointed iron stakes, or were tortured with electric wires and pincers before being killed, a perverse mercy considering the barbarity they endured. Some had their fingers chopped off. The luckier ones were executed immediately.

From the comfort of his retreat in Irbid, hundreds of miles away from Baghdad, Shawket Najim had watched the rise of the Ba'ath Party with disgust. The past three years of his self-imposed exile in Jordan had been ideal. Majida was happy living on her family's property where she could watch her daughters safely grow up close to their grandfather and uncles and aunts. She had planned on being home for a long time, but Shawket's idyll was interrupted five weeks after the coup with the arrival on 23 March of a telegram from Iraq's new president, Abdul Salam Arif, the very same man who had been Shawket's mentor at the military academy in Baghdad when he first enlisted in 1942.

Arif's telegram was to the point. 'Return to your

country', he had written. Arif needed Shawket and wanted him to resume his retired rank in the Iraqi army. Arif, according to Sandra Mackey's *The Reckoning*, was 'a military man determined to preserve the authority of the Army' and the Ba'ath's control of government was intolerable. With the telegram came an order reinstating Shawket to the position of colonel.

Arif's telegram offered no alternative, so Shawket heeded his country's call. He despised the savagery and gratuitous bloodshed of the Ba'ath Party in the streets of Baghdad. It was a threat to the Iraqi people and their army, and he firmly supported its expulsion from the political infrastructure of his country. Three days later he was back in Baghdad. It was 26 March, and Shawket noted his arrival briefly and without any emotion with a one-line entry in his diary. Shawket left Majida and their two daughters in Jordan for the time being, worried about the level of safety in Baghdad.

Arif rewarded Shawket's loyalty with a subsequent Order of the President, dated 12 July 1963, giving him back-pay from the date of his official retirement in September 1959. Shawket was delighted. President Arif's munificence was a clear vote of support for him and not only restored him to his rank, but also returned to him the many privileges he had given up when he left Iraq, not to mention the prestige that comes from being a member of the officers corps.

Majida and the children stayed in Irbid for six months while Shawket settled back into Baghdad. He moved into a brand new American-style house in the upmarket Al Yarmouk area, not far from the Arabian Knight Monument and the Grand Mosque. The two-storey home had three bedrooms, three bathrooms, a lounge room, a salon for watching television and a huge kitchen which looked out over a beautiful garden. There was also a live-in gardener and cleaner. Flush with his back-pay, Shawket decided to splurge and went on a shopping spree, buying all new furnishings for the house. It was perfectly presented when his wife and daughters arrived in September.

Those were hectic days and Shawket's attentions were divided. While readying his house for the arrival of the women in his life, he was in command of a regiment in Baghdad. President Arif was planning a new coup to remove the Ba'athists from government. The always shaky alliance had become totally unworkable. Arif regarded al-Bakr's Ba'ath regime as wretched and ruthless and on 18 November, he mobilised the machinery of the military. They ousted the Ba'athists from their ruling position, effectively and unequivocally stripping them of office and quarantining them from the controlling end of Iraqi politics for the next five years. The new alliance had lasted a short nine months.

Shawket Najim's unit was involved and on 28 March 1964 he was awarded the state-struck '18th of November Medal' for his efforts. In the years that followed, Shawket was promoted through the army to the rank of general, receiving medals and recognition along the way. His stunning white officer's uniform with gold brocade would eventually carry more than eight medals for distinguished service.

'My father rose up and up in the army during those years,' Guzin remembers now. 'We lived a very good life in Iraq then. My parents were very educated people and they taught us the principles of how to act and think.

We travelled every year and sometimes twice a year. Everything was good. Everything in Iraq was very good. This was the only period in Iraq when there was no bloodshed – this and the royal period.'

Guzin was seven and Buthaina five when they returned to Baghdad. They spent a lot of time with each other and shared a bedroom on the top floor of the house in Al Yarmouk. Even though Majida and Shawket indulged their two girls, they insisted they live by their rules, which observed Arab traditions. The girls were forbidden from closing the bedroom door to their parents, and their mother entreated them to act with decorum at all times. They knew to take their social cues from her and their manners were impeccable. Majida was the consummate hostess and within weeks of returning to Baghdad she was back into the swing of her social set, organising glamorous soirees and cocktail parties in their new home. Majida allowed Guzin and Buthaina to skirt the periphery in their finery as long as they behaved like proper little ladies. The sisters loved playing grown-ups, especially when their mother threw sumptuous sit-down dinner parties for eight to twelve people from the upper echelons of society in which they moved.

The girls greeted guests and asked them questions about whatever happened to pop into their inquiring minds, and the guests responded in such a way that anyone would have thought that being interrogated by two little girls was the most natural thing in the world. Guzin and Buthaina radiated charm, and they had plenty of opportunity to polish their social skills. Majida, with her formidable family background and connections, frequently opened the house to a range of people from commanders in the military and heads of government to members of the Jordanian royal family. She also had a spare room which was frequently used by guests and friends from Europe. Guzin remembers that Majida took her and Buthaina to the local social clubs where she played bingo with her society friends. They squealed with delight when their mother won, shouting out 'bingo' and taking home a little prize, usually a box of chocolates, which she shared with them. It was a wonderful life, and truly international. They were fully exposed to the prestige of their father's life but they saw little, if any, of the chaos of Baghdad.

Once enrolled at the Al Khansaa school in their neighbourhood, the girls' lives became more regimented. They were up each day by seven for school at eight. From Saturday through Thursday, the family chauffeur would drive the girls in the blue Mercedes to the front gates of the school. Even though it was just a few streets away, the girls were not allowed to walk on their own. It was a cultural tradition. Wearing navy blue uniforms accented with a white collar, Guzin and Buthaina took classes until 1.30 pm, when school broke up for the day. Everyone looked forward to Thursdays because they were 'short days' and classes were dismissed at 12.30 pm.

Guzin loved school. She was a high achiever and before the first year was out she was dux of her class, a feat she repeated every year right through to high school. Her father, ever proud, bought her a gold bracelet to celebrate. She was self-confident and loved having the attention of her teachers, particularly when they complimented her on how European she looked. Buthaina was just as bright, if not more so, Guzin says now, and she too would eventually go to university to study physics and then psychology.

Just as the mornings flowed according to a certain routine, so too did the afternoons. At two o'clock every day without fail, the family driver would be leaning against the Mercedes with his arms crossed, waiting for the Najim sisters in the same spot outside the school gates. Once in the car, Guzin instructed the driver to stop at a nearby shop and buy her a large Kit Kat bar. She gobbled all four slender chocolate fingers as fast as she could before arriving home, making sure she wiped away the evidence from the corners of her mouth so her mother would not be cross with her for spoiling her lunch. After lunch the girls took a nap. Depending on the time of year and the heat, it lasted anywhere from one to three hours. It is a habit Guzin retains even now. Their father usually arrived home around 3.30 pm and would sit down for lunch around 4 pm before helping the girls with their homework.

Dinner, too, was a ritual and, more often than not, an elaborate feast beautifully cooked and presented by Majida. She and Shawket sat at opposite ends of a fully laid table in the dining room, complete with napkins and silverware, and Guzin and Buthaina sat between them, facing each other across the table. If it was summer, dinner would be served within the walled garden of their house with the trees rustling in the breeze and Guzin's cat, Foo Foo, prancing around underneath the table. It was formal but comfortable. Shawket listened as his daughters chatted about their adventures at school, and they fell silent, listening with awe as he filled them in on the events of his day and the direction his country was going. With no boys, Shawket Najim treated his eldest, Guzin, as something of a confidante, and the way he raised his children was a reflection on his own childhood. Shawket's mother died when he was just eight years old and his father remarried. As a young boy, he dearly missed his mother's love and grieved for having lost the deep bond that inextricably ties a parent to his or her firstborn. He wasn't about to miss it with his own child.

'My father would say that in Middle Eastern society they treat girls as something very weak. He wanted his daughters to be strong enough in the future so they would never need anything, not even from their husbands,' Guzin recalls, tears filling her eyes. 'He always said, "I don't want anybody to make my daughters cry, not even one day in their lives". He wanted to protect us from anything he had suffered as a child, but in a way it hurt us because as we grew up we could never hear the word "no". Everything had to be "yes". My mother was just as protective. Every night she would come into our room just to be sure that we were alive – and I am the same with my own children now.'

Reflecting on her childhood now, in her small flat in Sydney which has few of the accoutrements she was accustomed to in Iraq, Guzin is not sure if the manner in which her parents indulged her and Buthaina was sensible. 'Now I feel very sad about myself because I have nothing. Everything is gone', she says. 'I know they didn't know all these things would happen to me, but they did all these things for me and they were happy to do them. But now I feel very sad . . . You know, I think the right thing is not to do this for my children. It's a very wrong way to raise children like this, in luxury, because nobody knows what will happen, especially in bad countries, nobody knows, not one hour later. I don't tell my children these things because they will be sad. It's just inside my heart. Sometimes I feel that my heart will explode.'

Chapter Five

If Shawket Najim was all erudition and urban sophistication from having been brought up on the right side of the tracks and mixing with Baghdad's elite, Saddam Hussein was his polar opposite. Uncultured and tribal, the man who would later become the world's most hated dictator, dubbed 'the Butcher of Baghdad', was thirteen years younger than Shawket and existed in a parallel universe in the hierarchy of Baghdad society and politics. Yet throughout the sixties each was making his own way through the ranks and, before the decade was out, their paths would intersect.

It is crucial to understand the importance of Iraqi culture and its sharp class and religious divides to comprehend the bitterness and divisions that have long existed in this wondrous land, home to desert tribes and five-star hotels. Saddam Hussein was born in 1937 into a poor Sunni family in a mud-hut village of Al-Ouja on the banks of the Tigris River in Tikrit, in north central Iraq. The son of a peasant and a member of the al-Bu Nasir tribe, he was abandoned by his father as a child and sent to live with relatives. Depending on the source, his mother was either the village whore or a clairvoyant. His name Saddam means 'the one who confronts' and he was doing that from an early age. He was an uneducated street thug who never shied away from a fight. To educated people from Baghdad – people like Ra'ad and Guzin – Saddam was of lowly peasant stock and would never amount to anything more than the sum of his family background, even when he emerged as a ruthlessly powerful dictator in the Arab world in 1979.

Saddam entered the political fray with the bare-knuckled panache he developed as a child growing up in a violent and impoverished world. Tikrit was known as a haven for river bandits who robbed the barges that trafficked goods on the Tigris. As a youngster, Saddam was something of a bandit himself. He was forced to steal chickens and eggs to help feed his dysfunctional family and, by all accounts, he thrived on it. 'Saddam's clan was called al-Khatab and they were known to be violent and clever. Some viewed them as con-men and thieves,' an Iraqi defector told author Mark Bowden in May 2002. A victim of bullying, Saddam quickly developed a reliance on brute force and thuggery to survive. He carried an iron bar to defend himself whenever he left the mud-brick hut that was his home and, when challenged, was quick to rise to violence.

When he was about five or six, Saddam was tattooed as part of a tribal ritual to mark his roots, as many Iraqi children who come from rural backgrounds. He has worn the three small dark-blue dots on his hand near his right wrist all his life, and although they have faded with age they offer a telling commentary on his origins. More significantly, they are a sign of his family's low social standing.

Urban Baghdadis do not brand themselves to show their origins. Similarly, Saddam's mother, Subha, had several small black dots tattooed on her face, which is the tradition for young Iraqi peasant girls. The decorative tattoos are made up of dots, crosses and circles and can be placed on the face, hands or breasts.

Various authorities point to Saddam's innate sense of tribalism as his driving force. Writing in the *Atlantic Monthly* in 2002, Mark Bowden tells of a meeting in London with the Iraqi defector Saad al-Bazzaz, during which he offered a compelling insight into Saddam's tribalism:

> *Those who grow up in the villages are frightened of everything. There is no real law enforcement or civil society. Each family is frightened of each other, and all of them are frightened of outsiders. This is the tribal mind. The only loyalty they know is to their own family, or to their own village. Each of the families is ruled by a patriarch, and the village is ruled by the strongest of them. This loyalty to tribe comes before everything. There are no values beyond power. You can lie, cheat, steal, even kill, and it is okay so long as you are a loyal son of the village or tribe. Politics for these people is a bloody game, and it is all about getting or holding power . . . He (Saddam) is the ultimate Iraqi patriarch, the village leader who has seized a nation.*

In an interview in 1979 just weeks after his ascent to power, Saddam told one of his many official biographers, Faud Matar, that he felt 'no social disadvantage' even though he was a peasant's son whose father had abandoned him. He was initially raised by an uncle on his mother's side, Khairallah Tulfah, whose daughter, Sajida, Saddam eventually married. Tulfah was replaced for a short time by a stepfather, Hassan al-Ibrahim, after his mother remarried. Violence was part of the young Saddam's life and he saw it meted out frequently by his uncle, who would become his first political mentor. 'If he got angry he beat his relatives, but they gave back as good as they got. As a matter of fact, they hit him much more often than he did them,' Saddam told Matar. His stepfather, who was known in Tikrit as 'Hassan the Liar', was also violent, and frequently delighted in beating a young Saddam with an asphalt-covered stick, forcing him to dance in the dirt to avoid being hit.

Despite the violence, or perhaps because of it, Saddam revered his uncle Khairallah, who instilled in his young nephew a rabid nationalism and a contempt for the royal family and the British who backed them. As Saddam told Matar: 'My uncle was a nationalist, an officer in the Iraqi army . . . He always inspired us with a great nationalist feeling, which is why I never isolated the socialist program from my national outlook. The nation's problems were part of my conscience and the (Ba'ath) Party was a part of me before I became a member.'

Saddam did not learn to read and write until the age of ten. After that his education was sporadic, even though he would become a voracious reader. The most significant thing he gained from his uncle and his education was membership of the Ba'ath Party. When Saddam was in his teens, Khairallah replaced his stepfather as the authority figure. Khairallah moved from Tikrit to Baghdad, taking his son and nephew with him, and before long Saddam was running a street gang in Karkh on the western side of a bend in the Tigris near the Presidential Palace. As Con Coughlin writes in *Saddam: The Secret Life*, he was skilled in 'intimidating political opponents or, as a true son of Tikrit, anyone else who caused him offence'. He went to the Karkh high school with his cousin, but there is no proof – other than his word – that he graduated. Saddam was an academic underachiever. He failed the admission exam for entrance into the Baghdad military academy but, years later when he had risen to a reasonable level of power in the Ba'ath, he 'graduated' with a law degree from the prestigious Baghdad University. As graduations go, it was highly unorthodox, but for Saddam, using his Tikriti stand-over tactics which threatened violence at every turn, it was entirely appropriate. There are stories of him arriving unannounced at the end-of-year exams and menacingly displayed his side-arm while demanding to sit the test. The law lecturers knew that to fail Saddam could mean violence.

Through Khairallah Saddam met Ahmed Hasan al-Bakr, who became the leader of the Ba'ath Party in its unworkable alliance with President Arif in early 1963. It was Arif who ousted the Ba'ath from power on 18 November 1963, effectively humiliating the leadership and sending it to political purgatory for the next five years. Throughout this time Saddam Hussein was working his way up the party ladder, equipping himself with vile torture skills and ingratiating himself with al-Bakr, who needed a henchman. Saddam, already notorious for having murdered a rival of his uncle years before in Tikrit while in his late teens, was said to have been involved in rounding up the communists during the sadistic Ba'ath witch-hunts in the months leading up to the November coup in 1963. He also established the party's ferocious paramilitary wing, the Jihaz Haneen.

Kenneth M. Pollack, in his critically acclaimed book *The Threatening Storm*, writes that by the time Saddam took control of the Ba'ath Party on 16 July 1979, he had already cemented 'his image as the most ruthless and thorough of Iraq's dictators'. It was, writes Pollack, 'a reputation that was already well established from the brutal purges he had conducted as Bakr's second-in-command. During his years waiting in the wings, he had developed a host of methods to maintain his power, and these he now deployed to their fullest extent.'

There is an old Arab proverb that says 'he who speaks about the future lies, even when he tells the truth'. In other words, the future is unpredictable. It was a fitting adage in Iraq, where the government was a house of cards. In 1964, Saddam Hussein and fellow members of the exiled Ba'ath Party once again began plotting to assassinate President Arif. But by October, the plot was betrayed and Saddam was arrested. The conspirators were jailed while waiting to stand trial before a military tribunal on charges of attempting to overthrow the ruling regime.

Shawket Najim, who had been promoted to the rank of general, was on the military court to hear the charges but, as in most countries, the wheels of justice turned slowly, and on 23 July 1966, after eighteen months in jail, Saddam escaped. According to Coughlin, he either befriended his guards en route to the court and persuaded them to let him escape – a theory propagated by Saddam's biographer Faud Matar – or he feigned an illness in jail and escaped while on his way to hospital for treatment.

For the next two years the leadership of the Ba'ath Party was hard at work secretly planning another coup they nicknamed *rashad*, which translates as 'guidance'. Saddam

Hussein was among the revolutionaries. At 3 am on 17 July 1968, civilian Ba'ath members and Ba'athists inside the military toppled the regime of President Abdul ar-Rahman Arif, who had succeeded his brother in 1966 when Abdul Salam Arif was killed in a helicopter crash. Tanks rumbled through the streets of Baghdad and surrounded the Republican Palace where the president was sleeping. The palace was one of Baghdad's most impressive buildings. Built on the banks of the Tigris after the fall of the monarchy in 1958, it was the nerve centre of Iraq's government and the ultimate seat of power. The entrance hall to the main palace building is mounted by a huge turquoise dome that rests over an eight-sided room soaring three storeys high. A giant gold-and-crystal chandelier hangs from the top of the dome. In the decades that followed the coup its carved white marble walls would be decorated with poems in praise of Saddam Hussein, etched in huge gold letters. The leaders of the coup fired artillery over the palace to warn the president that his time had come. Realising he had no options, the president surrendered. 'The Ba'ath Party has taken control of the country,' he was told. Not a single life was lost in the coup.

General al-Bakr was named president. Saddam Hussein was rewarded with the plum role of ensuring national security. Not only had Iraq's leadership been ousted, but the army that had supported and protected the regime for the previous five years was about to undergo a major restructure. General Shawket Najim would not be spared. He was of the old order and the old order had not been kind to the Ba'ath Party. Guzin recalls the coldness of her father's dismissal. 'On the first day of the revolution of Saddam Hussein, they sent my father a letter that said, "You are not acceptable, you are retired". They said "go home".' At the age of forty-four and after serving his country for twenty-six years, Shawket Najim's army career was over.

Guzin, who was twelve years old at the time, remembers that her father was shattered at the regime change and the reversal of fortune of his beloved military. The next day at 7 am, Shawket was sitting at the breakfast table with Majida and their two daughters, trying to understand how the Ba'ath Party had succeeded. He was still wearing his pyjamas and listening to the radio when two men from the intelligence service knocked on the front door of the house in Al Yarmouk. They told him he was being transported to the Republican Palace, a short distance away. The girls were not too young to fully understand the awfulness of what was about to happen. Majida, too, must have been terrified. Memories of the torture of communists and leftists at Qasr al-Nihayah during the Ba'ath Party's brief flirtation with power in 1963 would have struck a chill in her heart.

After allowing Shawket the dignity of changing from his pyjamas into civilian dress the two men, who Guzin now believes were from Saddam Hussein's Jihaz Haneen, escorted him outside to a parked white Volkswagen Beetle. His horrified wife and children looked on. They did not know if they would ever see him again. The former General Shawket Najim was blindfolded and the nameless men forcibly folded him into the back seat of the tiny car and drove to the Republican Palace, newly occupied by President al-Bakr and surrounded by his loyalists and henchmen.

Twelve hours later, Shawket returned to his family but, according to Guzin, he never said a word about what had happened inside the palace and no amount of prompting could cajole any answers to their questions. All Shawket said he knew was that a relative of Majida's well-connected family in Jordan who was a high-ranking member of the Jordanian Ba'ath Party had intervened and saved his life. Fearing he had suffered the same fate as so many enemies of the Ba'ath Party years before inside the notorious Palace of the End, Majida and Guzin asked over and over if Shawket had been tortured or physically threatened. Shawket insisted he had not been hurt at all, probably as a result of Majida's family connections; such connections, in Arab societies, count for a lot.

Whether he was protecting his family from the truth or just telling it straight, Guzin will never know. What she did know, even then as a young girl of twelve, was that her Iraq had changed irrevocably. It had begun its slow and steady descent into a dictatorship. A decade later, Iraq would be a country ruled by fear.

Chapter Six

Guzin Najim had been bold all her life. The word 'compromise' was not in her personal lexicon and if there was a hidden challenge, she would find it, embrace it and conquer it. She was a natural leader and came with personality enough for two people, maybe even three. It took only one look to know that she was the type of girl who would take a dare and then, with a cheeky glint in her eye, raise it some, not to throw down the gauntlet to anyone else, but to test herself. In fact, Guzin was so adventurous and sassy that she believed there was absolutely nothing she couldn't do. Which made it all that much more difficult to swallow when she discovered that she couldn't follow in the footsteps of her adored father Shawket.

While growing up, Guzin, like many girls, saw her father as all knowing, all doing – an omnipotent figure who cast an enormous shadow – and she wanted to be just like him. Throughout her childhood she asked, 'Baba, why can't I be like you, why can't I join the army?'. To a girl who had been brought up fully believing that she was equal to any man, it didn't seem fair that she couldn't retrace her father's footsteps and it seemed doubly unfair, a right insult even, that her country didn't share her opinion. Her father would laugh and tell her that she should focus on her studies and get a good education and, the way he said it, it sounded more than reasonable, so that's exactly what she did. Guzin had always dreamed of becoming a leader, a role she naturally assumed among her friends and peers at school, and she knew to achieve that she had to be educated.

Guzin graduated dux from high school at the age of sixteen in the company of her best friend Sana. Long ago the girls had formed a durable friendship typical of teenagers and they shared their hopes and built their dreams in tandem, imagining what it would be like to fall in love and travel the world. Their dreams were rich and colourful and they took on a life of their own because at that age and in their Arabic society, when it came to boys, dreaming was all they had. Teen romances of the sort that their western counterparts enjoyed were simply unheard of.

Shawket's daughters were not allowed out on their own nor were they permitted to visit the homes of their friends for social events, no matter how well chaperoned they were. It wasn't that Shawket didn't trust Guzin and Buthaina, but somewhere deep in his heart he didn't trust the inflexible expectations of their culture, which meant that his daughters' futures would be secure only if he could guarantee their virtuousness. It was all stitched into the intricate code of Arab honour.

'Until I went to university my parents didn't let us go to our friends' houses at all, they just let the others come to us because they wanted to be sure we were not doing the wrong things. This is our society,' Guzin says. 'Nobody touches us. We don't have boyfriends. We don't go out together like Europeans. In our society it's not allowed and we didn't do anything without our parents knowing, never, not until we married.

'We can see boys but just with our families – just like old English families – and we have to be virgins. Our husband must be the first man in our life. I like this. I like this very much and I believe in it. This is important. Every society, of course, has its beliefs and it doesn't mean that others are wrong and I am right, no, no, no. It's just our society and our traditions.'

Shawket had not worked since he was forcibly retired from the Iraqi army by the Ba'ath Party in 1968, but he didn't need to. He was a man of independent wealth and his income was further supplemented by Majida's own prosperous background. To escape the changes and uncertainty in Baghdad in the aftermath of his dismissal, he took the family on a four-month holiday through Europe. Guzin remembers the tension at home while Shawket waited for the new government to approve the visas which would allow the family to travel beyond Iraq's border. It was a dicey proposition. As soon as he had secured them, Shawket gave the family a few hours to pack and they were on the road by three o'clock that afternoon.

They travelled first to Jordan via the Baghdad–Jordan road across the desolate western desert of Iraq, but their Mercedes sedan broke down just past Ar Ramadi en route to Ar Rutba. They were towed several hundred kilometres into the city centre, where Shawket paid a premium to have the car exhaust fixed immediately. He was secretly worried that the new regime would act capriciously and revoke the visas so he wanted his family out of Iraq as soon as humanly possible. They reached Jordan at eleven o'clock the next morning. Guzin didn't know it then, but she would take that same route in a daring escape exactly thirty years later. They stayed one night at her grandfather Ali Neyazi Al Tell's home in Irbid before leaving for Syria, a journey which involved another nerve-racking experience, this time at the border between Jordan and Syria.

Thirty-five years later, Guzin is reading her own hand-writing in the journal she shared with her father. 'I have written, "We were frightened because maybe the Syrian Government will not let my father, a retired Iraqi general, go through their country". We were very frightened, but thank God, they did.' Raising her eyes to the ceiling and clasping her hands before her as if in prayer, Guzin says, 'We said, "Insh'Allah, maybe they will". It means if it is God's will, they will let us through. And they did.'

For four months they travelled through Turkey, Bulgaria and Yugoslavia, then to Salzburg and on to Frankfurt, Stuttgart, Munich and Bonn. Shawket permitted Guzin to take her best friend Sana for company, possibly thinking her presence would confirm to suspicious government officials that this was to be a family holiday, not an escape. Even now, when they speak Guzin and Sana revert to the girlish-ness they once shared so effortlessly and laugh at the memories of the holiday in which they noticed boys for the first time. Both are in their late forties now, but back then boys were a complete mystery.

By the time the family arrived back in Baghdad, the country was on its new course under the Ba'athist govern-ment. Everything and everyone Shawket had once been so familiar with was gone and he never truly felt at home in

Iraq again. He and Majida were still a couple of considerable means and influence, but things had changed markedly. He once orbited the axis of power in Baghdad and now he did nothing. The only way Shawket found he could distract and distance himself from his old life was to focus almost exclusively on his family, particularly his clever Guzin.

In November 1971, Shawket enrolled his daughter in the American University in Beirut for a year-long bridging course between high school and university. The course was a reward for her achievement in high school but, more significantly, it marked Guzin's transition to womanhood, because it would be the first time she was ever away from the sanctuary of family life. Shawket and Majida took Guzin to Beirut to ensure she settled in safely, and before leaving he wrote in the journal: 'Dear Guzin, you are going to Beirut to study. I feel that I cannot live without you because I am very close to you, but I am sure you will be good and strong and you will make me proud. I trust you very much and trust that you will be well behaved. I am weeping because you will not be here, and your mother is crying also.'

It was only a brief note but Guzin understood its meaning and welcomed its weight of responsibility. She was Shawket Najim's firstborn and, even though she was a girl, she had been treated with the customary respect and privilege usually accorded to a firstborn son. She carried Shawket's name and always would – even after she married. As much as Guzin did not want to disappoint her father, she desperately did not want to dishonour his family reputation. That she could never undo.

Guzin's year in Beirut was a success and before she knew it she was living back at home in Al Yarmouk with her parents. She started a bachelor degree in international law and politics at the medieval Al Mustansiriya University on the eastern bank of the Tigris in the old part of Baghdad. The majestic sand-coloured building with high arched doorways and finely carved masonry was built in 1233 to promote an ecumenical form of Sunni Islam. The grand edifices and the stores of knowledge held inside gave Guzin a deep sense of her country's history. Baghdad in the thirteenth century had been the beating heart of a growing Islamic empire and the university played an integral role in ensuring the city's intellectual and religious preeminence in the region.

More recently, Al Mustansiriya has been projected into the international spotlight for other reasons. Since the end of the first Gulf War in 1991, the university has twice been bombed by allied forces. The first time was during the US administration of President Bill Clinton in 1998 after Iraq, in breach of the UN sanctions, expelled United Nations' weapons inspectors. The second attack came on 23 March 2003 during the second Gulf War to remove Saddam Hussein from his dictatorial reign of terror over the country.

Perhaps poetically, and maybe even defiantly, the hallowed halls and ancient corridors of academia at Al Mustansiriya remain standing even now. For Guzin, the resilience of the glorious building would become a metaphor for her own life.

◆ ◆ ◆

Ra'ad Mohammed Said Khamis Al-Qaysi was born on 12 July 1947 in Istanbul, the beautiful port city of Turkey located on the mighty Bosporus, which separates the two continents of Europe and Asia. Ra'ad, whose name meant 'thunder' was the elder of the two sons of Mohammed Said and Fakhira Abdul Latif Nouri. They were an upper class family and well respected in the community. Ra'ad's father was an Iraqi diplomat whose career was propelled to stellar heights during the years of the constitutional monarchy of King Faisal II. His grandfather was a member of the first all-Iraqi ministry under the first King Faisal. Ra'ad's grandfather took up a position in the defence ministry, which was arguably one of the most important departments in the new government.

With his paternal pedigree, Ra'ad came to appreciate the finer things of an old, imperial Baghdad, which was heavily influenced by the genteel and proper presence of the British. It was an era when men of standing never stepped out in anything other than jaunty bowler hats and sharply tailored suits of the finest wool lined with silk, accessorised with gold fob chains and wind-up watches. Starched handkerchiefs with fierce edges peaked out from the top pockets of their suit jackets. In summer, the men wore snappy straw boaters and crisp white suits cut from the softest Egyptian cotton. Women, if they did not adhere to the hijab, wore chic frocks in sumptuous fabrics, seamed stockings held up by suspender belts, and elegant hats. They carried dainty handbags over their forearms as if they had stepped from the pages of fashion magazines.

Ra'ad's mother, Fakhira, was born in Baghdad in 1927 and educated at the exclusive Adhamiah Secondary School for Girls. She later became an artist and was known for her signature landscapes and seascapes. Her vibrant oil paintings captured brilliant, fiery red sunsets on the horizon over the Dead Sea and ice-blue waterfalls cascading from the

Turkish mountains. Mohammed was posted to the Iraqi Embassy in Turkey, so that was where the newlyweds made their first home. There in Istanbul in 1947, she gave birth to Ra'ad and, two years later, to another son she named Mohanned.

A striking woman with fine features and long, elegant fingers, Fakhira completed her studies at the American Cultural Institute in Istanbul in 1959 while her husband worked in the potentially explosive world of diplomacy. Eventually, Fakhira would be employed by the United Nations in the United Arab Emirates and Canada. Based in Abu Dhabi, she was an expert instructor in women's handicrafts and worked with thirteen women's community groups under the International Labor Office. She taught women how to improve the standards of traditional Arab dressmaking. Part of her brief was to adapt the trademark handmade decorative elements that adorn the fabric known as *tallies* and embroideries.

The first thirteen years of her eldest son's life were spent in Turkey. Ra'ad was educated at a succession of prestigious international schools where he learnt several languages, including English, which he spoke with perfectly rounded vowels. Ironically, he hadn't learned to read, write or speak Arabic, the native language of his parents. Fakhira Nouri and Mohammed Said spent their time in Turkey as part of a glamorous circle of expatriate diplomats. But the glittering life came to an end abruptly when Mohammed was recalled to Baghdad in 1959. A few months earlier, the bloody revolution had deposed the monarchy, beginning a decade-long era of coups and rickety regimes. From 1959 to 1964 the family lived in Baghdad but they were hollow years. Ra'ad tried desperately to catch up on his Arabic but the language barrier meant his studies were disjointed and he ultimately lost three years of schooling.

In 1964 the Iraqi regime packed his father Mohammed Said off to the embassy in Cairo where Ra'ad finally completed his secondary education just a few years behind schedule. His mother made the best use of the posting and took a four-year degree at the Fine Arts Academy in downtown Cairo. Four years later, the Ba'ath Party came out of the political wilderness and into power and once again the family was recalled to Baghdad. Swings and roundabouts.

This time the chances were strong that Mohammed Said would not receive another foreign posting under Ba'ath rule. Ra'ad, with his international schooling and high school diplomas, decided to study law at the prestigious Al Mustansiriya University.

He was well into the fourth year of a five-year degree when he spotted Guzin Najim standing in the students' union hallway looking at a noticeboard with her best friend, Sana.

Guzin was a petite and striking eighteen-year-old with sultry, almond-shaped eyes that recalled the beauty of Cleopatra. Ra'ad was short and chubby and his baby-faced looks were soft and kind. He wore huge dark-framed spectacles and had his thick black hair cut in a short style combed to one side. Ra'ad was shy, considered, and on paper he was no match for Guzin's boundless enthusiasm, but from the moment he spotted the auburn-haired beauty, he knew he never wanted to let her out of his sight.

Part of the attraction was her infectious laugh which was so easy and free that it swept up anyone who was within earshot. But a bigger part of it was the way she carried herself. Guzin was self-indulgently high-spirited and had a rare confidence. She wore her dark hair cut short and tucked behind her ears in the style made popular by the English model Twiggy, and she preferred the contemporary European fashions of the time – mini-skirts and colourful shirts, high heels and stockings. She was not alone but plenty of other women at the university wore the abaya, the traditional long dress of Iraq. That was the beauty of modern Iraq – it was a religious and ethnic melting pot. Just an hour out of Baghdad were the holy Shi'ite Muslim cities of Najaf and Karbala where women are totally covered and men flagellate themselves with chains as part of the holy festival of Muharram. It was a world away from the more western lifestyle of Ra'ad and Guzin and their contemporaries in Baghdad.

As serendipity would have it, Ra'ad's and Guzin's families travelled in the same circles of Baghdad's high society and were friends. Their fathers were both moderate Sunni Muslims. They came from privileged backgrounds and, sharing similar political beliefs, suffered the same vicissitudes of fortune under successive regimes. Even so, Ra'ad had grown up in Turkey and later Egypt, while Guzin was raised in Baghdad and Jordan, so their paths never crossed until the early 1970s when both lived in the heart of the Iraqi capital.

Guzin recognised the 26-year-old Ra'ad from a previous social event they both attended with their parents, and noticed him noticing her. He was always smiling but Ra'ad was too shy to make a move and, even though Guzin was wilful and not short of an opinion, it was not her style to approach him. She was too sophisticated and cool to do that. So she waited. Ra'ad finally plucked up the courage to chat, and his opening line showed a certain degree of resourcefulness which impressed her. She also noticed he had eyes the colour of dark honey.

'He said to me, "Your name is Turkish, are you Turkish? You certainly don't look Iraqi", and so we began to speak in Turkish,' Guzin says now, blushing, still enchanted by the memory and flattered that Ra'ad knew the origins of her unusual name. 'He was very nice. His father was a diplomat and he lived a very good life, a diplomat's life. He has a very nice mother, very intelligent and very polite. She acts just like a princess. Ra'ad was very polite and had excellent etiquette – it means a lot to him and his family, so he knew how to deal with me.'

Their romance started slowly, but Ra'ad confessed later that he was instantly besotted with Guzin. She was dynamic and he was drawn to her purposefulness and leadership. She was the pivot around which her circle of friends rotated – always the centre of attention, whether it be organising picnics or study groups with fellow students. Where Guzin was ebullient and outspoken, Ra'ad was reserved and shy. She was a natural beauty, and he was a man of average height and looks, but what he lacked in looks he made up for with his intellect.

Ra'ad pursued Guzin relentlessly, spending as much time as he could with her walking around the grounds of Al Mustansiriya. The spectacular architecture, with its fretwork and long archways that carried the whispers of ancient history, was conducive to romance. Even though it took Guzin a little longer to understand her emotions, she had no doubt she was falling in love. They had coffee in the students' café and spent time poring over books in the 700-year-old library. But while ardent in his pursuit of Guzin,

Ra'ad never tried to steer her from the strict morality of her upbringing. They were never alone, and they never held hands. Guzin couldn't and Ra'ad wouldn't dare. It was not the way she had been brought up. 'He knew I mustn't cheat my father at all. He respected me very much,' Guzin recalls.

Sure enough, Ra'ad's persistence paid off and the young couple were soon in love. It was a brand new feeling for Guzin, the first time she had ever felt butterflies when she saw a man. When Ra'ad finally summoned the courage to tell her how he felt, he was so nervous that he went red in the face, started to stammer and dropped his books. Guzin reverted to type and took the lead: 'I can't understand what you want to say, just say it,' she insisted. Then he did.

'He said, "From the first day I knew I would marry this girl, or I would never marry". He said to me, "You know, Guzin, we are the same level, our families are good families", and then he stopped. I have more courage than him so I said, "Okay".' That was Guzin's way of saying yes. 'He went by car directly to his mother to tell her. The second day after that his mother began to send to me, with Ra'ad, some cake, a thermos of tea, sandwiches. Every day I had something from his mother.'

Guzin, however, didn't quite know how to broach the subject with her parents. She didn't want them to think that she had spun off their moral compass by falling for a young man at university, and she certainly didn't want them to think that she had done anything that would make them doubt her integrity. But she wanted them to know that she had her sights set on a man from the same background as hers and who was known to their family, and that he similarly had his sights set on her. As it happened, just at that time Ra'ad's mother was interviewed in an Arabic lifestyle magazine not unlike *Vogue Living*. Guzin decided to show the magazine to her mother, Majida, on the off-chance that she would read the article featuring Fakhira. Guzin thought it was a clever plan, and she was right. Majida turned the page and instantly twigged, demanding: 'What's happening? Do you know her son? Tell me!' Guzin admitted that she did and that she liked Ra'ad. It was enough to set the wheels in motion. After all, Guzin was now eighteen, an age when many Middle Eastern girls think of marriage and motherhood.

Once Ra'ad and Guzin told their parents of their affections for each other, Fakhira Nouri began to accompany Ra'ad on visits to Guzin and her family in Al Yarmouk, building on the longstanding acquaintance between the two families. She could see the attraction between the young couple and, after a time, knew that they had both agreed to be husband and wife. Finally, after weeks of visiting, Fakhira told Majida, 'We want Guzin to be Ra'ad's wife'. To seal the decision, Fakhira gave Guzin a delicate antique diamond bracelet with an intricate filigree design.

Many girls in Arabic countries do not date in the same sense that western women do. If two people show an interest in each other, their families meet and if everyone is of the same opinion, they agree for the couple to marry. After the official engagement, the couple begin a courtship during which they get to know each other, but it remains chaste. The process is elaborate and not always entirely successful. After all, the map of the human heart is not easy to chart.

The next step is even more elaborate and confronting. Guzin was worried that her father would say no to the agreement because she had met her future husband at the university, but she had the luxury of tradition to fall back on.

It's customary for men who know the prospective groom to join him in a visit to the father of the prospective bride. Ra'ad's father, together with his two sons, convened a group of male relatives and friends and took them to Shawket Najim's house. They stood behind Ra'ad as he asked for Guzin's hand in marriage. There were more than forty men inside the home – all of them from very high positions in Baghdad society. Their presence was meant to assure Shawket that the young man asking for his daughter's hand in marriage was one of the finest fellows around. By simply being there, each and every one was personally vouching for Ra'ad's integrity and honour – but also that of his family. It is an important tradition. Among their number was Ra'ad's uncle Hassan Rydha, a high court judge, who spoke directly to Shawket. 'We want Guzin to marry Ra'ad. Are you going to say yes or no?'

'When anybody in our society comes to ask somebody to marry them they send the men first of all. Of course, the agreement between the women has been made, it's okay, then the men will come,' Guzin says. Fakhira came too but she remained with Majida and Guzin in another room while the men conducted their business. Once Shawket said yes, that he agreed, Fakhira offered flowers to the family and they celebrated with sweet Iraqi tea. The men chatted, pleased that they had successfully fulfilled their function.

In the days that followed, Ra'ad, Guzin and their mothers went shopping for jewellery as is the custom in Iraq, and Shawket and Majida hosted a sumptuous banquet to officially announce the engagement. Table upon table was laid with traditional Iraqi food and guests from both families joined in the festivities. Guzin was deliriously happy. She wore a new long baby blue dress made from the softest, shimmering chiffon with patterned circles embroidered with white flowers circled in silver thread. It had a modest round neckline, showcasing perfectly an exquisite gold necklace that featured stunning round medals with arabesque designs strung together by an elegant chain. Ra'ad was more than generous with his gifts of gold, prompting Shawket to comment during his speech to the families: 'Why did you bring all of these things? We didn't sell Guzin and we don't want jewellery. We just want our daughter to live in peace, calmly, with your son'. Guzin remembers that Ra'ad's mother Fakhira replied: 'No, we must bring more than that for her'.

Fakhira's riposte was a compliment, the essence of it being that she and her husband respected Shawket Najim and Majida Al Tell. They were more than happy that their families were merging. In Iraq, when couples marry, so too, in effect, do their families. Fakhira didn't actually have to say as much, for it was understood by everyone there. To a man, and a few good women besides, they all believed this marriage would work – in more ways than one.

The engagement would last less than a year but it didn't give Guzin and Ra'ad a licence for intimacy. In fact, the same rules applied. They were passionately, intensely in love but they were rarely alone. They could spend hours together at university, but they were always with friends and could never steal a private moment. It was driving them crazy, so Ra'ad developed a system whereby he would ring Guzin at home every night at six o'clock. Guzin rushed to answer the phone before anyone else got to it, always nervous that her father would pick it up and expose their game. When she answered, Ra'ad simply said: 'Is this Woolworth's?'. It sounds terribly corny but, as Guzin admits now, it was the only way they could share a private moment. 'I said, "Yes" and he said, "Okay" and hung up. He said it was just to hear my voice.' The secrecy added to the frisson.

The lovestruck couple devised other ways to spend time together. While playing games in the garden at Guzin's home, where they would be discreetly chaperoned by her parents, Ra'ad would accidentally fall over her just so he could brush her arm or touch her face. One time Shawket and Majida drove house guests to the airport for a flight back to London. They left at 6 am and were expected to be gone for two hours. Ra'ad had timed the trip down to the last second. As soon as the car pulled out of the garage and turned into the street, he was on the phone to Guzin. 'We spoke for two hours, just about silly things,' Guzin says, laughing. 'Just like young teenagers.'

Whenever Shawket and Majida took their daughters out, Ra'ad would miraculously appear, as if by pure chance. Without fail, Guzin's parents politely asked him to join them, believing that to do otherwise would be rude. Guzin is sure her mother knew, but Majida didn't say a word, and if her father was any the wiser, he didn't let on either. They had probably done the same thing themselves years before.

The only hiccup for the couple came soon after Ra'ad graduated from Al Mustansiriya University. Buoyed by the excitement of finishing his law degree, he asked Guzin to go alone with him to his home. She was outraged, and told him so. She considered Ra'ad's invitation crude and thought it showed a lack of respect for her. 'For one month, I didn't speak to him. I told him, "I am not your girlfriend, I am not like these girls who do these things. You must respect me". He said, "Please, Guzin, I am sorry", but I refused. He brought his mother to ask me to forgive him. She respected me for it. In our tradition it must not happen. If a man respects a woman he will wait for marriage.'

The faux pas rattled Ra'ad to his very bones. He was terrified that Guzin wouldn't forgive him and that he'd lost her. It took months before he could muster the courage to kiss his betrothed and, when he did, it was a quick peck on the lips while they stood in her family kitchen. It was a monumental risk because Guzin's and his parents were both sitting in the garden sipping tea, just a few metres away, separated by only a pane of glass. Guzin was worried her father would walk in and catch them, but it gave her an enormous thrill just the same. The next kiss was even more daring. They arranged a secret rendezvous near the Baghdad International Airport so they could spend just five minutes alone. Guzin drove in the family Mercedes, and Ra'ad got there under his own steam. They kissed, nothing more, and drove back to Guzin's house in separate cars. Guzin was red-faced and nervous, worried that she would get caught for her innocent indiscretion. The next time Ra'ad tried something, she ran away.

Guzin and Ra'ad were married on Thursday 20 June 1974 at an extravagant function at Ra'ad's family home in Al Mansour. She was nineteen. He was twenty-six. He was the love of her life. She meant everything and more to him.

Guzin wore a fashionable white dress with a seven-metre train that fanned out and followed her like a billowing cloud. Before the ceremony, a tearful Shawket asked his daughter if she was sure that Ra'ad was the right man for her. She said yes, and he cried some more – heartbroken at losing a daughter, yet happy that she was now a woman. During the wedding service Ra'ad gave his new bride a turquoise and gold necklace and his relatives gave her exquisite gold bracelets, and an assortment of rings and necklaces. Majida gave her daughter a diamond. Her father gave her advice: 'If a girl is not happy, this jewellery will do nothing.'

The reception was held in the garden, which was in full bloom. The infernal heat of an Iraqi summer had held its fire and a gentle breeze kept temperatures down. Tables were covered with fragrant red rose petals. Waiters served guests an endless array of food, some of it European and some of it traditional Iraqi, such as *masgouf*, a fish speciality, and *quzi*, lamb stuffed and roasted with a special blend of spices. Some revellers ignored the custom of their Islamic faith and enjoyed a spirituous drop or two and in this prestigious company, no one seemed to notice or, for that matter, mind. The Iraq of Ra'ad and Guzin was fashionable and progressive, more European than Arab. Guests danced well into the night. Artists mixed with politicians who chatted with businessmen who hobnobbed with diplomats. It was just like the old days. Guzin radiated charm and grace as she greeted her guests. Those who had known her as a winsome girl now saw her as an accomplished woman. Ra'ad was chuffed, wearing his pride in a grin for all to see. Until now, he was an unfinished man, but with Guzin he felt complete.

Once married, Guzin and Ra'ad wasted no time. The next day they were on a plane heading for their honeymoon in London. Their destination couldn't have been more different from Baghdad. In the streets at home they heard the familiar reedy sound of the oud, a traditional fretless 13-string instrument which is strummed using a feather, or the voice of a meuzzin calling Muslims to prayer from the minaret of a nearby mosque. In London, Guzin and Ra'ad were accosted by cheeky cabbies shouting, ''allo, guv,' and barrow-boys near Leicester Square selling their goods with an "ow's ya fahvver?' They had landed in the middle of a cultural and political watershed. Glam rock and punk rock were emerging from the musical 'underground' and had catapulted over the sixties icons like the Rolling Stones and disbanded Beatles. Discos were the new new thing and feminism was the old new thing. Television had gone colour, a female was about to become leader of the Tories and terrorism went public in the streets of London. Accustomed to Iraq's ubiquitous armed militias and menacing intelligence service officers, they were shocked to see unarmed bobbies on the beat in the streets of London, wearing funny helmets and carrying nothing more than a truncheon to keep miscreants at bay. Women could drink in pubs and bars and stay out late – and they could do it on their own. Fashions were come as you please.

London was another world, and Guzin and Ra'ad were hooked. They visited Madame Tussaud's Wax Museum, swam at Brighton Beach, had dinner in fancy restaurants, posed for pictures in front of red telephone boxes and next to Beefeater guardsmen, and went shopping on Bond Street and in Harrods and Selfridges.

The honeymoon turned into an extended family holiday when Guzin's parents and sister finished their own European vacation and joined the newlyweds in London. Together they walked through the sites they had come to know on the Monopoly board, toured Piccadilly Circus and strolled along the Thames. Guzin insisted that they drop into a disco on Queensway and she led the charge down a steep stairwell into a darkened, crowded, noisy room with a mirror-ball spinning from the ceiling, then straight back up again. 'I didn't like it.'

In Soho they walked past a strip club and adult shop, 'something strange', she says now, meaning it was completely different to the stores in the better streets of Baghdad. Guzin, who usually carried herself with such elan, became surprisingly coy. Ra'ad nipped inside to buy a nudie magazine to show her. 'When we got back to the house I couldn't look at it. I was always very shy about those things and my husband laughed at me and I said, "I can't, I can't", and I never looked. Even now, I can't look at these things. I feel these are very special things, and always I feel sorry for those who do these things just for money.'

For once, Ra'ad had the upper hand.

Chapter Seven

Preparing for the challenges of life after marriage can be exhausting, but for Guzin, it took a sum total of four hours the day before she and Ra'ad tied the knot. She didn't need to house hunt or shop for furniture at bargain-basement prices like so many pending newlyweds, because after the honeymoon she moved into her new husband's family home. All she had to do was pack some personal effects and a few suitcases of clothes, load up her car and drive the short distance from her home in Al Yarmouk to Ra'ad's in the upmarket Al Mansour district. With Buthaina as her chaperone – Ra'ad was in the house – Guzin spent a few hours establishing a niche and finding the right spot for her belongings. She put her clothes in a cupboard and set picture frames on the dresser and wandered around exploring the house with her sister. There was little else to do. Ra'ad's mother, Fakhira, had told her that furniture and other essentials would be taken care of as part of their wedding present. As for new clothes and other knick-knacks, she suggested that

Guzin go on a shopping spree during their honeymoon in London and she gleefully agreed.

The house on Princess Street, or *Shari Al-Amirat* as it is known in Arabic, was big enough to accommodate the newlyweds without cramping their style or invading their privacy. Built on a massive block of land set back behind a huge brick wall, the two-storey villa had five bedrooms – three upstairs and two downstairs – three bathrooms, a kitchen large enough to feed an army, and three luxurious salons in which they could read, watch television or simply lounge around and talk. Entry was through a grand hall, the walls of which were hung with Fakhira's landscape paintings. A verandah ran along the front of the house and in the front garden sat an old swing surrounded by a rhapsody of colourful blooms. The backyard was studded with fruit trees producing a small harvest of lemons, limes, oranges and olives and tended to by a regular gardener. Ra'ad's parents had their own section of the house and he and his bride were given another area that was almost completely self-contained. The custom in Iraqi is to live in extended families, and the upper-class lifestyle Ra'ad and Guzin were accustomed to meant that they would rarely, if ever, dine alone, which was fortunate for Ra'ad, because his wife admitted she was not a very good cook. When pressed, she confessed that she actually hated it.

When they returned from their honeymoon, Ra'ad's family made good on their promise and the newlyweds were presented with several flawless pieces of Louis XV furniture which had been imported from France. The gift included a sofa and dining setting upholstered in plush red velvet with ornately carved arms and legs painted gold. As well, they were given an exquisite French provincial styled armoire.

The only thing Ra'ad and Guzin bought was a matching bedroom setting in a rare white timber. Guzin had an eye for style. She decorated their quarters with antiques from Paris and covered the floors in sumptuous kilims from Turkey and Persian rugs she spotted in the teeming bazaars of Baghdad. Like many Iraqi brides of a certain social standing, Guzin had been given a lot of gold as wedding gifts, and by the time they were settled in the Princess Street house, they wanted for nothing.

Al Mansour was then, and still is now, one of the most fashionable and exclusive districts in the thriving metropolis of Baghdad and was named for the caliph who built Baghdad and conquered the surrounding lands for Islam. Members of the old upper class who were educated in the days of the monarchy had long ago established themselves in the area, and by the 1970s the district had become something of a mini United Nations. Embassies and diplomatic residences filled the pretty streets that ran between the two main thoroughfares, Al Mansour and Al Fallujah, which serviced the neighbourhood. A villa in the suburb was coveted by the growing bourgeoisie and affluent middle class, most of whom had graduated with degrees from leading American, European and Middle Eastern universities and spoke near-fluent English. Cafés, chic restaurants and elegant shops lined the wide, tree-shaded boulevards, and the expensive homes were tended to by a small army of hired help. Clubs and five-star hotels were frequented by the locals, many of whom were transported in chauffeur-driven cars. It was nothing to see a high-powered government official stepping out of a limousine escorted by boundary riders to meet with a foreign head of state.

When Guzin and Ra'ad moved to Al Mansour, Iraq was

under the leadership of Ba'ath Party President al-Bakr, who had risen to power in the bloodless coup of 1968. The country was in a period of comparative stability and growing prosperity, even if Machiavellian politics were still being played out behind closed doors and would erupt later that decade. The Ba'ath Party nationalised the oil industry, removing it from the hands of international petroleum companies, and a subsequent oil boom promised much to many. Iraq was able to produce three million barrels of oil a day, and the wealth it generated helped the Ba'ath fund programs which linked villages to the national electricity grid and gave free televisions and refrigerators to the poor. Thanks to the oil reserves lying deep below Iraq's scorched and ancient earth, the country was one of the richest in the Middle East. As well, it was emerging as a dominant political force in the region.

Throughout the decade the standard of living for ordinary Iraqis had been rising, food was cheap and education was free from kindergarten through to university. The general feeling of well-being in Iraq crossed almost all levels of society. It had been years since Iraq had had any real sense of constancy and, even though the political structure of the nation was fragile underneath, on the surface most of its people felt a relative sense of calm.

Rich Baghdadi gentlemen bought their suits from Haroot, an expensive tailor in the city's Chaakia district. They socialised at al-Alwiya, a club which had been made famous by the British during the halcyon days of the monarchy. Guzin and Ra'ad became members at the ritzy Al Rasheed hotel on the western banks of the Tigris, which was then the epitome of style with exclusive stores lining the lobby. It gave them access to a swimming pool – a veritable luxury in the desert climate – and elegant dining facilities which they often used.

Ra'ad landed a job at the department of foreign affairs. He had enjoyed his childhood abroad and loved immersing himself in exotic cultures, and had always wanted to follow in his father's footsteps. Ra'ad understood the importance of diplomatic relations, particularly in the Middle East, which was so volatile. His father had shown him how the diplomatic world worked first-hand and no matter which way he looked at it, the prestige and prominence of a life of diplomacy appealed to him. Diplomats were refined and cultured; they knew how to entertain and behave. They travelled and were involved in politics. What's more, to a boy who grew up with fluid borders, diplomats looked as though they were never bored. Relying on his strong academic performance and with a little help from his father, Ra'ad joined the department of foreign affairs as a junior officer in 1974. By now he was fluent in Arabic, having studied hard throughout the latter years of high school and at university. It was his first job as a married man and Guzin was proud of her new husband. For her, his entry into diplomatic life was not only a professional achievement, it was a social one as well.

Ra'ad spent nine months studying the arcane world of diplomacy at a special course set up by the department in its building in downtown Baghdad. He had to learn numerous protocols for dealing with dignitaries from a vast array of foreign countries – each with its own set of customs and philosophies. He was taught the finer points of leading delegations on behalf of Iraq, which included advice about what to say and when to say it. It was heady business, but also incredibly serious. One wrong gesture, one slip of the tongue, one misplaced wink or nod, and the gossamer connections of international relations could be destroyed.

Guzin, who would graduate with a degree in international law and politics in 1977, settled effortlessly into life in Al Mansour. She spent her days at university, reading magazines and keeping fit by swimming at the Al Mansour Club.

She visited her parents daily. They were a ten-minute walk away, and even though she was now a married woman, she missed them desperately. If she wasn't having lunch with them, she would corral a group of friends from school and university and spend hours in chic cafés chatting over kebabs and coffee. She got to know the local markets and every nook and cranny in the crowded bazaars where vendors sold everything from household utensils to leather goods and jewellery. Guzin ferreted out the best places to find the most luxurious carpets at the most competitive prices. After oil, carpets are the Muslim world's best commodity, and Guzin could tell the real McCoy from a cheap impostor at some distance.

At every opportunity Guzin drove into the heart of Baghdad to meet her husband for lunch on the banks of the Tigris near the department of foreign affairs. They were a young couple in love and every minute together was precious. Their favourite restaurant was Al Ena'a Althahaby (The Golden Plate), and they soon became regulars. The waiters knew their order by heart: grilled lamb chops followed by special Iraqi tea. The evenings were spent socialising and, more often than not, Guzin and Ra'ad would join his cousin Manahil and her husband, Amer, at a local Lebanese café. Guzin lived the life of a pampered princess and Ra'ad let her. To his mind, she deserved it and, like her father and grandfather, Ra'ad quickly realised that he could never deny her anything. Not that he wanted to. For Ra'ad, Guzin's happiness was a source of immense pride; in his culture, it was his job as the man of the house to ensure she was properly looked after.

They were surprised to discover three months after the wedding that Guzin was pregnant. They hadn't planned on starting a family so soon, but they were over the moon. From that moment on, Ra'ad insisted that Guzin do everything slowly, from walking down steps to getting out of bed. Pregnancy was a mystery to him and he didn't want anything to happen to his wife or unborn child. 'He said to everyone, "She's a small girl and she's pregnant and she's spoiled",' Guzin says now. 'I slept all the time and I didn't want to do anything. Ra'ad was very good.'

A daughter they named Lina was born on 22 April 1975 at a hospital in Al Mansour. Ra'ad was present for the birth and was astonished that his young wife seemed so calm, so stoic. In fact, Guzin was embarrassed at having so many people around while she was in labour. She didn't want the doctors and nurses, let alone her husband, to hear her screaming and moaning so she did her best to keep quiet, bearing down and biting her lip. 'When I gave birth to my children I was very brave, I didn't shout or scream or cry, I kept quiet. I walked the corridor all the time, and sometimes the pain came and I'd hug my husband and my mother would say, "Don't lie, you want to hug him, so you pretend that it's painful".' Guzin laughs. 'It wasn't true. It was painful.'

Ra'ad was ecstatic. The birth of Lina gave him something to smile about at a very black time. His father, Mohammed, died suddenly of a heart attack when Guzin was eight months pregnant, leaving a huge hole in his life. Ra'ad grieved for the fact that his father would never see him receive his first diplomatic assignment and he felt a blanket of sadness fall on him knowing that his daughter, the first grandchild in the family, would never know her grandfather. He was heartbroken and his grief was compounded when, soon after the birth, his mother, Fakhira, announced she was moving to London. But when he took Lina and Guzin home from hospital a few days later, the house didn't feel nearly as empty. As Ra'ad looked at his daughter sleeping in her crib, he could see a future.

Chapter Eight

With a new wife, a new baby and a new job, Ra'ad had his hands full. He was already confronted with a steep learning curve in foreign affairs, particularly in the geopolitical landscape of the Middle East, which was forever changing. And now he had an equally steep one in negotiating the even more foreign world of first-time fatherhood. Ra'ad understood the intricacies of policy papers on international treaties and trade with relative ease, but the art of putting a nappy on a baby had him stumped. Despite this small technicality, he took to fatherhood like a duck to water.

Ra'ad was crazy about Lina and spent as much time with her as his job would allow. In fact, his daughter's growth mirrored his own. He was quickly learning the ropes in the foreign ministry, and as Lina grew into her toddler years, so too did her father grow into his role in diplomacy. Before long, he was making his mark. It seemed that each time Lina hit a developmental milestone, her father was hitting a professional one, working his way up the bureaucracy, much to Guzin's delight. She knew how much her husband wanted to emulate his father's diplomatic career, and with each new step, he inched closer.

Soon after Lina turned three in April 1978, Ra'ad received his first posting as second secretary to the Iraqi Embassy in London. It was a relatively junior position, but the embassy in London was, in diplomatic terms, one of the most prominent. If handled the right way, it could make or break a novice diplomat. Ra'ad was intent on making his tour of duty a success. He flew out of Baghdad in August while his wife stayed behind to finalise some family business.

Guzin joined her husband in early November and, by the 20th, had been issued a 'Certificate of Identity' card by the Protocol and Conference Department at the Foreign and Commonwealth Office in London. It was the colour of a deep blue sea and about the size of the palm of a man's hand. Inside, typed on the right-hand page, it stated:

This card is issued to
Mrs. Kzain Shawkat Najim
Wife of
Mr. Rad M.S. Khames
Second Secretary
at the
Embassy of Iraq
in London.

The department had misspelled Guzin's name and those of her father and Ra'ad, but she didn't complain. There is no standard translation from Arabic to English and words were often taken down incorrectly. On the facing page was a photograph of the then 22-year-old Guzin. She has a Mona Lisa smile and dark eyeliner traces the outer corners of her eyes. Her hair is teased high at the back and kept short the way she liked to wear it. No matter how many times Ra'ad asked her to grow her hair past her shoulders, she refused, saying it was much easier to manage if kept short. On the back of the card was the address of the Iraqi Embassy at 21 Queen's Gate in the heart of London.

The document was more than just a card to prove who she was. It was symbolic – she and her husband were now members of an elite corps of international statesmen and women and, on a more personal level, she hoped it signalled better times ahead.

Ra'ad had left at the beginning of August and Guzin had spent the last three months in Baghdad alone. It had been hellishly emotional, the final week a frenzy of upheaval. Her mother died from a heart attack in April at the age of forty-six. Shawket was devastated. 'My lovely wife Majida died on Sunday, the 30th of April 1978 at 12.30 pm in the hospital in Baghdad', he wrote in his journal a few days later. 'She left me alone with my daughters Guzin and Buthaina and I will cry for her every minute of my life.' The family took Majida's body home to Jordan and buried her near the house in Irbid where she grew up.

Back in Baghdad, Shawket grew increasingly depressed. When told that Ra'ad had received his first official diplomatic posting to London and that Guzin and his granddaughter Lina would be leaving before the end of the year, he sank into a bigger hole. Apart from his second daughter Buthaina, he was alone, and not a man enjoying his retirement. Shawket had never accepted the Ba'ath Party as the legitimate government of Iraq and quietly seethed at having been forced to retire from the army. He was only fifty-four but the anger and bitterness made him feel much older. He had spent the decade since his retirement reading the monthly *Al Arabi* news magazine or listening to the BBC World Service and bemoaning the fate of his country under the Ba'ath Party which, as time went on, became increasingly repressive.

Saddam Hussein had been increasing his power base within the party since the coup of 1968 and was appointed vice president in 1975. While in this position he restructured the secret police into a vast and fearsome Medusa-like apparatus with competing organisations which controlled the population and the military. He also established the hated intelligence service, the Mukhabarat. Brick by brick, Saddam was building a cult of personality. He demanded to be called 'Mr Deputy' and even published his phone number asking Iraqis to call him if they had a problem. Few did. Saddam *was* the problem. Saddam and his president al-Bakr loaded the upper ranks of government with their fellow Tikritis, uneducated men from peasant stock, and limited entrance to Shawket's beloved military academy to members of the Ba'ath. To mask the rampant tribalism in government, the bureaucracy decreed that men should no longer use their family names – such as al-Tikriti – which indicated clan, tribe or area of origin. Shawket's disgust was palpable. He told Guzin that if she was leaving Iraq, then he would go as well. But it was not as easy as it sounded.

By the late 1970s, Baghdad had been divided into security zones run by *al-Amn al-Amm* (general security). Al-Amn was staffed by petty thugs who harassed and brutalised Iraqis in order to keep them in line. People were prohibited from living in one zone and owning property in another. If they did, they were forced to sell the property at a price set by the government. Their movements within and between the zones were strictly monitored by surveillance cameras which sat atop buildings or were hidden in statues and public monuments. Under Ba'ath laws all citizens had to register their address and telephone number at the nearest police station. Citizens had already been issued a document called Shahadat al-Jinsiyyah (witness of citizenship) – they needed government permission to leave the country temporarily and permanently. Very few were ever granted exit visas. Yet Shawket was insistent. He did not want to stay in Iraq any longer.

Guzin was booked to fly Iraqi Airways on an overnight flight from Baghdad to London, where she would be reunited with Ra'ad in the early hours of 19 November 1978. The day of her departure started early. The department of foreign affairs had already organised removalists to ship the family goods to London and she still had to pack suitcases for herself and Lina, who was now three. But Guzin had more pressing matters to deal with. A couple of days before she was due to leave, Shawket and Buthaina had flown to Jordan for what appeared to be a holiday. Shawket left his car in the garage and the house in Al Yarmouk in a condition that looked as if he would be back soon. But once he was out of Iraq, Shawket had no intention of returning – ever.

On her final day in Baghdad, Guzin sold everything in the house, including the furniture and her father's car. There was nothing she could do about the house itself at such short notice, so it would remain empty for the time being. Shawket had transferred the house into his daughters' names long ago, to protect the property and ensure their ongoing independence should anything happen to him. Guzin later rented the house but that day, she was relieved that no one asked any questions and she managed to finalise everything without raising suspicion. When Guzin was done, she and Lina raced to the airport to board their late-night flight to London.

Ra'ad was waiting for Guzin and Lina at Heathrow Airport. The flight had been uneventful and luxurious. As the family of a diplomat they travelled first class, and it was sumptuously plush, even for Guzin, who had always enjoyed the finer things in life. Ra'ad had an official limousine and took her home to the two-bedroom flat he had rented in Gloucester Terrace in Bayswater, always one of the better suburbs of London. They unpacked the bags while Lina, bubbling with excitement at seeing her father again, told Ra'ad about their trip, with Guzin filling in the missing pieces. He felt guilty that he hadn't been there to help her. At midday Ra'ad took his 'girls', as he called them, to a restaurant he had taken Guzin to on their honeymoon. He figured it would make the transition to London infinitely more pleasant, particularly after the gruelling weeks his wife had just lived through without him. Guzin was touched by the gesture, but she had come to expect no less of him – it was Ra'ad's way. He was kind and thoughtful, a gentleman's gentleman. After lunch they popped into a Mothercare shop and Guzin bought a tiny bed for Lina. She kept the receipt – a memento of her first purchase as a resident in London.

Guzin's husband was a diplomat for a country that was of vital importance in the Arab world and here she was living in what was then one of the most dynamic cities on earth. Within the year, the Shah of Iran would fall to a fundamentalist cleric; in Iraq, a new president would rise unchallenged to totalitarian power; and in the United States and Britain respectively, a former actor and a baker's daughter would emerge victorious from the polls.

London was bound to be an adventure. As well as the use of a diplomatic limousine, Ra'ad had his own car to negotiate London's nightmarish traffic and its crowded, snaking streets. While the first few days behind the wheel were an experience of anxiety and frustration, Ra'ad and Guzin soon adapted to driving on the wrong side of the road. They had all the perks of life on the diplomatic circuit which came with a built-in social life and offered precisely the connections they needed. Ra'ad's English was fluent, and Guzin's English was good even if the nuances and context of words sometimes stumped her. And she didn't have to worry about being isolated or making new friends.

Guzin landed in London with impeccable connections, none being more important than the Iraqi Ambassador, Dr Hisham Al-Shawi, to whom Ra'ad would ultimately answer. Al-Shawi had been a close friend of Guzin's uncles, the assassinated Jordanian Prime Minister Wasfi Al Tell and his brother Said. As young men they had studied together at the American University in Beirut and, years later, before he entered Iraq's diplomatic corps, the then Professor Al-Shawi taught Guzin the art of diplomacy as part of her bachelor degree in international law and politics at Al Mustansiriya University in Baghdad. Although they didn't know it at the time, Al-Shawi privately opposed Saddam Hussein's regime and when he moved to his next posting in Canada, he sought political asylum. Although he was refused, he eventually settled in London and joined an Iraqi opposition group dedicated to ousting Saddam. He was just one of dozens of Iraqi ambassadors and representatives to the United Nations who fled Iraq during Saddam's reign.

As the new kids on the diplomatic block, Ra'ad and Guzin dazzled in their vitality. Ra'ad's family background gave him an aura of gravitas even though he himself was in a relatively junior position. Guzin was a novelty in the gossipy world of diplomacy, so steeped in intrigue. Thin, exotically beautiful, well educated and naturally outgoing, she was noticeably younger than the wives of other diplomats and attachés, who were thickened by middle age and wary of the exuberance of youth. It was a lifestyle made for Guzin. She was equally at home making small talk about families and fashion with cliquey wives and low-ranking secretaries while sipping champagne in stately halls as she was discussing the minutiae of international relations with aristocrats and diplomats at dinner tables in consular homes. She was the perfect diplomat's wife.

The first order of business for Guzin and Ra'ad as the diplomatic *arriviste* couple was to attend an official welcoming dinner in their honour hosted by Ambassador Al-Shawi at his residence near Knightsbridge. The house was stunning. It had belonged to the deposed King Faisal II who used it as his London *pied-à-terre* while studying in the United Kingdom, but was appropriated by the Republic of Iraq after he was assassinated in the coup of 1958. Ra'ad used the evening to network, as every good diplomat does. Guzin mingled and positively shone. She wore an elegant cocktail dress in a subtle shade of sea-green that she had bought on a recent holiday in Spain. It was tightly fitted and had a modest décolletage. The ambassador's wife, assuming a motherly role, fussed over Guzin and tried to entice her to eat from the banquet tables laid out before them. Guzin desperately wanted to, but couldn't. She was afraid her dress would split.

The evening was a huge success, not least because it was so unusual for the ambassador to host an official function for the second secretary to the embassy, a point everyone silently noted. Such were the dividends of Guzin's family name and her connections. A succession of 'welcoming' dinners and receptions followed, hosted by the various consular generals and high commissioners of Iraq's neighbouring countries.

Away from their official life, Ra'ad and Guzin quickly resumed a family routine. Ra'ad left the apartment each morning at eight o'clock to be in the office by eight-thirty. If the weather permitted, he walked. It was a beautiful stroll across Hyde Park to the embassy on Queen's Gate near the Royal Albert Hall and Kensington Palace. Ra'ad preferred the walk because it helped him manage his weight, a lifetime problem that caused him no end of angst. He had an insatiable sweet tooth and Guzin often caught him raiding the kitchen at night. It was a constant source of aggravation between them, though when she was pregnant with Lina, their joint midnight sorties to the kitchen on Princess Street made her laugh. Ra'ad had lost 30 kilograms when he married Guzin, but over the years several of those had crept back on.

Guzin fell in love with the Bayswater apartment even though it was small compared to her homes in Irbid and Baghdad. The third-floor unit at 31-33 Gloucester Terrace had two bedrooms and two bathrooms and a generous combined dining and lounge room. Large windows let the sun in whenever it managed to sneak through London's notorious low grey skies. They had respectable neighbours, essential in Ra'ad's line of work, and the flat was ideally located. Gloucester Terrace started at Porchester Road to the north, crossed Bishops Bridge Road and ended a stone's throw from the Marlborough Gate on the northern side of Kensington Gardens. To the east was Marylebone, to the southeast Mayfair, Piccadilly Circus and Charing Cross, and to the west Notting Hill. Harrods was a little further south on the other side of Hyde Park, but with Lina in a stroller, Guzin could travel the distance on foot in no time. Soon, she was familiar with the shops on Knightsbridge and Sloane Street as well.

The only thing the apartment lacked was a garden, but with so much parkland around her, Guzin didn't mind. She had also forsaken the hired help she had in Baghdad – with the exception of a cleaner. The owner of the apartment gave her the name of an old lady from Wales who agreed to come in once a week. She spoke with a lilting Welsh accent and quickly grew fond of Lina, who was a pretty little girl with huge round brown eyes and jet black hair and who loved being taught new words. Guzin didn't have a cook and so her culinary skills gradually improved with time, much to Ra'ad's amusement and delight. She started with a Jordan-ian rice dish, which she perfected and finessed, and moved on to Iraqi specialties which were comfortingly familiar.

While Ra'ad worked, Guzin and Lina went sightseeing. She visited places she'd been on her honeymoon, such as Madame Tussaud's Wax Museum and London Bridge, and she took Lina to performances at the Royal Albert Hall. On weekends the young family took day trips to places like Stratford-upon-Avon to visit Shakespeare's birthplace or, in summer, Brighton Beach, where she would swim, astonished that the beach was made of pebbles and horrified at the bleak colour of the ocean, so different from the cerulean waters of Aqaba. They went to Oxford and Cambridge and laughed so much while punting that they almost fell out of the flat-bottomed boat Ra'ad was trying, unsuccessfully, to steer.

They had their first white Christmas in London that year, just a few weeks after celebrating *Eid el fitr*, which marks the end of the fasting month of Ramadan. And on New Year's Eve, Ra'ad and Guzin partied like a couple of teenagers with the raucous crowd in Trafalgar Square and Piccadilly Circus. Meanwhile in Jordan, Guzin's father was happy and her sister, Buthaina, was about to be married in a dress bought by Guzin from Harrods. Life couldn't have been more perfect.

◆ ◆ ◆

On 16 July 1979 Saddam Hussein convinced Iraqi president Ahmed Hasan al-Bakr to remove himself from office and he readily complied. There was no struggle or bloodshed but, almost immediately, a reign of terror descended on the small oil-rich country. On 20 July Saddam convened a Ba'ath Party executive meeting that turned into a purge. The meeting was videotaped and copies eventually made their way to the western world, which was horrified at the calculated and cold brutality of the new president. Puffing on his signature cigar, Saddam Hussein sat on a stage overlooking the auditorium. Many of those who had been loyal to him were betrayed as 'traitors' and marched out of the hall. When one tried to defend himself, Saddam shouted 'Itla', itla' [Get out, get out].'

Those led out of the auditorium were executed at gunpoint by those in the upper reaches of government whose names had not been denounced. The hunters had been hunted, and their comrades were their killers, yet they were not willing executioners. 'Neither Stalin nor Hitler would have thought up a detail like that. What Eichmann-like refuge in "orders from above" could these men dig up in the future if they were ever to marshal the courage to try and depose their leader?' writes Iraqi Kanan Makiya in his book *Republic of Fear: The Politics of Modern Iraq*. 'Can anyone devise a more brilliant tactical move to implicate potential foes in their personal ascent to immorality, assuming brotherly love is put aside as a consideration? With this act, the party leadership was being forced to invest its future in Saddam, just as previously it had herded the whole populace into investing their future in the party . . . The terror had turned against its perpetrators, as it is wont to do, but the circle of guilt and responsibility was closing . . .'

By the beginning of August one-third of the highest-ranking Ba'ath members had been executed at Saddam's behest, and hundreds more were jailed. 'The purges were designed to transfer already existing bonds of complicity away from the party and firmly into the person of Saddam Hussein', Makiya writes. A murderous megalomaniac and cold political pragmatist had been revealed on the public stage. Saddam's actions announced, without censorship, that Iraq was now ruled by the iron fist of a tin-pot dictator.

Soon, Iraq was turned into a national gallery for Saddam Hussein. Every household displayed a picture of him, its inhabitants too fearful of being arrested if they didn't, and every village erected at its entrance larger-than-life cut-out images of him, some showing Saddam in a spiffy white suit. A myth was being created. Statues went up, billboards displayed Saddam as a knight riding a white stallion and liberating his people. Every public speech evoked his name. Every nightly news bulletin began with a song honouring him. He was showered with honorific titles that were more grandiose and ego-driven than his many official ones: 'the knight of the Arab nation', 'the daring and aggressive knight', 'the father leader', 'the God father' and 'the great leader', among others.

But for all that, Saddam Hussein did enjoy a short honeymoon of popularity. The nation had experienced a level of prosperity from its oil resources and the 1973 oil embargo which sent Iraqi oil prices into the stratosphere. The oil wealth was shared across the country, even with the usually downtrodden Shiah majority, many of whom lived in the south. Still, as the biographer Saïd K. Aburish writes in *Saddam Hussein: The Politics of Revenge*, 'everybody whispered about how the achievements were built on the bones of the hundreds of people who dared to oppose him'. They were just too scared to confront him.

Iraq's international reputation was also about to explode with the begining of its eight-year unwinnable war against Iran. The Iraqi war effort was partly funded and aided by London and Washington; the British and United States governments feared the spread of Islamic fundamentalism preached by Iran's new leader, the firebrand Ayatollah Ruhollah Khomeini. In 1979 when the Shah of Iran was overthrown, the ayatollah branded the United States an enemy, the 'great Satan'.

Ra'ad, in his role in the London embassy, would have been acutely aware that the new leadership of Saddam

Hussein was involved in sensitive diplomatic negotiations with the new British conservative government of Margaret Thatcher and that of the newly elected Republican President of the United States, Ronald Reagan. But he never talked about it with Guzin. Ra'ad was deliberately secretive when it came to his work, both out of respect for the office and also to ensure his family was always protected from being in possession of potentially dangerous or sensitive information which could jeopardise their safety. He was disdainful of those in the diplomatic corps who drank too much, fearing they would reveal a state secret in a reckless moment of inebriation or make themselves vulnerable to bribery and extortion. For her part, Guzin had enough on her mind. She was busy raising a three-year-old and helping her sister organise her wedding in another country. She had little interest in the political machinations back home. As well, she was pregnant with her second child, a boy they would name Mohammed in honour of the grandfather he never knew.

Shortly after their second Christmas in London in 1979, Ra'ad received notice that his next posting would take him to Yemen, the Islamic country attached to the southern border of Saudi Arabia on the Gulf of Aden, across the Red Sea from Ethiopia and Eritrea. They had a final farewell at the ambassador's residence in London which was attended by more than one hundred guests. Guzin looked radiant in an elegant maternity dress that showed off her expanding stomach, and was relaxed about the future and the baby growing in her belly. Ra'ad was less enthusiastic. He didn't relish the idea of giving up the cosmopolitan lifestyle of London for the under-developed backblocks of the third world.

Ra'ad and Guzin spent the final weeks of a freezing London January visiting their favourite restaurants and tourist sites and packing up their flat. Every moment counted. Ra'ad was flying directly to the dust bowl of Sana'a, the capital of Yemen, and Guzin was flying back to Jordan, where she would spend the last few months of her pregnancy before giving birth in a Roman Catholic hospital in Irbid. The arrangement was not ideal, but in the circumstances it had to do.

The Iraqi representation in Yemen was significant politically and strategically, but not large. Ra'ad was appointed chargé d'affaires of the embassy. With preparations for the war with Iran mounting, he also assumed the responsibilities usually delegated to a military attaché. Ra'ad spent hours flying back and forth to the Iraqi Embassy in Saudi Arabia for military briefings and organisational meetings. On 22 September 1980, Saddam Hussein declared war on Iraq's Persian neighbour. He sent the first squadrons of Iraqi MiG-23 and MiG-21 fighter jets to bomb Iran's airfields and military installations while fifty thousand Iraqi troops attacked the country at four points along the shared border. Several jets were launched from a Yemeni airbase in Sana'a where they had been quietly stationed for weeks. The personnel who manned them had posed as Iraqi tourists, waiting for their orders to strike. Ra'ad had organised the accommodation and supplies for military personnel in hotels throughout the capital.

The war was not the shock and awe campaign the Iraqi regime expected. It dragged on for eight long years. In mid-1988, Iran's Ayatollah Khomeini made the decision he described as 'more deadly than drinking hemlock' and agreed to a United Nations cease-fire with Iraq. The cost of the war was enormous on both sides, in terms of money and morale. But an even greater toll could be found in the casualties: an estimated 200,000 Iraqi soldiers were killed in battle, and another 500,000 were wounded. The financial cost was estimated at more than US $200 billion. Iran reportedly lost 300,000 lives and sustained 500,000 casualties.

Ra'ad despised Yemen. With the outbreak of war, he worked around the clock in conditions that were less than salubrious. He looked down his nose at the culture of the small developing country on the southwestern corner of the Arabian peninsula. At one point Ra'ad told Guzin – largely in jest – that he would commit suicide if he couldn't leave. Before she left Jordan after the birth of Mohammed, he telephoned her and told her not to come: 'There is nothing here but dust, there are no trees'. She would have none of it. She valued the family and would fight to protect it and keep it together.

When Guzin arrived with their two children in tow, the heat of summer had slammed down on the dustbowl desert airstrip in the heart of Sana'a. As the plane made its descent on approach to the airport, she looked out the window and saw sand for miles and miles and eddies of dust swirling around in the heat haze. She panicked and thought the aircraft had overshot the runway. When she realised that she was landing on a dirt airstrip, she laughed. So *this* was what Ra'ad had been complaining about, she thought to herself.

Despite what she saw and in spite of Ra'ad's antipathy, Guzin couldn't help but be charmed by Yemen. Old buildings rose three storeys high and magically, subtly, changed colour as the sun travelled across the sky. In old Sana'a soaring white belltowers were backdropped by the bluest of blue skies, which contrasted with the beige dirt of the streets. Guzin loved to watch robed merchants carrying their goods on their shoulders as they shuffled their dust-covered feet down alleys that seemed impossibly narrow, en route to bazaars that were a kaleidoscope of colour and a potpourri of smells. But more than the architecture and street scenes, Guzin was amused by the blithe attitudes of the people in power, and the Yemeni themselves: the highly educated diplomats and heads of government dressed casually in trousers and wore shoes without socks, or open-toed sandals! There was also the Yemeni tradition of wasting an entire afternoon chewing a leaf with amphetamine-like qualities called *qat*. The dress standards were fanciful fashion aberrations to Guzin's stylish eye, but Ra'ad dismissed the laconic attitude as an embarrassment to the diplomatic corps and international relations. The national *qat* habit also repulsed him. Guzin, who could easily be described as a cultural adventurer, just laughed and wanted to try it for herself to see what all the fuss was about.

Qat, dubbed 'this evil plant', or *catha edulis* in Arabic, has been chewed by Yemenis for more than seven centuries. It is to the Yemeni what the siesta is to the Mexicans and transcends regional, religious, sex and class divides. Every day some time past noon, the little shiny green leaf becomes the country's social lubricant, the opiate of the masses. Yemenis gather together in private rooms for a '*qat* chew' during which they masticate the raw leaves especially grown in the outer regions of Yemen. As they chew, marijuana-like qualities take effect, and while waiting for them to wear off – which can take several leisurely hours – Yemenis sit around and talk. And talk. And talk some more. Obviously, to engage in this daily social reverie they needed to stop work, totally, and almost everyone did, including the public service, a habit which flummoxed Ra'ad. The only exceptions were the *qat* traders and growers, who kept working while chewing on a mouthful of their product. *Qat*, however pleasant, had its associated problems: chewers lose their appetite afterwards, and often can't perform the next day.

Guzin marvelled at the daily ritual and wanted to experience it. She tried to convince a Japanese diplomat to let his wife attend a *qat* chew with her. When he discovered that there were significant health effects that the cavalier Yemenis paid no heed to – insomnia and anorexia being the two most prevalent – his response was, unsurprisingly, 'No.' Guzin's days as a *qat* chewer were over before they began.

Ra'ad and Guzin's house was commodious by Yemeni standards. It had a backyard that had been turned into an abundant market garden by an enterprising Egyptian gardener whom Ra'ad had employed to provide fresh fruit and vegetables every day. Guzin's cooking had improved markedly since her first faltering attempts in London, and she made the most of the home-grown produce. Guzin hated to be alone and with her husband putting in so many hours in the office, she threw parties and organised get-togethers. Almost by default, she became something of an Arabic Martha Stewart, an *éminence grise* of the Sana'a international social scene. As ever, she made friends easily and, with the influx of Iraqi personnel to Sana'a to help in the war effort against Iran, Guzin had an ever-increasing pool to choose from in addition to the regular circle of diplomats and Yemeni officials.

A regular guest to Guzin's soirees was a junior member of Ra'ad's staff at the consulate, a 27-year-old man named Ali Al Delamy. Ali was a member of Saddam Hussein's dreaded intelligence service, the Mukhabarat, and his presence at the consulate during a time of war made perfect sense. Under normal circumstances, Ra'ad would have been reluctant to breathe the same air as Ali Al Delamy. But, in the prelude to war before Guzin and the children arrived in Sana'a, he shared his house with him and one other official. Oddly, Ali and Ra'ad developed a friendship. A case of opposites attracting, the real benefits of which would not be realised for nearly two decades.

Ali was seven years younger than Ra'ad and came from a village outside of Baghdad. He was unsophisticated and uneducated. Something as common as a bed on castors astonished him and he pushed it around the house as if he were a child with a go-cart. He was used to sleeping in a barn with the sheep, cows and donkeys, not an opulent home fit for diplomats. As a child, when he wanted to wash he walked from his hut to the muddy banks of the Euphrates River and splashed around in the water. He had to walk up the same muddy banks to get home, which he did with mud rising to his ankles like baked-on socks, impossible to remove. In Sana'a, Ali could wash with running water.

Ali quickly became attached to Guzin too. She was the same age and yet she was so different. She was a mother. He was single and desperately wanted to find a bride and have children of his own. She was from an upper-class family with a direct line to politicians and ties to the royal family of the Hashemite Kingdom of Jordan. He was a peasant who, under the rule of his 'great leader' Saddam Hussein, was forced to drop his family name. Guzin recalls Ali's wonderment at the changing fortunes of his life. 'Always in English he would say, "My childhood compared to

SANDRA LEE

Guzin's!", she says, imitating Ali by throwing her arms in the air as if in mock defeat.

Ali's background did not define him nor would it limit him. Ra'ad and Guzin never saw in Ali the blind thuggery and peasant mentality that signified so many of Saddam's Mukhabarat brutes. Nor did he insinuate his way into their lives. They knew who and what he was from the moment he arrived in Sana'a and if they had to do a balance sheet of Ali's attributes, few, if any, were what they expected. He was gentle with Lina, who had turned five and was in her first year of kindergarten, and he doted on the baby, Mohammed. Ali's was an affection that could not be faked, and the truth-tellers were the children. 'They loved him very, very much. He was very faithful and honest,' Guzin says.

Shawket arrived to visit Guzin six months into Iraq's first campaign in the Iran–Iraq war. He brought with him news of Iraq and, of course, his opinions of Saddam Hussein. Guzin had never been one to contain her opinions and with her father in Sana'a, she let forth. With the war in full flight and Yemen a strategic base for the Iraqi offensive, Saddam had sent an acting ambassador, Abdul Al Wadoud Jado'o, to Sana'a. It was crucial to have a titular presence in the country but, as had become the standard under Saddam Hussein's one-man reign of absolute power, the ambassador was, Guzin and Ra'ad believed, another of the uneducated yes-men who were swelling the ranks of upper government.

Guzin looked down her nose at him. Ra'ad considered him less than a rank peasant. 'He was complaining that when his father was a diplomat they were all from good families and they knew how to behave and eat and speak. But most of them then, and now, in the Ba'ath party are not used to this life,' Guzin says. 'Sometimes he spoke to me about the regime. Most of them in the Ba'ath have not studied to be diplomats so they don't behave like diplomats.'

Ra'ad, Shawket and Guzin spoke about their increasing enmities toward their president in private, but they never knew who was listening. They had come to trust Ali, the known Mukhabarat agent, but any number of the Iraqis in Sana'a could have been enlisted as one of Saddam's army of spies. He relied on a broad informer network which involved the largest number of people possible in the terror of the regime. As the Iraqi writer Kanan Makiya asks in his book *Republic of Fear*, 'who is an informer? In Ba'athist Iraq the answer is anybody.' Makiya writes that the entire membership of the party 'are a mass under discipline, expected to inform on all acquaintances, including other party members'.

In 1984 the *New York Times* quoted a European diplomat in Baghdad saying 'there is a feeling that at least three million Iraqis are watching the eleven million others'. Even members of the Iraqi Women's Federation joined the queue of informers. Fast forward two decades and Joseph Braude, writing in his book *The New Iraq*, states that:

> . . . in 2003, available Iraqi intelligence documents surveyed suggest that more than 500,000 people spanning the country's 18 provinces were serving as sometime snitches for the five principal services: special security, general security, general intelligence, military intelligence and military security. This figure does not include the many more who assisted the Ba'ath party's internal security agencies, the civil police forces, and various paramilitary wings.

Ambassador Jado'o, says Guzin, was jealous of the extensive social and political network she and Ra'ad had. He was also suspicious of Guzin's three-monthly trips to Jordan when her baby Mohammed had to be immunised. The ambassador wrote a series of negative reports about Guzin and Ra'ad, stamped them 'top secret' and sent them back to Baghdad. Ali Al Delamy saw one of the first reports. Loyal, he told Guzin and Ra'ad. They knew it was too late to do anything, and they also knew that with the war and Ra'ad's role in it, little would be done. They hunkered down. From that moment on, Ali Al Delamy had become Guzin's best connection. She just didn't know it yet.

Chapter Nine

In the second half of 1982, seven-year-old Lina Ra'ad Said entered the second grade at the Westmount Park School in the city of Montreal in the province of Quebec in Canada. A few months earlier in Sana'a, she had passed her first grade exams, scoring a distinction in Arabic and religion, and a 'very good' in each of mathematics, science and English, as well as for conduct and effort. 'She is a good and obedient student', her teacher at the international Azal School wrote in her end-of-year report. In Montreal, where Ra'ad had been appointed consul at the Iraqi consulate, Lina's Jamaican teacher, a robust-sized Mrs Jackson, advised her that she needed to learn her times-table but otherwise, she was 'progressing nicely'.

Back in Baghdad, Iraqi children Lina's age and younger were being taught an operetta written by an Iraqi poet, Faruq al-Sallum. Called 'The Leader and the Future', it was part of the myth-making machinery in which Saddam Hussein was being crafted as the undisputed and unchallengeable leader of all Iraq. Children learnt it off by heart. A second poet, Ghazay Dir' al-Ta'I, wrote a song for children which helped further the myth and inculcate the belief by Iraqi youth that there was no higher authority on earth than Saddam:

We are Iraq and its name is Saddam;
We are love and its name is Saddam;
We are a people and its name is Saddam;
We are the Ba'ath and its name is Saddam.

The cult of personality which demanded the indoctrination was pervasive. Children were named after Saddam; they wore t-shirts with his face emblazoned on them as if he were a rock star; and they stood to attention in class and said prayers of thanks for him. A joke doing the rounds at the time in Baghdad was that the country's population was 28 million – 14 million Iraqis and 14 million pictures of Saddam.

Life for children in Baghdad was the photographic negative of that of Lina and her eighteen-month-old brother, Mohammed. In the family's penthouse suite at 34 Drummond Street in the heart of downtown Montreal, they had the life every western child dreams of. Each afternoon after being discharged from the care of Mrs Jackson with scores of other students from around the world, Lina paid one Canadian dollar to the bus driver to take her home. Strung over one tiny shoulder was a school bag stuffed with notebooks and an empty lunch box, and over the other hung a heavy bag loaded down with her snazzy white leather ice-skates. This being Canada, where ice hockey and winter sports are a national pastime, if not a religion, Lina was learning to skate as part of her school curriculum.

As soon as she hopped off the bus, a concierge darted out and took her bags, escorted her to the elevators and sent her up to the penthouse. People were like that with Lina; they felt inclined to protect her. She was a skinny little girl and she had a gentle contemplative nature and an old soul. Canada was her fourth country of residence and she spoke with an international accent that could not easily be identified. The concierge thought she was adorable.

Lina's brother Mohammed spent his days with his mother. As she had with Lina, Guzin took Mohammed out for breakfast each morning, ferrying him through the streets of the French-speaking city in a pram and finding swish cafés where they didn't mind her beginner's fractured French. Instead of bargaining in Arabic in bazaars and shopping for exquisite handmade fabrics and traditional antiques as she had in Sana'a, she shopped at Miracle Mart and Kmart while practising her French and, on the odd occasion, her English.

The Drummond Street apartment, which was paid for by the Iraqi government, as were all diplomatic residences, was spectacular, and from its vertiginous height it offered magnificent views of the city, from Mount Royal to the St Lawrence River. The master bedroom had an en suite and opened to a balcony, and Lina and Mohammed had a bedroom each. With the children as young as they were, the lounge and dining rooms had been surrendered to the accoutrements of childhood. A swing-set was erected in one corner and toys overflowed from boxes in another. Guzin used the indoor swimming pool on the ground floor every day, living up to her childhood nickname of Froggy. They had a navy blue metallic Oldsmobile and a well-thumbed tourist guide. During school vacations the family travelled to Niagara Falls to watch the ice floes crash with a thunderous roar over the edge of the famous waterfalls. They went skiing outside the capital of Ottawa, and visited the revolving tower and restaurant in Toronto.

Quebec is the only French-speaking province in all of Canada and as difficult as the language is, Guzin and Ra'ad tried. They had arrived in Montreal from a four-week vacation in France where they practised their French every day. Had Lina's teacher from Sana'a been with them, she probably would have graded their effort as 'very good'. However, their achievement left a little to be desired. In Paris they gave up after negotiating a fare with a small, beret-wearing taxi driver who erupted into a Gallic rage when they asked to be taken to the Eiffel Tower. Shouting something indecipherable, but clearly profane from the look on his agitated face, he swung the astonished family around and pointed furiously in front of them. There, just a few hundred metres away from them, rising into the sky in all its engineering glory, was the Eiffel Tower. Guzin and Ra'ad burst out laughing at the absurdity of it, and decided it would be better to wait until Montreal to sharpen their language skills. They toasted as much with a glass of champagne on the Champs Élysées later.

Ra'ad's diplomatic postings were limited to two years in one destination. It was the Iraqi standard for all members of the department of foreign affairs who served abroad. After two years the foreign ministry would either recall the representative or assign him or her to another country. Canada was Ra'ad's third and most senior posting yet, and he hoped it would be followed with another.

As idyllic as it seemed, Guzin was not happy in Montreal. She barely saw her husband and had two children to raise, which she did practically on her own. Ra'ad left the apartment around five o'clock each morning to be at the consulate by five-thirty. Iraq, at that stage, had hospitable relations with the western world, including the United States, the United Kingdom and Canada. Saddam's army was still in the grip of its long war with Iran. The war was being waged in phases that involved attack, counterattack, retreat, stalemate and attack again. It was bloody and ugly with no end in sight. Saddam Hussein was also in the middle of acquiring nuclear arms and the materials to build them. The diplomacy of the political wheeling and dealing had to be handled with kid gloves and, as was Ra'ad's style, he never revealed the exact details of his work to Guzin or the children. Sometimes, it drove her to frustration.

At the end of a punishing day in the consulate, Ra'ad went to McGill University, where he resumed studies in English, which is the international language of diplomacy. He felt at a distinct disadvantage when talking with western dignitaries because he had lost his elegant fluency during the two years in Yemen, where he spoke mostly in Arabic. He wanted to recapture the nuances of the language. As a result, Guzin was alone for more than twelve hours each day. She coped that first summer and autumn, when the weather was mild and invited outdoor activities, but the Canadian winters were as long and brutal as the Iraqi summers. Temperatures plummeted to minus thirty degrees Fahrenheit and wicked, icy winds tore through the city and belted against the windows of the penthouse. The sun set before three-thirty in the afternoon, and with so many hours cooped up in the apartment with only the children for company, Guzin sometimes felt claustrophobic. On top of this, Ra'ad's diplomatic engagements and social calendar were infinitely more sparse than they had been in Yemen. Guzin found that in the smaller countries, members of the international community developed a close-knit camaraderie. They spent more time together socialising, however informally, because there was less to do and their work commitments were less restrictive.

In Montreal, Guzin felt isolated, although when Ra'ad was recalled after two years, the news was greeted with mixed emotions. Guzin was happy to be leaving Montreal, but the directive from the ministry of foreign affairs in Baghdad was a double-edged sword: for the first time in six years Ra'ad was not reassigned. He was recalled to Baghdad. Neither he nor Guzin wanted to go home. In their absence Iraq had undergone a radical change under Saddam Hussein and was descending deeper into a republic of fear. Politically, the couple were neither Ba'athists nor Ba'ath supporters. Ra'ad had always considered himself a member of an international community and Guzin remembered her best days as those she spent in Irbid as a child, or when her father had a respected position in the community in the pre-Saddam Hussein period from 1963 to 1968. She had also inherited her father's undying affection for and loyalties to the deposed royal family.

'All the time we were talking about the situation in Iraq with the Ba'ath Party in 1982 and 1983,' Guzin says now. She is staring into an Australian version of Iraqi coffee in a pretty, petite cup in front of her, explaining how the situation was for her and Ra'ad. 'It was the first time we thought about running away. The people in the Ba'ath Party were very difficult to deal with and our point of view was different from theirs. We didn't like them. We believed in the politics of our families – we always supported the royal family. We didn't like the left wing and the Russians and the socialists. We preferred to live in freedom. We had more liberal ideals and we believed in free market forces and democracy and allowing people to live in freedom. It must be a law – not a false freedom like in Iraq, where it's forced. There must be some freedom for people to feel free about how to think and to believe in anything they want. We believed that everyone has the right to believe in anything if they don't hurt others. My father taught me this.'

As highly educated Iraqis with a global outlook, Ra'ad and Guzin saw the intellectual degradation of their country as unforgivable and unlivable. Because they lived abroad they were not affected by it on a day-to-day basis, but they recognised in their fellow Iraqis an endemic acquiescence mandated by fear and a real lack of choice. According to Kanan Makiya, by 1983 Iraqis had become more gullible and less political.

Wave after wave of propaganda left Iraqis deadened and cynical, and they believed that politics was, as Makiya writes, 'invariably associated with cheating and lying'. Ra'ad and Guzin did not want the same gullibility or cynicism that flattened their fellow Iraqis to infect their family or the minds of their children.

From an emotional perspective, Guzin had few if any personal ties in Iraq. Her father Shawket and her sister Buthaina, who was now married with two boys of her own, were in Jordan where they had been since they slipped out of Iraq in 1978. Neither had set foot in the country since that day, and neither would ever again. Ra'ad's mother had moved to Abu Dhabi in the United Arab Emirates with her second husband, Hikmat Draz, and would soon resettle in picturesque Kent in the English countryside. As far as Ra'ad and Guzin could see, there was no compelling reason that would draw them back to Baghdad.

After much discussion they decided to flee Iraq and seek political asylum. If they succeeded, they knew it would be final. There was no going back while Saddam Hussein held absolute power. There were other risks too. For diplomats from dictatorial countries, seeking asylum is like a game of Russian roulette. If one officially seeks it and fails, they can never return home, particularly to a country like Iraq where to do so would mean death or torture or, at the very least, imprisonment. Secret inquiries are needed either with a trusted contact or within an unofficial underground of sympathisers. A mere whiff of defection by a suspicious informant was a potential death sentence.

Ra'ad carefully investigated the options with a fellow Iraqi who was taking a doctorate at McGill University. His oft-repeated mantra was that 'there is no hope in our country' and he advised Ra'ad to leave, just as he had. However, Ra'ad was told that Canada would not grant asylum to diplomats. The conundrum was similar to the one that faced Ra'ad's and Guzin's old friend, the former professor and Iraqi ambassador to London, Dr Hisham Al-Shawi. He requested asylum from Canada while serving as Iraq's ambassador there, but was refused. He found refuge in London instead. Ra'ad turned to the Arab world and sought preliminary assistance from a trusted contact in the department of foreign affairs in the United Arab Emirates. A reply came back that amounted to another rebuff. Guzin and Ra'ad were shattered. They were mortified that an Arab nation would turn its back on fellow Arabs.

Guzin's father Shawket Najim desperately wanted his daughter and grandchildren to move to Jordan with him and waged a strong but ultimately futile campaign to convince them they would be safe. He repeatedly argued that he had not been harassed or victimised since making Jordan his home. But then his late wife Majida had been a Jordanian with impressive ties to influential people in the upper echelons of society. This time, it was Ra'ad who refused. Had he been granted asylum officially, he would have the protection of the host nation who had taken his family in. But simply absconding to Jordan guaranteed no safety at all. And Ra'ad couldn't risk making another inquiry. So far he had been lucky and his inquiries about defecting were known only to two people outside his family. He worried that the next time he would not be so fortunate and the secret would be revealed, endangering his family. Ra'ad's internal barometer and understanding of what Saddam's regime was capable of rang warning bells.

'My husband said, "They will kill my son if we don't go back", and they would. It's happened many times. Many times,' Guzin says.

So they went home to Baghdad. It was 1984.

Chapter Ten

The Sveriges Kreditbank in the commercial district of Stockholm is as bland as big buildings get, but at fifteen minutes past ten on a quiet Thursday in 1973, a criminal twist of fate propelled it to infamy. Two prison escapees, armed and dangerous, rampaged through the bank screaming 'the party has just begun'. They stormed the tellers' counters and pointed automatic weapons randomly at three women and a man working behind them. For the next 131 hours the criminals held the employees hostage in a small vault half the size of an average-sized bedroom in the bowels of the bank. Despite the terror of what they were going through, something strange happened. Some of the victims began to bond with their captives and refused attempts by police and hostage negotiators to rescue them. After the ordeal was over, two of the women accepted proposals of marriage from the criminals and raised money for their legal defence.

Experts were astonished at the behaviour of the hostages.

How could they identify with the two hardened criminals who had threatened their very lives and whom they believed would have killed them if they needed to? Not only that, how could the victims have formed such strong attachments to the perpetrators? Psychological tests and a series of interviews revealed the captives began to identify with their captors as a way to endure the violence and the imminent threat of death. Under psychiatric inspection, their behaviour was seen not as an aberration, but rather as a survival mechanism in a situation of extreme emotional and physical duress. Any act of kindness from the bank robbers – however small – was perceived by the captives as a huge gesture because, as hostages, they were dependent on the criminals for their lives. Furthermore, the hostages were isolated from outsiders, so the only view they had about what was taking place outside the vault came from the hostage-takers themselves.

The victims' reactions to the bank robbery and their behaviour during it did not constitute an isolated incident. When victims who had survived other hostage situations were interviewed, their responses were similar. The four hostages in the bank vault at the Sveriges Kreditbank were not, it turned out, alone. The experts subsequently concurred that the behavioural responses they identified were not an uncommon human reaction to extreme threats of violence. In fact, victims of cults, prisoners of war and victims of domestic and ongoing sexual abuse also reported similar emotions toward their captors or those who had abused them. Psychiatrists named the behaviour 'the Stockholm Syndrome' after the location of the bank in which the four hostages were taken.

Baghdad is three thousand miles and several countries

away from the Sveriges Kreditbank, but when Ra'ad Said and Guzin Najim returned home from Canada in 1984, the people of Iraq were collectively in the thrall of Saddam Hussein. Much of the population was, in its own way, suffering from Stockholm Syndrome. Saddam's political police force used 'torture, kidnapping, murder and rape to intimidate dissenters and malcontents. Its agents became ever vigilant to discover the faintest sign of disaffection', writes Dilip Hiro in his book, *Iraq: A Report from the Inside*. People were powerless to do anything other than what they had to do to survive. They were caught between a rock and a hard place. Publicly, the population supported the leader who ruled with an iron fist but, privately, many held him in contempt.

Where possible, they turned a blind eye to the precarious nature of life. They found comfort in fulfilling their daily routines. They continued taking their children to school and maintained business as usual. Artists and musicians kept feeding the soul of Iraq, painting and performing in electrifying currents which moved below the surface, while providing portraits and plays in homage to Saddam, 'oh great leader', above. Merchants found haven in their tiny patch in the crowded bazaars, and those who had enjoyed life under the old British empire shook their heads in disbelief and dreamed of recapturing the better days of times past. Overall, they hoped not to be double-crossed or fall foul of Saddam's cancerous network of informers and spies.

Ra'ad and Guzin moved back into the house in Al Mansour and noticed that the suburb had grown in the years they had been away. Not only had it become increasingly trendy with the growing middle class frequenting the Al Mansour club, but it was home to Saddam Hussein's favourite social haunt, the Nadi al-Said club, which translates as the 'hunting club'. There he sucked on his pungent Cuban cigars and imbibed his preferred beverage, Mateus Rosé, a limp drink hardly worthy of tyrants and potentates.

Al Mansour was also a vital cog in Saddam's terror machine. The general intelligence department (GID) and the Mukhabarat headquarters were located in the district. The GID concentrated on rooting out political opposition to Saddam Hussein within Iraq and across foreign borders. The main office for the intelligence service was located on busy Al Mansour Street, which formed a T-intersection with Ra'ad and Guzin's leafy Princess Street. The proximity was unnerving. It was a pustule in the pretty neighbourhood. People walked by the multistorey edifice studiously averting their heads, as if by ignoring the elephant in the corner it somehow would not be there. But self-deception can only go so far. Iraqis knew the terrible fate of those who were dragged inside, even if they tried to deny it to themselves. Dilip Hiro writes of the GID's activities within the building with a clinician's cool remove. The reality is that the deeds he describes need no embroidering:

> Besides resorting to well-known methods of torture – administering electrical shocks to genitals, caning the soles of feet, hanging suspects upside down, burning sensitive parts of the body with cigarettes, immersing the head into water for oppressively long periods, depriving the suspect of sleep for days on end – the GID specialised in administering slow-acting poison to the suspects and holding hostage the families of the dissidents who proved elusive, often raping their young female relatives.

Ra'ad Said returned to work at the ministry of foreign affairs on the banks of the Tigris. Lina was enrolled in the Dejla Primary School near their home and, like her mother years earlier, continued to thrive academically. Mohammed was too young to go to school but started kindergarten around the corner. Guzin desperately missed her father, who was in Jordan, and she did not see him for nearly three years.

As a family, they reacquainted themselves with the upscale lifestyle they had left six years earlier. They renewed their membership at the Al Rasheed hotel, which, in March 2003, was one of several hotels used by the international media covering the second Gulf War, as it was in the first war of 1990–1991. After that war it featured a broken mosaic of former American president Geoge Bush captioned 'Bush is criminal' laid into the lobby floor. Guzin was soon back swimming in the pool. When time permitted, she would take on Ra'ad in a game of tennis, his favourite sport. If they needed a break, they booked a suite at the hotel – one room for the adults and another for Lina and Mohammed – and stayed for the weekend. Sometimes they packed the car and headed out of town for picnics with Ra'ad's brother, Mohanned, and his family and other friends hoping to escape the oppressiveness of Baghdad, however temporarily. The men played poker and those who drank took whiskey. The women sang and danced as if they were teenagers again.

Guzin and Ra'ad also decided to build a second smaller house on the massive Princess Street property – a project which took up much of 1985 and 1986. Guzin oversaw the construction and ensured that it blended in with its location. When the house was finished, they rented it out hoping for a steady, ready source of income. It was a good life, considering. But no matter how much they tried to fit back into Baghdad, and regardless of the efforts they took to resume a normal existence, Ra'ad and Guzin could never conform to the rigidities of life imposed by the personal autocracy of Saddam Hussein. When they left Iraq in 1978, the country was ruled, nominally at least, by the comparatively benevolent President Ahmed Hasan al-Bakr. Now, for the first time ever, they were living under the direct rule of a dictator whose goodwill to his citizens was capricious at best.

Unlike most of their fellow citizens who needed government permission to leave Iraq, Ra'ad and Guzin had been spoiled by the freedoms of living abroad. They felt the claustrophobia of Saddam's rule as if he personally were wrapping his hands around their necks. They were hemmed in. What was once welcomed as vital debate among the Iraqi intelligentsia was now outlawed as provocative anti-Ba'ath hate-speech, punishable by death. Even to protest would be a death sentence. Like all Iraqis, Ra'ad and Guzin could do nothing but watch their backs. As privileged as they were, their elevated position in society potentially made them more of a target for snake-eyed informants hoping for a big kill.

Saddam Hussein's Iraq had two faces. One was the international face. Saddam at that time had diplomatic, economic, political and military ties with several foreign countries including the United States, Great Britain, various European countries, and Arab neighbours such as Kuwait and Saudi Arabia. Some relationships were tenuous and others rested on a thin tissue of pragmatism, but however solid or questionable they were, they existed. Iraq was still at war with Iran, whose fundamentalism was seen as one of the greatest threats in the Middle East. During the war Saddam's ego grew exponentially and his audacious myth-making machine went into overdrive. He had been cultivating the warrior image for years and now seemed the perfect moment to proclaim himself the 'Knight of the Arab nation'. Iraq bought arms and materials capable of building chemical, biological and nuclear weaponry from France and Germany. The United States, Britain and France lent their military might to the Iraqi war effort against Iran. In exchange, Iraq offered its support for a negotiated peace settlement between Israel and the Arab world, paid off its loans to the US and offered it discounted oil.

Meanwhile, the dictator in Saddam Hussein was permitted to run wild as his people 'willingly' sung hymns to praise him and men grew luxuriant moustaches just like his. The genie had been let out of the bottle. Between 1974 and 1978 a series of death-penalty decrees ensured lifetime loyalty to the Ba'ath Party from its members. In 1982 members of the Iraqi national assembly wrote a pledge of loyalty to Saddam, using their own blood as ink. By 1986, the penalties had been ratcheted up and now included 'insult' as a criminal offence. Saddam signed the law himself, a personal flourish, delighting in its monstrous scope. 'Anyone insulting publicly in any way the President of the Republic, or his office, or the Revolutionary Command Council, or the Arab Ba'ath Socialist Party, or the Government, is punishable by life imprisonment and the expropriation of all his property both movable and immovable. The punishment will be execution if the insult or attack is done in a blatant fashion or is designed to provoke public opinion against the authorities,' it thundered.

The irony is that the Ba'ath Party of the 1950s actually stood for freedom of speech. Saddam Hussein was a revisionist and opportunist. Ostensibly, the decree outlawed public debate, public dissent, public discussion, public ridicule and, of course, public interest. The only interest worth serving was that of Saddam Hussein, the paramount ruler. In a 1990 television interview broadcast on America's ABC network six months before the first Gulf war, Saddam told journalist Diane Sawyer that he saw nothing wrong with the law: 'Does not the law in your country punish whoever tries to insult the president?' he asked Sawyer through an interpreter.

'No, Mr President, half of the country would be in prison,' Sawyer replied somewhat mischievously.

'And no measures are taken against anybody who insults the president?'

'No, they are even given their own TV show,' she retorted to the stunned Iraqi leader.

'Well, in Iraq the president is regarded by the people as a symbol representing something.'

Saddam Hussein had a death-grip on the Iraqi population and no one was capable of fighting it. People found it easier to choose the path of least resistance, and that was how Guzin and Ra'ad survived. They kept their heads below the parapet and hoped and prayed that Ra'ad would receive another posting that would spirit them away.

Their prayers were answered, not once but, blessedly, twice in the next five years.

Chapter Eleven

As the hottest months of summer started to pummel the Iraqi landscape in the middle of 1986, Ra'ad Said herded his family onto an Iraqi Airways Boeing 747 jumbo jet and waited anxiously for take-off. His wife Guzin sat beside him, absent-mindedly fingering the seatbelt tightened across her lap as if it were a protective talisman. The children were seated side by side, one row back. Within six hours they would be touching down in New Delhi, the capital of India. They had planned a short holiday before heading to Ra'ad's next posting as under-secretary to the Iraqi ambassador in Kabul, Afghanistan.

Once in the air, Guzin asked the flight attendant for two glasses of champagne. She was, after all, travelling first class. Guzin wanted to toast a simple matter of their survival, which was no mean feat in Baghdad. They had deliberately flown below the radar for two years and it had worked. Now, they were returning to the international life that fitted them like a glove.

Like all tourists in India, Guzin and Ra'ad visited the Taj Mahal, a white marbled palace of love built by a Mogul emperor in the seventeenth century in memory of his favourite wife. They rode elephants that had their faces decorated with white chalk flowers. Guzin loved watching the rituals of religion when recumbent cattle would spread their bovine mass lazily across a street and cars would stop, waiting patiently – without honking their horns – for them to be mobile once more. Guzin and the children loved everything about their trip to India, so much so that they returned every few months while living in Kabul, which was only a few hours away by plane.

Kabul was another world altogether. The family settled in the Wazir Arkbar Khan district a few kilometres north of the Old City Wall and slightly northwest of the Kabul River which trickled through the city during the summer months. The four-bedroom two-storey house was in a good neighbourhood, not far from where the American, British and German embassies now stand. Guzin had a staff of four to help her with the household – two cleaners, a cook and a gardener. Staff were cheap in Kabul in 1986.

Ra'ad's job as under-secretary was one of the least taxing he had had while working in the department of foreign affairs, but it would be the most rewarding. Iraq was still at war with Iran, which shared half of its easternmost border with Afghanistan. Before 1991, the north was bordered by the former Soviet Union but that same stretch of border is now shared by the independent states of Tajikistan, Uzbekistan and Turkmenistan. Strategically located in a valley surrounded by mountains in the central-east near the Pakistan border, Kabul is Afghanistan's seat of government while Herat, on the western border, is the financial heart of the country and its major trading region.

When Ra'ad and Guzin arrived, Afghanistan – which is a devoutly Muslim country – had been under the control of the USSR since the Russian invasion on 26 December 1979. A night-time curfew of nine o'clock was enforced, but diplomats were exempted if travelling between embassies and consular residences. Basically, the same restrictions that governed the locals did not apply to the diplomatic corps, which was probably just as well because it supported an even more active social life than Ra'ad and Guzin had experienced in Yemen six years earlier.

Guzin made friends with people from India, Egypt, Saudi Arabia, Cuba, Spain and the Philippines, all of which had official representation in Afghanistan. They spent every day in each other's company, either for official business at the United Nations Staff House (which had a swimming pool, much to Guzin's delight) or socialising at the Hotel Intercontinental. The wife of the Japanese ambassador taught the women how to make origami, and Guzin taught them all about the weaves and textures of Afghani rugs and how they were not to be confused with those from across the border in Pakistan. Both Lina and Mohammed were enrolled at the United Nations' International School, where they mixed with the children of the diplomats. They also had a dog, a German shepherd they called Tiger.

Ra'ad had never been happier in a foreign posting. He worked well with the Iraqi Ambassador, Burahan Ghazal, and they formed a close bond, much of it founded on their shared political beliefs. Ghazal came from a similar background to Ra'ad and Guzin and he and his wife, Shatha Ahmed Ayoub, held the same low opinion of Saddam

Hussein, a fact so simple and yet so big that it forged their relationship as if it were cast in steel. The two couples confided in each other. Guzin thought to herself that it was almost incredible how so many of the Iraqi elite, when safely outside the country's borders, felt free enough to give an honest point of view. It made her realise how terrified they all were of the regime.

Even though they trusted each other with their opinions, they were ever vigilant and guarded in their comments when in outside company, assiduously watching out for the informers who lurked in their ranks, waiting for any crumb of dissent. Embassies are a hotbed of intelligence and are routinely infiltrated by covert agents who use a range of covers to disguise their real purpose. They could be education or information attachés, consuls, or even high commissioners. Some might be mere pen-pushers. The point is, as under-secretary to the ambassador, Ra'ad knew they existed and he knew to be cautious.

'Burahan Ghazal was eight years older than my husband, but we spent a very nice time together. He is a very intelligent man, a good man. He was a friend and he often spoke with Lina and Mohammed. Always, always, we spent our time in a very nice way,' says Guzin, tears filling her eyes. 'He always asked my children about their problems, and whether they needed anything. He treated us as more than family. I will never forget that. Shatha was a good friend to me, very supportive, and she was very intelligent. Our children also played together.'

The information attaché assigned to the Iraqi Embassy, however, was another matter. Guzin believes he was part of Saddam Hussein's labyrinthine network of informers, if not a covert member of the Mukhabarat itself. He fitted the bill.

He was uncouth and ill-placed among the more refined folk of the diplomatic corps, and his wife was full of the arrogance of authority. They were conspicuously awkward and Guzin could see them bridling at how easily she and Ra'ad fitted in wherever they went.

'One day his wife said to us, supposedly joking, "You are not good people". I made out as if I knew nothing. But I was not fooled. She said it many times, as if she was joking, "You are not good people", but I knew what she meant. I knew about Sana'a,' Guzin says, recalling the incident in Yemen when Ali Al Delamy, the intelligence service agent from the Mukhabarat, told Ra'ad and Guzin that the ambassador had sent a negative report about them back to Baghdad.

Ra'ad was reassigned in 1988. The Soviet Union would withdraw from Afghanistan in 1989, leaving it on a crash course to a prolonged civil war in the hands of the communist regime of Najibullah. Guzin was sad to leave. There was little she didn't like about Afghanistan. The locals were so accepting of foreigners, even women like Guzin who did not conform to traditional Islamic dress, and were passionate about their country's rich heritage, with its well-trodden trade routes and temperate climate. 'We left Kabul when the country was going to war,' Guzin says, sitting in her flat in Sydney with the television tuned to CNN, sound on mute. 'It was very sad. I liked these people and I was sad for them.'

It is Monday 31 March 2003. As Guzin recalls her exit fifteen years earlier from Afghanistan, her own country is once again at war. The irony stings. Dawn is breaking in Iraq on the twelfth day of the American-led allied assault on Iraq, which is progressing steadily. The first Tomahawk missiles hit key targets in Baghdad and, within the first twenty-four hours of war, sixty missiles had been fired. The next day, Saddam Hussein's Republican Presidential Palace on the western banks of the Tigris was bombed, effectively knocking out the nerve centre of the regime. In southern Iraq, 60,000 American troops were pushing north, and in the United States, President George W. Bush announced he would send 120,000 more. Australian troops had taken Umm Qasr and were defending it from Iraqi fire in preparation for the humanitarian aid mission that would bring food and water to Iraqi civilians. Next to fall was the port town of Al Faw on the Persian Gulf. Then Nasiriyah. Basra. And Najaf, the holy shrine city for Shi'ite Muslims on the Euphrates River. And on the towns fell until Baghdad toppled with the fall of Saddam's statue in Firdos Square and its subsequent beheading.

The television camera cuts to Iraq's irrepressibly cocky information minister, Mohammed Saeed al-Sahaf, the man the western world dubbed 'Baghdad Bob' for his calculated swagger and wild, implausible exaggerations of Iraq's successes against the rolling might of the allied armed forces and its superior air power. With his insurmountable braggadocio and a pistol worn jauntily on his hip, he could pass as a gunslinger from the Wild West, but Guzin looks at him with disgust. She is unable to disguise her contempt at the propaganda Baghdad Bob has been disseminating and which he blithely delivers as either a sermon or a stand-up comic routine. Today, he is still talking about the Iraqi suicide bomber who detonated a bomb-laden taxi at an American checkpoint north of Najaf, killing four American soldiers the previous Saturday.

'For twelve days now the Iraqi people have had this criminal telling them lies,' Guzin says, her anger rising as

Baghdad Bob's theatrics continue in the corner. 'It has been happening ever since Saddam Hussein took power from the Iraqi people, destroying their lives. My country is a very ancient country and we are very proud because we have a very ancient civilisation. We are good people, intelligent people, well-educated people. But he, Saddam Hussein, is a criminal.'

Guzin has been thrown into a war zone just as if she were still in the heart of Baghdad with the bombs raining down around her. She has barely slept, staying up overnight to watch the BBC and CNN broadcasts for news of her friends trapped in the city. She doesn't know if Princess Street has been hit by allied missiles aimed at the general intelligence department and Mukhabarat headquarters around the corner from her home. She shrugs and says, 'I don't know. I don't know. But they must find him, this Saddam Hussein. They must.'

Twelve days earlier on the first day of war, the Sydney skyline had turned an ugly brown colour, as opaque as the Yarra River in Melbourne. A dust-storm had blown in from the drought-ridden southwest of the state. It reminded Guzin of the *turab* that frequently brought Iraq to a standstill. A blinding sandstorm that sweeps across the Iraqi desert, the *turab* can cut visibility to an arm's length. It was what had slowed the progress of the allied forces in the early days of war when soldiers and tanks were being pelted by tiny pebbles of sand.

The television silently broadcasts images from Baghdad. Red and white tracer bullets streak across the night sky followed by noiseless fiery explosions. Guzin stares into the dusty distance outside her window as tears splash down her cheeks. 'I want the Australian people to know what heroes their soldiers are,' she says, crying harder. 'They are not going there to kill my people. They are going to free them from this evil man.' Her hands are clasped at her chest and she prays out loud in Arabic before speaking in English.

'The Iraqi people want Saddam dead – even those who are fighting for him want him dead. They are only fighting for him because they are too frightened of him not to. He is a criminal. How many love stories have been destroyed by Saddam Hussein in my country, Iraq?'

Chapter Twelve

Next stop Athens. Ra'ad had been representing Iraq around the world for ten years when he landed in Greece in the summer of 1988 to take up his fifth diplomatic assignment. He was forty-one years old, had been happily married to the same woman for fourteen years, almost to the day, and had two children, a girl and a boy aged thirteen and eight respectively who, he boasted with pride, never gave him a moment's trouble. His tennis was a bit rusty and his weight wasn't getting any easier to manage, but he still had a thick head of hair and his health. Ra'ad Said was enormously happy. The international stage was his natural home and he was the perfect character actor for it.

Ra'ad's postings over the previous decade had given him a range of experiences in diplomacy and, as a result of his accumulated knowledge, he was a multifaceted expert in foreign affairs. As under-secretary to the ambassador in Afghanistan, he had been in a penultimate position of power in a critical posting and had gained a comprehensive understanding of all the issues concerning Iraq from a global perspective. He knew where Iraq stood politically, economically and militarily. Ra'ad was abreast of trade issues, security and cultural matters. As a consul, he was also responsible for the welfare and safety of Iraqi citizens in whichever country he was then engaged in. It was a job he took very seriously. His personality, too, was perfectly suited to the diplomatic life. Dignified and polished, multilingual and educated, he was, in a way, accessibly aristocratic without being superior or patronising.

Ra'ad took the sum total of his experiences and seniority with him to Athens, where his position as consul gave him responsibility for Cyprus as well as the Greek mainland and all of the surrounding islands. He was kept extremely busy and his long hours often resulted in him sending magnificent sprays of flowers to Guzin to apologise for his absences. Ra'ad was so sincere and so committed to his job that Guzin could never stay angry with him for long, even if it did rile her when he missed his cherished evening ritual of dinner and helping the children with their homework.

As usual it was Guzin's job to settle the family into a new home and she chose historic Feylothai. Known as a diplomatic enclave and located at the foot of the Acropolis, it was one of Athens' most prestigious districts. They were just a few kilometres away from the Panathenian Stadium, home to the first modern Olympiad in 1896. Guzin decorated the house with exquisite furniture imported from China and Hong Kong, and brought in European white-goods from Copenhagen.

Guzin enrolled Lina and Mohammed at the prestigious Green Hill School at 17 Kokinaki Street in Kifissia. The principal, Ms Sbeiti, was pleased to have them. Over the previous years at the International School in Kabul, Lina had scored straight As in English, French, mathematics, physics and biology, and was described as 'very quiet, ambitious and hardworking'. The report card could have been describing Lina's father, for those were the very qualities he was renowned for and, clearly, she had inherited them from him. Lina was just like Ra'ad. In fact, her close relationship with her father mirrored that of Guzin with Shawket.

Lina's younger brother Mohammed was only eight but he too was showing early promise with excellent reports from his first teachers in Kabul. By the time he was eighteen and ready to sit the academically rigorous international Baccalaureate Examination in 1998, Mohammed was a straight A student in the sciences. In the Baccalaureate, he scored a total of 651 out of a possible 700 in the scientific section. It was a mighty achievement.

Once the house was established and the children were settled, Guzin set about investigating the social scene. By now she was an old hand at securing an entrée to the international world of diplomats and dignitaries and the glamorous receptions they threw. By the third week in Athens, Ra'ad had run into a British diplomat whom he had known a decade earlier while he was second secretary at the Iraqi Embassy in London. They had also crossed paths when both were posted to Yemen. The British diplomat, as one would expect, had strong ties with western diplomats and Ra'ad, being something of an international citizen, immediately accepted an invitation to a small, informal soiree at a local restaurant. He and Guzin welcomed the company and were happy to extend their social network.

One of the guests was an American named Samuel Spencer, who was assigned to the United States Embassy in

Athens. Introduced as Sam, he was married to a much younger woman named Charlotte, a beautiful woman with elegant features. The couples had several things in common and hit it off instantly. Sam, who was two years older than Ra'ad, was a tall, thin man with an earnest expression. He spoke with the unique rounded sounds of a man who hails from the northeast coast of the United States. Charlotte was eight years younger than Guzin and did not have children of her own but was quickly drawn to Lina and Mohammed. The two families frequently got together to play Monopoly and other board games, and Charlotte went along with Guzin to watch the children at skating practice at the local ice-rink, where two 85-year-old Australian parrots with clipped wings chattered away all day.

On weekends Guzin and Ra'ad continued their custom, when in new countries, of exploring their surroundings, showing their children the Greek islands and Grecian ruins, which reminded them of the antiquities of Mesopotamia in their homeland. The trips also allowed Lina and her father to indulge their shared passion for seafood – something Guzin and Mohammed couldn't stand. On the picturesque island of Mykonos, Mohammed's eyes almost dropped out of his head when he saw a nude woman for the first time, soaking up the sun. Even though he had been brought up in a secular westernised world, for a young Arab Muslim it was something of a shock.

◆ ◆ ◆

The Iraqi Embassy in Greece was riddled with agents from Saddam Hussein's dreaded intelligence service, the Mukhabarat. It was no secret that they operated abroad spying on suspected dissidents and gathering intelligence.

Until now, though, they had mostly been anonymous or, at the very least, kept a low profile and did not draw attention to themselves. In Athens they were so conspicuous that Guzin was able to tell an agent at ten paces. Their inordinate presence was a by-product of Saddam Hussein's foreign and weapons policies.

Throughout the 1980s, and particularly since the end of the Iran–Iraq war, Saddam Hussein had been building his capabilities to produce weapons of mass destruction (WMD). His policy on non-conventional weapons was of paramount concern to the United States and its allies. He aimed fixed Scud missile launchers at Israel, tested a space-launch vehicle loaded with a cluster of Scuds and, in 1990, began building a uranium enrichment facility at the isolated Iraqi town of Tarmiyah. Then, in a much publicised meeting with fellow Arab leaders in Amman on 24 February 1990, Saddam Hussein gave a speech calling on Arab unity to withstand American and Israeli power. Two months later in a speech broadcast on Iraqi radio and quoted in the biography *Saddam Hussein* by Efraim Karsh and Inari Rautsi, Saddam directly threatened Israel, saying 'we will make fire eat half of Israel if it tries to do anything against Iraq'. Over the coming months more deadly weapons, the devices to fire them and materials to make them, would be found in Iraq. The final straw would come in August 1990 when Saddam Hussein invaded Kuwait and ignored all subsequent United Nations resolutions to withdraw, putting Iraq irrevocably on a path to war.

Meanwhile, Iraq was ten years into developing what it called a 'supergun'. Saddam Hussein had engaged a Canadian-born American citizen and astrophysicist named Gerard Bull to design a massive 40-tonne weapon which could fire missiles loaded with chemical, biological or nuclear warheads several hundred kilometres – effectively from Baghdad to Israel. Codenamed Project Babylon, the weapon was never completed, but not for want of trying. Bull was assassinated in Holland in March 1990, at the height of the western world's renewed concerns about Saddam's WMD capabilities. To this day Bull's murder remains unsolved, but all fingers point to Israel's spy agency, Mossad, as his killer.

Shortly after Bull's assassination, American and British customs officials intercepted shipments destined for Iraq which contained sophisticated electrical devices that could be used to trigger nuclear arms. As well, massive steel tubes that were believed to have been built as barrels for the Bull 'supergun' were intercepted in transit in the Athens harbour, and other weapons materials were discovered in Turkey.

Ra'ad, as the Iraqi consul in Athens, learned of the discovery of the WMD material in Greece on the BBC and the new American channel, CNN, which were broadcasting the story live. Guzin, who never asked her husband the precise nature of his job, does not know how deeply involved Ra'ad was with the ensuing diplomatic and political crisis. 'I don't know if Ra'ad had something to do with these tubes, but this shipment was to arrive in Iraq without anybody knowing about it,' she says now. 'Ra'ad was just saying that Saddam Hussein is mad. Always, he said to Sam, "He is very mad, he is importing these things while my people are hungry".'

The Mukhabarat responded to the western world's discovery of the Project Babylon hardware in Athens by ratcheting up pressure on members of the diplomatic corps, particularly Ra'ad. They questioned him at length about his connection with Sam and Charlotte Spencer, and instructed him to cut all ties with them. 'They kept asking us all the time, "Why are you friends with the Americans? Why are you so close with these Americans?"' Guzin says now, drawing deeply on a cigarette, her hand trembling. 'My husband was afraid. We loved those people, they were good people.

'Every weekend we got together for lunch and dinner and we watched videotapes together with the children. I showed them many books about my family. I told them that we were against the regime but Ra'ad wouldn't be as clear about it as me because he was a diplomat.'

Ra'ad had become agitated, Guzin recalls, and extremely nervous. He started drinking heavily, which caused fights with his wife. The pressure was immense. Even though he and Guzin had become close to Sam and Charlotte since arriving in Athens, Ra'ad insisted that Guzin sever their relationship on orders from the Mukhabarat.

'Ra'ad said we must cut everything off with them. He said, "If they call you, you must say to them that we don't want any relationship with them",' Guzin says. It was one of the most emotionally difficult things Guzin had ever had to do.

Sam and Charlotte Spencer, meanwhile, had been recalled to Washington DC by the American State Department. They were scheduled to fly out in September, just when the autumn temperatures make life bearable but still hold warm memories of summer. Guzin rang Charlotte and, using the sternest voice she could muster, told her that she and Ra'ad wanted nothing more to do with her and Sam. Charlotte was shocked and hurt and wanted to know what she had done to offend Guzin. Likewise, Guzin was a sea of roiling emotions. She was upset and angry that she had to end their friendship, and hated hurting Charlotte. But as Ra'ad pointed out, they had no choice; one doesn't say no to the Mukhabarat.

Sam and Charlotte suspected something, because as Guzin tells it now, twelve years on, Charlotte telephoned Guzin and asked to see her and Ra'ad before she and Sam returned to Washington. Guzin said no, but it didn't put Charlotte off from trying one more time. 'Charlotte phoned me from the airport and said, "I have something for you here, just come and see us and say goodbye", but I said, "No, do not call us again". We couldn't do anything, we couldn't call them or go and see them. Why? The regime of Saddam Hussein.'

A few weeks later, a fax addressed to Ra'ad Said arrived at the embassy in Athens from Iraq's department of foreign affairs. It was concise. Ra'ad's mission in Athens had been terminated. He must return to Baghdad.

War was looming.

Chapter Thirteen

They didn't return to Baghdad straight away, as per the orders printed on the thermal paper facsimile with its curling edges and imperious logo of Saddam Hussein's foreign ministry. Instead, Ra'ad sent Guzin and the children to the safety of her father's home in Jordan while he remained in Athens for a few days, sorting out their personal business and packing up the apartment in Feylothai. When Ra'ad arrived in Jordan, Guzin's father Shawket Najim told his son-in-law that he did not want his daughter and grandchildren returning to Iraq on the eve of a war. Shawket insisted that they stay with him, and Ra'ad readily agreed. The last thing he wanted was to put the lives of his children and wife at risk in a war zone.

Privately, Ra'ad was also terrified of repercussions from the Athens 'supergun' incident and from the friendship he and Guzin had shared with the Americans Sam and Charlotte Spencer. He hoped that his immediate acquiescence to the orders of the Mukhabarat to sever the relationship with the Spencers had been the end of it. Yet it was impossible to know. The Mukhabarat were legal outlaws who operated with Saddam Hussein's imprimatur. In their hands, the laws of the land were extremely elastic and the Iraqi citizenry was powerless to stop them. By keeping the children and Guzin in Jordan, Ra'ad could, at least, quarantine them from any risk that might exist in Baghdad. The Mukhabarat had their own methods and, at that moment, it didn't bear thinking about.

Three days after arriving in Jordan in mid-December 1990, Ra'ad received a telephone call from the Iraqi Embassy in Amman. He had no idea how they'd found him because he'd left no forwarding address or contact details upon leaving Athens. His worst fears were realised when an officious consular staff member told him that foreign affairs were ordering his immediate return to Baghdad. It was an order from the top, he was told.

Ra'ad was shaking when he replaced the receiver but he calmed himself as he relayed the news to Guzin. 'I have no choice but to return to Baghdad. Foreign affairs know our phone number and where we are staying,' Ra'ad said, his voice stiff, an attempt to mask the fear in his heart. 'I'm going back to Baghdad immediately. You and the children will stay with your father in Jordan. It's for your own safety.'

Shawket stood to one side, listening solemnly. Finally, he looked Ra'ad in the eye and told him to ignore the directive and stay in Jordan with his family, where he belonged. Ra'ad would not be drawn into the debate. Of course he wanted desperately to stay but he knew he couldn't. Shawket was relentless, like a dog with a bone. 'Stay,' he implored. 'Stay.'

The stress of the past few months coupled with the phone

call was too much, and Ra'ad exploded. 'They will kill my son. I have to go back to Baghdad,' he said.

The words ripped through the house like a bomb. It explained why Ra'ad was so distressed after the phone call. Mohammed's life had been threatened. He was just a boy of ten. Ra'ad was terrified. Foreign affairs had already found him. Who knew if the Mukhabarat would be next? At that moment their future was clear. Guzin knew Ra'ad had to return to Baghdad, and yet she refused to let her beloved husband go back alone or split her family during a time of crisis. If Ra'ad was returning to the gates of hell, then she would go with him. No amount of rational argument from Ra'ad or her father was going to change her mind. She was defiantly obstinate. 'I remember I said, "I will never stay, I want to go with my husband to Baghdad",' Guzin says now, showing the fierce independence and loyalty for which she has been known all her life.

With little choice but to support his daughter, Shawket prepared Guzin for her return to a war zone. A retired general, he, more than most, knew what provisions would be needed to survive a long, drawn-out battle which would knock out the main facilities in the city. They were a family of considerable means so money was not an object. He and Guzin's brother-in-law, Dr Mohammed Al Tell, hired a truck and loaded it with an assortment of basic foodstuffs, bare necessities and medical supplies: 100 kilograms of rice, 200 kilograms of flour, dried beans, milk powder, soft drinks and chocolate for the children, cooking oil, detergent, candles, matches, water, gasoline. A range of medicines came from Mohammed's pharmacy.

Shawket told Guzin to pack her most precious things in a bag which should always be ready and waiting near the car in case they needed to flee urgently. She packed her gold and diamond jewellery, a mink coat, and small antiques that were given as wedding gifts – all things that could be used as currency, if needed – and of course, photographs and passports. She would never be emotionally prepared for war, but at least she felt ready on a practical level.

Guzin returned to the Princess Street house with Lina and Mohammed in time to welcome in the New Year. She silently noted how modern and rich Baghdad looked, built on the profits of the oil that ran deep below the surface. Ra'ad had returned two weeks previously, straight after receiving the telephone call from the Iraqi Embassy in Amman, and had resumed work at the department of foreign affairs. The incidents in Athens, for now at least, were behind him, and his duties were tailored around the impending war.

The full might of international diplomacy was working towards finding a peaceful resolution to Iraq's illegal occupation of oil-rich Kuwait. Arab leaders sought what became known as the 'Arab solution' to obtain Iraq's withdrawal, but concluded that Saddam Hussein was unwilling to leave Kuwait and relinquish his grip on its oil reserves and vital access to the Gulf. President George Bush personally warned Saddam that if he fired chemical or biological weapons 'you and your country will pay a terrible price'. A coalition of twenty-eight countries led by the United States and the four-star General Norman Schwarzkopf were ready and waiting at well-defended bases in Saudi Arabia for their orders to remove Saddam Hussein's forces from the tiny, neighbouring Kuwait.

The wait was excruciating. Iraqis were on edge. Schools were closed, and more than one million of the three and a half million who lived in the capital fled from Baghdad. They feared that Israel, one of the allied forces in the coalition, would drop a retaliatory nuclear warhead on the city if Saddam fired a chemical or biological missile across its border. Guzin noticed the streets, especially around her fashionable neighbourhood, were much quieter and the traffic had slowed dramatically. But, oddly, the nearby race-track – which was built after Saddam reintroduced horse-racing as a national pastime in the 1970s – was a hive of activity as jockeys continued their early morning workouts on their mounts.

While Iraqis had hoped the last minute diplomatic negotiations would succeed, Saddam Hussein revelled in pre-war machismo. He believed the coalition would fall apart. He had himself photographed in a replica of the war chariot used by the Babylonian king, Nebuchadnezzar, who destroyed Jerusalem in 587 BC and drove its inhabitants into seventy years of captivity. He greeted his soldiers and told them they would prevail and be heroes to their fellow countrymen and women. But a huge contingency of allied forces was waiting in the wings, ready to strike when so ordered. This time it was Saddam Hussein who was ignoring the elephant in the corner, and the elephant was a multinational coalition from five continents about to embark on Operation Desert Storm. It would take just forty-three days of warfare to drive Iraq from Kuwait.

The first bombs screamed through the silence of a freezing Baghdad night and found their targets just after two o'clock on 17 January 1991. Fired from allied fighter planes which roared through the blackness, they struck key military installations and vital political and economic targets in Iraq and Iraqi forces in Kuwait. Guzin

Najim woke up to the wailing of air-raid sirens and the thunderous roar of bomb blasts, aircraft, fires and panic as Al Mansour was rocked by explosions. The bombs hit bridges, destroyed roads and power stations, and took out weapons facilities. She heard deafening blasts in quick succession and felt their home shake from the vibrations. She remembers the time as twenty minutes past two o'clock. She was terrified for her life and those of her husband and children.

Guzin and Ra'ad had been waiting for the bombs. The day before, Ra'ad came home from the foreign ministry at nine o'clock in the evening and told Guzin they should sleep on the floor that night because the war was about to begin. She chose to ignore the warning and they slept in their bed, hoping Ra'ad's information would turn out to be wrong. Lina and Mohammed went to sleep in their own rooms. 'I was sleeping but I woke up suddenly and I said to my husband, "Wake up, wake up, there is a revolution, they have killed Saddam Hussein". There were many fires in the city. Ra'ad said, "No, this is war",' Guzin remembers, her mind flashing back to the outbreak of war twelve years earlier. Lina was fifteen and Mohammed ten. Guzin prayed they would survive the night. 'I ran to the children and took them to the lobby and we sat in the entrance of the house under the wooden doorframe. We stayed there for one hour listening to the bombs. I was very afraid, very much, and I worried for Lina. She kept falling down. She couldn't walk, she was so scared. She was crying hysterically.'

The bombing campaign eased as dawn broke to reveal a devastated Baghdad caught in the flames of war – a pattern that would be repeated for the next forty-two days and nights. Two hours after the first American missiles hit Baghdad, the 41st president of the United States, George

Herbert Walker Bush, sat at his desk in the Oval Office and addressed the American people on a live television broadcast. It was exactly one minute past nine o'clock in the evening, American eastern standard time:

Saddam Hussein systematically raped, pillaged, and plundered a tiny nation, no threat to his own. He subjected the people of Kuwait to unspeakable atrocities – and among those maimed and murdered, innocent children . . . This is an historic moment . . . We have before us the opportunity to forge for ourselves and for future generations a new world order – a world where the rule of law, not the law of the jungle, governs the conduct of nations . . . We have no argument with the people of Iraq. Indeed, for the innocents caught in this conflict, I pray for their safety.

President Bush had just finished his television address when, from somewhere in Bagdhad, Saddam Hussein spoke to the few Iraqi people who were tuned in to the state-run radio at that hour of the morning. It was eighteen minutes past four. Dawn was about to break but Saddam's rhetoric was as preposterous as ever. 'Oh great Iraqi people, sons of our great people, valiant men of our courageous armed forces . . . Satan's follower Bush committed his treacherous crime, he and the criminal Zionism. The great duel, the mother of all battles, between victorious right and the evil that will certainly be defeated has begun. God willing.'

Iraq's war propaganda was a magnificent ballet choreographed by the ministry of information with all the finesse of a country hoedown. Its headquarters were located on the western banks of the Tigris, not far from one of Baghdad's major bridges and a cherished landmark, the Al Jumhuriya, which was bombed by allied missiles three times during the war and was therefore unpassable – although this significant fact was conveniently ignored by the ministry. It continued spewing forth lies to the Iraqi people about Saddam's war successes, a habit that would be repeated by Baghdad Bob in March and April of 2003.

The first onslaught in the American-led coalition's air offensive against Baghdad went unchallenged and destroyed the Presidential Palace, the ministry of defence and the Ba'ath Party headquarters. Massive explosions rocked the capital all night. The morning after, the minister for information told journalists the battle had 'been settled in our favour'. The Iraqi people were well and truly used to the thick tapestry of lies that passed for truth in modern Iraq, and instead of focusing on Saddam's fantasy, they focused on their own survival.

Their reality was entirely different from the Iraqi 'successes' being touted by the government. The electricity supply was in tatters, which meant stockpiled foodstuffs and meat perished in refrigerators. Water stopped running clean and turned into a murky dribble as water treatment plants were bombed. Cars stood still because the gas lines had stopped pumping fuel, and people were forced to walk. These memories of war are still fresh for Guzin, years after the last bomb was detonated. She is sitting in her Sydney apartment, staring blankly at the images of the second Gulf War on her television screen. Every now and then, tears roll silently down her face as the pictures from the BBC reveal yet another terrible toll of death and destruction in her country.

Guzin and her husband remained at home during the war, as did most Iraqis who hadn't fled to the bomb shelters in the north, or weren't in Saddam's army fighting on the frontlines. They chose to stay because their house was adequately if not generously supplied. They buried drums of water in the backyard and, thanks to Shawket Najim's strategic pre-war preparations, had enough food and supplies to survive. They were, as Guzin says proudly, 'well prepared for war'. But that didn't prepare them for the psychological trauma of being under siege in their own home in one of the most dangerous neighbourhoods in Baghdad.

Ra'ad and Guzin lived in what the coalition had dubbed a 'high value target' area. The headquarters for the general intelligence department and Mukhabarat were around the corner on Al Mansour Street, as was a major communications and television tower – always a priority target in a time of war. The latter was successfully demolished by missiles in the first two days of hostilities, putting an end to Saddam Hussein's state-run television station.

'In the first days of the war we were very frightened. We didn't know what would happen to our children. I can't explain how frightened we were. I had an ulcer and I began to vomit blood because of the explosions,' Guzin says, shifting between the past and the present as she speaks. 'We can't sleep at night – the bombing sometimes starts at 8 pm and went all night till morning. The second day we slept outside in the garden – it was freezing cold. We had been told it was safer to be outside the home where we would be protected if the bombs hit the house. But we didn't know what to do because of the bombing near my house. All of the walls and ceilings were shaking.

We sleep and sit on the ground and I feel that the ground is shaking beneath me like an earthquake. This area was very, very bad. Even now, the same area, Al Mansour, is being bombed,' she says, talking about the 2003 Gulf war. 'We were just sitting, like this, hugging ourselves, waiting for the bombing.

'We have a clock on the wall – tick, tick, tick – it was very quiet, we were just waiting – tick, tick, tick – and we all became very nervous from it. Then when the bombs hit, it was like disco colours going off in the sky from the explosions. You would see the light of the blast before you heard the sound. At night the children were very scared, especially Lina.' When the air-raid sirens stopped wailing, neighbours dashed outside to do a head count and make sure everyone had survived before scrambling for safety when the sirens announced another air assault. While never directly hit, Guzin's home was badly damaged from the fallout. Two missiles detonated at the end of Princess Street, shattering windows and putting baseline cracks in the walls. The kitchen cupboards were shifted from their mounts and all the crockery and glassware were destroyed. One night the bombing was so relentless that the children were screaming in terror and Guzin shepherded them to a corner in the garage and covered them with her body as the entire house shook around them. 'We thought the bombing would finish all the people,' she says.

'Ten days later, we noticed that the Iraqi people were not the target of the war, but the problem was Saddam Hussein. He decided to put the most important military people and services among the property of the people and he knew very well they would be the target of the war,' Guzin says. When talking about the war, she becomes detached, as if it hasn't really happened to her, but the tears that fall from her eyes betray her. 'He even put anti-aircraft guns in the market, knowing that when people went to buy their vegetables, they could die.'

To cope, Ra'ad and Guzin fell into a peculiar rhythm of war. During the nights they stayed awake with their children and prayed that their home would not be bombed, and every morning they walked to the front of their home with their hearts in their mouths to see who had survived the night. And yet as terrorised as they were by the war, a bizarre atmosphere emerged during the daylight hours. Once the macabre head count had been done, the days were spent socialising with neighbours in the streets outside their homes, pooling their wartime stockpiles and talking about their shared experiences. Thankful for a daylight reprieve from the bombing, they met at a makeshift communal table and ate a breakfast cooked on a sidewalk barbecue. The children played ping-pong and shuttlecock while the adults, most of whom were educated professionals, discussed a future without Saddam Hussein. 'It was a very nice atmosphere during the daytime. There were no cars in the streets and all of our children were playing because the Americans gave us a break during the day,' Guzin says. 'During the day there were no rockets. But at night it was horrible.'

The days and nights bled into each other. Those with access to a radio capable of picking up the frequency for Voice of America relayed the relevant information to those who didn't. The death toll was mounting, the casualty rate accruing, the coalition was winning. Saddam set fire to the oilwells in Kuwait and began pumping oil into the Persian Gulf. By the end of February, nearly 20,000 Iraqi soldiers supposedly loyal to Saddam Hussein had raised white flags of surrender and willingly turned themselves over to the coalition forces.

Guzin and her neighbours spoke derisively of their leader, substituting words, evoking the name of the American President George Bush when they really meant Saddam Hussein.

'We would say things like, "Oh, I hope America will die", which meant I hope Saddam Hussein dies,' Guzin says now.

It gave her and Ra'ad and their neighbours a sense of sat-isfaction knowing they were so united. They clung to the hope that their time would come, that Saddam Hussein's reign of terror would be defeated. But their greatest hope became their greatest disappointment. 'I was hoping that this war would be the end of Saddam Hussein. But at the end, we felt hopeless, every Iraqi, because they did not kill Saddam Hussein. I love people, I love to be with people. I don't have any enemies, only the Iraqi regime. After the war Iraqi people never trusted the Americans. They said, "They cheated us, they didn't kill him, they didn't remove him",' Guzin says.

'When the war ended we were still scared for no reason other than because everything stayed the same, nothing happened. After the war, everything was destroyed. The people of Iraq became more against Saddam Hussein because he was the reason for the war. We wanted a trial for him. You know, we are not criminal people but we want a trial for him, he is a criminal. What will he say? We want to hear why he did all of these things. We want to know.'

At five-thirty on the morning of 28 February 1991, exactly forty-three days after Operation Desert Storm began with the bombing of Baghdad, a formal cease-fire was declared. Saddam Hussein's armed forces were crushed, and he withdrew from Kuwait. The war was over, but Saddam had just begun another battle against the Iraqi people.

Chapter fourteen

The Persian Gulf war was the second of Saddam's warrior follies to fail in the space of three years, but its impact on the population was horrific compared to the Iran–Iraq war, which ended in 1988 and had little effect on daily life in Baghdad. With the cessation of hostilities and the continuation of the comprehensive United Nations sanctions against Iraq, Saddam Hussein had added to the oppressive hold on his country. What was once a republic living in a constant state of fear was now a republic of fear. Life had been tough enough for the Iraqi population under Saddam's hostile police state, but in post-war Iraq, things were worse.

Devastation after devastation fell upon Iraqis like a slow drip of acid rain. The Iraqi currency, the dinar, collapsed. People suffered malnutrition and pawned their jewellery and other possessions in order to buy food. Unemployment spiralled out of control. Thousands of people were homeless. Hospitals were ill-equipped and unable to adequately care for the sick. Crime increased. Oil stopped flowing and the economy crashed. Phone lines were cut and communications were limited to the propaganda provided by the state and the eldest son of Saddam Hussein, Uday, who had opened a television and newspaper company lavishly named Babel. The people of Iraq were, effectively, isolated from the outside world. And Saddam was not in a giving mood. The United Nations rations and a later oil-for-food program were managed – and mismanaged – by the regime, giving it even greater control over the people as it siphoned off supplies for its own ends.

Saddam, of course, got richer. By the end of the 1990s his wealth was reported to total a staggering six billion American dollars. He built more than fifty palaces for himself, all of which were decked out with gold taps and crystal chandeliers, the walls painted with gaudy murals and the grounds decorated with artificial lakes and rivers – water being the ultimate status symbol in the desert region. He extended his largesse to his personal army of loyalists and cronies, who also profited handsomely. 'A class of fabulously wealthy *nouveaux riches* has arisen among those engaged in smuggling, virtually all of whom are connected to the regime. However, the middle class has been wiped out,' wrote Kenneth M. Pollack in *The Threatening Storm*. Ever paranoid about being deposed, he gave his sons Uday, the brutal one, and Qusay, the strategic younger one, more and more power, effectively restricting control of the country to his immediate and extended family, those he believed he could trust.

Uday had witnessed executions as a child and, by his mid-twenties, had killed several people himself. His father had made him head of the Iraqi Olympic Committee and he

Even at the age of three, Guzin was style-conscious and insisted on changing her outfits three times a day.

Guzin with her favourite doll in Irbid, circa 1960.

Every Christmas, a doting Shawket gave his daughters a Santa doll. The girls are en route to a family gathering in the north of Jordan.

General Shawket Najim, in full military dress in the late 1960s. Shawket served his country for more than two decades.

Guzin and her sister Buthaina climbing the trees on her grandfather's property in Irbid.

Guzin with her best friend, Sana, at university. Despite her Muslim faith, Guzin favoured western fashions, opting not to wear the traditional floor-length Iraqi abaya.

Guzin graduated with a degree in law and politics from Al Mustansiriya University in Baghdad in 1977, and later received a Masters degree in international law. She met her husband Ra'ad at university in 1973.

Ra'ad Mohammed Said graduated with a law degree in 1974, just before he married Guzin.

As is customary in Iraq, Ra'ad gave his bride-to-be a piece of gold jewellery on their engagement in 1973. Guzin's delicate sky-blue chiffon dress was bought especially for the occasion. Guzin and Ra'ad were married in a traditional ceremony on 20 June 1974, but Guzin left her wedding photos in Baghdad when she fled Iraq.

With her liberal upbringing, Guzin fitted right in to the London scene when she first visited on her honeymoon in 1974.

This card is issued to

Mrs. Kzain Shawkat Najim

**Wife of
Mr. Rad M.S. Khames
Second Secretary
at the
Embassy of Iraq
in London**

Sig

**Head of Protocol Department,
Foreign and Commonwealth Office**

When Guzin was issued this identity card in London in November 1978, she felt like she had truly arrived in the international world of dignitaries and politics. She was just twenty-two years old.

Ra'ad, the proud father, holding baby Lina, with Guzin by his side, in the front garden of their Princess Street home in Baghdad.

In 1978, Ra'ad received his first diplomatic posting to the Iraqi Embassy in London. Guzin is posing outside Buckingham Palace, with Lina on the left.

Guzin and Ra'ad enjoyed an active social life as members of the international diplomatic community. They are seen here at a reception in London in 1978.

Guzin dancing at a party to celebrate her sister Buthaina's imminent wedding in 1979. Guzin was living in London and bought her sister's wedding dress at Harrods before flying to Jordan for the occasion.

Guzin is playing with Lina (to her right) at a beach in Yemen, where Ra'ad had been posted in 1980. Guzin did not wear a swimsuit out of respect for the stricter dress codes of the Yemeni.

Ra'ad's third foreign assignment was to Montreal, where he was the Iraqi consul at the Embassy from 1982 to 1984. Here, Ra'ad (circled) was presented to the Quebec Parliament and officially introduced to the Prime Minister.

Shawket Najim with his grandchildren: Guzin's children Lina and Mohammed (front), and Buthaina's children Omar (on Shawket's lap) and Ramez, in Montreal, Canada, in 1982.

Ra'ad, Guzin, Buthaina and Mohammed (on the table) are helping Lina blow out the candles on her seventh birthday cake, in Montreal in April 1982.

With her love of life and sense of fun, Guzin loved to dance. She won a prize for her dancing at a New Year's Eve party at the United Nations Staff House in 1987. Ra'ad had been posted to the Iraqi Embassy in Kabul, Afghanistan.

Guzin's sister Buthaina with her two sons, Omar (left) and Ramez, and her husband Dr Mohammed Al Tell, circa 1987. Guzin and her family stayed at Buthaina's home in Amman, Jordan, for nearly three years after she escaped from Baghdad in 1995.

At the end of the first Gulf War, the United Nations imposed a series of tough sanctions on Iraq. Ra'ad was one of Iraq's delegates to the UN's Development Program held in Baghdad from October 1993 to January 1994.

Lina and her father shared the same tastes in music, food and books, and Ra'ad spent hours with his only daughter going over her homework and helping her plan her future. She wanted to follow in her parents' footsteps, and studied for a degree at the Al Mustansiriya University.

Mohammed and Lina in their lounge room soon after the family was placed under house arrest in December 1995. Their father had died in horrific circumstances sixteen days earlier. Lina could not go to university and Mohammed was prohibited from going to school. Guzin says Mohammed 'lost his smile'.

Lina Ra'ad Said and Ahmed Jamil Al Douri planned the perfect wedding on 1 September 1998. The only thing missing was Lina's father, Ra'ad. 'Most girls dream of this day and it was beautiful, but without my father, it was terrible.'

Lina with her three-year-old son, Abdullah, on the foreshore of Sydney Harbour just days after they arrived in their new home of Australia. Lina was pregnant with Abdullah when she fled Iraq.

Guzin now calls Australia home, and in September 2004 she will become an Australian citizen. 'I came to Australia because I want to point my children's feet in the right direction, in this free country, for their future.'

built a prison within its headquarters where he routinely jailed and tortured athletes who performed poorly. In 1994 he created his own vicious militia, the Firqat Fedayeen Saddam – otherwise known as 'Saddam's self-sacrificing division' – which he used to further terrorise an already terrorised nation. Even his idea of fun and friendship was based on terror and violence. He often hung 'friends' by their knees, upside down over a wooden pole as if they were on a monkey-bar, and, using a wooden club, beat the soles of their feet until they couldn't walk. When he was finished with the beating, he made his victim 'dance' in front of him to 'get the circulation moving again', as one of his former bodyguards told *Vanity Fair* magazine in 2003. Uday called this vile ceremony of violence and humiliation the *falaqa*, and he reserved it for those who had been late for an appointment with him, or perhaps a girl who rebuffed his advances. Uday's personal appetite for violence, rape, torture and murder was insatiable, and so too was that of his regime.

In the aftermath of the war, Saddam's legendary paranoia and fear of being usurped increased to genocidal levels. In March 1991, the Marsh Arabs in the south united with Shi'ite army deserters and rose in rebellion against him, believing that with the disaster of the Gulf war, the barrier of fear was broken. '*Hajiz al-khawf inkiser*,' they said. Uprisings began in Basra and the holy cities of Najaf and Karbala, and the Kurds in the north launched a popular uprising. Saddam's response was instant and comprehensive. He ordered the systematic destruction of the Shi'ites' ancient land by diverting waters from the Tigris and Euphrates, which were their only source of water, and Iraqi troops ran the Kurds into the mountains where many starved to death. According to an official government document quoted in *Time* magazine in 1993, Saddam also ordered 'the withdrawal of all foodstuffs, a ban on the sale of fish [and] prohibiting the means of transportation to and from these areas'. But it wasn't enough for the dictator. He also called for 'mass arrest, assassination, poisoning and burning of houses'. People were tied to tanks as human shields, and Shi'ite clerics and men in turbans and robes were summarily executed.

Evidence of the mass extermination was uncovered in April and May of 2003, at the end of the second Gulf war, which Saddam also lost. Mass graves filled with the remains of the Shi'ites were dug up in southern Iraq. At small towns such as Hilla and Mahawil, where more than 3000 bodies were uncovered, the remains of mothers were found lying next to the bones of their children, dolls and toys at their fingertips. All had been shot. A 1995 United Nations report also listed the cases of thousands of political opponents who had disappeared and remained missing after the March 1991 uprising, including more than 100,000 Kurds.

'Saddam Hussein stole the spirit of the people and the soul of the people, and now, the life of the people,' Guzin says of the terrifying atmosphere that prevailed in Iraq following the 1991 Gulf war. When it came to barbarism and ruling with an iron fist, Saddam Hussein's imagination was as boundless as it was brutal.

This widespread brutality was a theme addressed by President George W. Bush in his State of the Union speech in January 2003, as allied forces prepared for the second war against Saddam Hussein. 'Iraqi refugees tell us how forced confessions are obtained – by torturing children while their parents are made to watch. International human rights groups have catalogued other methods used in the torture chambers of Iraq: electric shock, burning with hot irons, dripping acid on the skin, mutilation with electric drills, cutting out tongues, and rape. If this is not evil, then evil has no meaning.' This was Iraq in the aftermath of the Gulf war of 1991.

Ra'ad and Guzin spent the first few days in the wake of the bombardment assessing the damage to their own home and the surrounding neighbourhood. There was no petrol and the roads had been bombed and were impossible to navigate, so they couldn't drive. The house was still standing, but it was without gas and electricity, which would take three months to be restored. The cracks in the walls and the concomitant damage caused by the constant bombardment they suffered would take months to repair. But, they would say to each other sombrely, they had survived.

The children returned to school within a month but in the following years, Iraq's state-based education system suffered as a result of Saddam Hussein's corrupt management of the United Nations aid programs.

Because Guzin was in the fortunate position of having family in neighbouring Jordan, which had remained a neutral friend to Iraq during the war, they had some help. Buthaina and Shawket regularly sent supplies by mail. Food supplies in Baghdad were minimal – anything that had survived the war had either perished or been looted – so people relied on the generosity of friends and aid programs. The food crisis provided Saddam's venal son Uday with another opportunity for cruelty: he ordered the resale of rancid meat and produce repackaged as fresh.

Two weeks after the bombing ended, Shawket and Buthaina sent Guzin thirteen boxes containing a range of foodstuffs. Considering the needs of children at a time of hardship and deprivation, they sent chocolate, Pepsi Cola, chickens – a popular staple of the Iraqi diet – and fruit. They kept the supplies coming for months. 'They sent everything, the boxes were like going to Woolworths. They even sent more detergent. I will never forget them for the help they gave us,' Guzin says.

A member of the International Red Cross arrived with a letter from Ra'ad's mother Fakhira, who by now was living in Dubai. It came with a huge box of chocolates for the children which they shared with their cousins Reem and Tara, who were the same age as Lina and Mohammed, who also survived the bombing of Baghdad. Ra'ad's younger brother, Mohanned, his wife, Nasrin, and their two daughters lived not far from Ra'ad and Guzin in Adamiya. During Operation Desert Storm, the two families had watched over each other like hawks.

Ra'ad returned to work soon after the war was over. The department of foreign affairs was one of the few government buildings that was not completely razed during hostilities, but in the immediate post-war days, there was little to be done. Iraq was an international pariah, so Ra'ad's diplomatic skills were hardly needed. Civil servants were also among the first victims of inflation as Saddam Hussein slashed their salaries to save money. Ra'ad earned just fifteen thousand Iraqi dinar a month, which, given the rate of inflation, amounted to less than ten American dollars. It was not uncommon for educated civil servants to earn significantly inferior wages to those of blue collar workers under Saddam's rule.

Despite the undercurrent of fear, slowly but surely over the following months and years, life returned to a version of normality. People fell back into their old routines and made do under the new order of things. Everyone found a way to cope in the post-war era, but life in Iraq would never be as it was. Ra'ad and Guzin were fortunate enough to have money to fall back on. Before the year was out, Guzin had hired a live-in housekeeper, Bessma, and driver, a Sudanese immigrant named Fathy, as well as a gardener who came once or twice a week. With unemployment escalating out of control, they were happy to have found work. Guzin paid them all out of her family money. Fathy earned fifty thousand dinar – more than three times as much as Ra'ad – and Bessma earned thirty thousand dinar. Guzin also bought them clothes and paid for their transportation. As members of the household staff, they ate the same food as the family. The gardener received ten thousand dinar per month.

Guzin also restored the family's social life, only on a much smaller and more frugal scale than that which they had been used to. They resumed their memberships at their favourite hotel, the Al Rasheed, overlooking Haleb Square and the festival and parade ground, and returned to swimming and tennis. They still dined at the National Restaurant in the Al Rasheed, although less frequently. To compensate, they began entertaining more in the safety of their own home, inviting friends for dinner parties and conversation fuelled with sweet Iraqi tea.

Among those who visited was one of Iraq's most famous poets and writers, Jabra Ibrahim Jabra, the author of a book about Al Mansour called *Shari Al-Amirat* or, in English, *The Princesses' Street*. After the war, Jabra visited

Guzin daily and she looked forward to seeing the old man because of his age and wisdom and, not least, his consummate skills as a storyteller. He regaled her with tales about moving to Baghdad in 1948 after the War for Palestine, and of meeting the mystery writer Agatha Christie at a dinner party at her home in Baghdad the following year. She was introduced as 'Mrs Mallowan', the wife of Mr Max Mallowan, an archeologist working on the ancient sites of Mesopotamia. In his book, Jabra described Mrs Mallowan as a somewhat large, virtuous woman with a broad face who 'was the only person in the room who does not suffer from the delirium of writing'. How wrong he was. Guzin also enjoyed debating religious and political issues with Jabra – topics close to her own heart – and because he was a Palestinian-born Christian Arab and his wife was an Iraqi Muslim, she drew on his experiences. 'I learned so much from Jabra Ibrahim Jabra,' Guzin recalls. He died in Baghdad in 1994.

As Saddam tightened his stranglehold on the nation, Ra'ad became more concerned about his job security and personal safety. By1992 he was spending longer hours at the office and some nights he stayed back until midnight. His fear was palpable, but he refused to talk with Guzin about it and never said what he was doing to keep such late hours. 'I became nervous and said, "Why don't you speak?", and he said, "I can't speak, this job is too dangerous",' Guzin says. 'But sometimes he spoke to me about the regime and what they did.'

In June 1992, Ra'ad's mother, Fakhira, organised a holiday to Jordan to see her family, because travel to Iraq was difficult in the post-war climate. Ra'ad applied to the government for permission to take his family on vacation but he was refused, although Guzin was allowed to take the children. Saddam's paranoia about defections – particularly from those in the upper echelons of government and the military, which he had turned into a personal militia force – meant that families were not allowed to leave Iraq together. Several defections had already taken place, particularly from Saddam's inner circle, and he wanted to stem the flow. Even though Ra'ad couldn't leave Baghdad, he insisted that Guzin take the children without him, saying he had much to do at the office. She did as he asked. The children needed a holiday and they hadn't seen their grandparents since before the war.

Guzin arrived in Amman with Lina and Mohammed and booked into a suite at the Commodore Hotel, which they shared with Fakhira. It was just like the old days. Without the spectre of Saddam Hussein hanging over them, Guzin and the children could relax and forget the privations under which they were currently living in Baghdad. She spent hours with Shawket and Buthaina and her family, discussing the situation in Iraq and what they could do about it. Guzin couldn't thank them all enough for everything they had done for them since the war ended. Naturally, they told her it was nothing, they were happy to help.

Lina and Mohammed had the time of their lives, swimming in the pool and playing with their two cousins, Ramez and Omar, who were eleven and ten respectively. Fakhira showered the children with presents and bought Mohammed a Raleigh bicycle. He was thrilled. For a small boy it was an expensive gift, but what made it more special was that he would be the only boy in Baghdad with a new bike. Since sanctions prohibited the importation of non-essential items, new bicycles had disappeared from

Baghdad's stores. The twelve days flew by and Guzin reluctantly returned to Baghdad. She remembers the time in Jordan as the last time she was ever truly happy.

The next year things went from bad to worse. In early 1993, America's new president Bill Clinton ordered an attack on Baghdad in retaliation for an attempted assassination on his immediate predecessor, George Bush, who was visiting Kuwait. Assassins from the Mukhabarat were suspected, and Clinton fired twenty-three Tomahawk cruise missiles from American warships stationed in the Persian Gulf. The bombs destroyed their targets, including the general intelligence department located in the heart of Al Mansour. Ra'ad and Guzin's house was just a few streets away and was damaged in the blast.

The fallout from the attack on Baghdad added to the strain at home. Ra'ad's behaviour had started to change, almost imperceptibly. Guzin couldn't put her finger on it, but he was becoming withdrawn in a way he had never been. As well, he was moody. Ra'ad had always been the emotionally stable member of the family, happy and forever smiling. He enjoyed socialising, in his official capacity as well as privately. He had an easygoing disposition and it took a lot to provoke him to anger. Initially Guzin put Ra'ad's melancholic behaviour down to a low-level depression as a result of the oppressive conditions under which all Iraqis were living. He had never, ever, supported the tyrant Saddam Hussein or his Ba'ath Party politics, and the deterioration of his country now shamed him deeply. Under the circumstances, Ra'ad's behaviour was not really surprising, Guzin thought to herself. Besides, Ra'ad was not the only person suffering a post-war lassitude, and at least he had a job which provided an income, however meagre.

There was one brief bright spot for Ra'ad between October 1993 and January 1994, when he took part in a United Nations training program on the UN's operations within Baghdad. Soon after Iraq invaded Kuwait in 1990, and in the years after the end of the war, the United Nations had increased its influence on Saddam Hussein's regime with the imposition of a series of tough resolutions and sanctions aimed at eradicating the country's weapons of mass destruction and protecting its citizens from their leader. The training program was part of the UN's ongoing efforts in Iraq. Ra'ad addressed the delegation and once again felt like the diplomat he had been trained to be. But his improved mood was short-lived.

In the months that followed, Guzin concentrated on making life the best it could be for the children. She did not want Lina and Mohammed to be permanently scarred by what the monstrous Saddam had done to their country. Ra'ad still helped his son and daughter with their homework, and spent time with them on the weekends. Being children, they were not acutely aware of their father's moods. Guzin, however, was increasingly worried about Ra'ad's unusual behaviour, and by the end of 1994 it became clear that something was very wrong with him. Ra'ad's working hours had become sporadic – some days he would leave at midday and return three hours later; other days he would be in the office burning the midnight oil. But his career in the diplomatic corps had, ostensibly, come to a standstill. Guzin took note and asked gentle questions of her husband, but she pushed on with life and never got to the bottom of it.

◆ ◆ ◆

Under Resolution 687 of the United Nations sanctions which were imposed on Iraq on 3 April 1991, five weeks after the war was officially ended, Saddam Hussein's government was to list, and then hand over for destruction, all of its weapons of mass destruction. From the outset the program had been a cat-and-mouse game of denial and subterfuge followed by piecemeal concessions. Saddam even established a Concealment Operations Committee which was headed by his second son, Qusay, who ordered that key components of the weapons programs be hidden at Saddam's villas and palaces in his hometown of Tikrit.

Despite these tactics, by 1995 significant progress had been made in the hunt by the United Nations Special Commission, headed by the Swedish career diplomat Rolf Ekeus, and the International Atomic Energy Agency (IAEA). The IAEA found highly enriched uranium and natural uranium that had not been listed and concluded that Iraq had a nuclear military program. Saddam Hussein also admitted having liquid nerve gas and chemical warheads, and officials conceded to Rolf Ekeus in 1995 that Iraq also had a biological weapons program and had produced anthrax and botulinum. Further, in August one of Saddam Hussein's top generals defected to the west and revealed that Iraq had kept some of the banned weapons in direct contravention of the UN sanctions.

Ra'ad observed the political brinkmanship from his position in foreign affairs. As Guzin tells it now, the situation angered him so much that he broke with his strict habit of silence on government matters and confided in her. 'He said the government was cheating these inspectors, they were putting the weapons in trucks and moving them,' Guzin remembers. Ra'ad didn't elaborate further.

It was around this time that Ra'ad's behaviour changed even more dramatically. Guzin remembers being stunned by it, but she felt at a loss to know how to help him. 'Suddenly Ra'ad began to sit alone. He sat in the salon where we had a music centre and he sat down with his cigar, smoking and listening to soft music. I saw tears, many times. Even one day in the bedroom I saw him sitting in front of the wall with his head in his hands, and I asked him what was wrong, and he said he was crying because his mother had remarried. But that had been twenty years earlier. I don't think after twenty years he would sit down and begin to cry,' Guzin says.

'He tried to pretend there was nothing wrong, but one day when I went to Jordan alone, he asked me to ask my sister's husband that if he (Ra'ad) wanted to come to Jordan what type of job could he get. He was thinking of getting out and I became very happy thinking we could get out of Iraq, but we didn't go.

'Always he was afraid. He said, "They will kill my son. If they don't kill me, they will kill my son". When I said why don't we go overseas to another country to live, he said it again, "They will kill me or my son". Always they were the same words. He began to be alone and he refused to go outside the house. He didn't want to invite anybody to our home. I was tired, I became sick, I was so nervous. Everybody who saw him will remember that he was not the same. He was preoccupied and he began not to sleep and he began to drink too much. He was under a lot of stress and anxiety and he tried to get us to live in Jordan, but I wouldn't accept it unless Ra'ad came with us.'

Guzin sent Ra'ad to a psychiatrist who prescribed sleeping tablets, but they had little effect. Ra'ad's listlessness worsened and he began drinking heavily during the day. He would drop into a bar on the way home from the office and polish off several glasses of whiskey, knowing that Guzin would not accept such excessive drinking in front of the children. By the time he returned home, his eyes were bloodshot and his face red from the alcohol, and they would fight. Guzin didn't mind the odd glass herself when socialising, but she abhorred drinking for drinking's sake and she absolutely despised drinking to excess. To make matters worse, Ra'ad was drinking to hide something from her. This was not the man she had married twenty-one years earlier. 'He cut off his relationships with people. He didn't want to see anybody and we began to have problems between us, many problems,' Guzin recalls. It was the first time the couple had had any serious conflict in their marriage.

'I remember one time I looked out in the garden and Ra'ad was standing there with the hose spraying the garden absent-mindedly. He didn't seem to be conscious of his surroundings. He started smoking cigars and drinking, drinking, drinking. He cut his tennis and swimming, even his relatives. For one year we didn't go to the Al Rasheed.'

In November of 1995, Guzin twice spotted a man loitering outside the house. Ever feisty, she confronted him and demanded to know who he was and why he was lurking in the street near her front fence. The man baulked, and said he was trying to sell makeup, a ruse so outlandish that she laughed at him, but she insisted on getting answers. The man refused to give his name and stumbled over his words as he tried to find an explanation. Finally, he said he was looking for someone in the house but he didn't know who. Guzin immediately recognised it as the work of the intelligence service. But she thought the bumbling old man, who was probably an informer, had mixed up his houses and was looking for somebody else in the street. She certainly didn't think it related to Ra'ad. Why would it? It did not make sense to her.

Every day for the past eight years, Guzin has replayed those anxious months over and over in her mind, trying to divine that one precise moment when she should have detected Ra'ad's crisis and the reason for it. After all, Guzin's love for Ra'ad was without end. They were blissfully happy together, so much so that the strength of their relationship was often commented on by their friends, who saw it as a model for how modern couples worked. And yet, no matter how many times Guzin revisits Ra'ad's tortuous months of anxiety, the drinking and the quarrelling, she doesn't know what went wrong. Her guilt is like a malignant cancer inside her.

'He knew something but I didn't understand, and that's my problem and this is very hard,' she says, tears streaming down her face. 'I should have understood, but I didn't. I am busy, I was busy with the children. I should have known.'

Chapter Fifteen

In 1995 the Al Shah Ba'a restaurant on Ramadan Street in the exclusive suburb of Al Mansour was a bustling little eatery frequented mostly by locals. Cosy and welcoming, it lacked the ostentatious design and glitz of the two-level rotating restaurant, Babil, which sat atop the newly built television tower a few blocks away. Nor did it have the five-star prestige of the National Restaurant at the Al Rasheed hotel on the western side of Zawra Park. Instead, it was renowned for its unique interpretation of Iraqi specialties including barbecued kebabs, kuba and masgouf. If you didn't have a reservation, you were guaranteed a long wait.

On the last day of November 1995, Ra'ad Said decided to take his family to dinner at the Al Shah Ba'a. It was around nine o'clock on a Thursday evening and he had a hankering for a traditional Iraqi barbecue. Lina and Mohammed chorused their approval, thinking it an excellent idea, and the sudden shift of mood in the house delighted Guzin. Privately she thought Ra'ad's enthusiasm for a family outing – the first they had had in months – augured well. Maybe, just maybe, he was emerging from the deep depression into which he had sunk.

The weather had turned cold so they rugged up against the chill before leaving the house. Ra'ad told Fathy, the family driver, that his services would not be needed for the evening and instructed Mohammed, who was then fifteen, to hop behind the wheel. Guzin began to protest, saying Mohammed was too young to drive on the main roads in the busy suburb, but before she could finish her sentence, Ra'ad said that he wanted to see his son drive. Mohammed, champing at the bit, implored his mother to agree, just this once. Even though the legal age for driving in Iraq is eighteen, Mohammed had taken his first spin in a car when he was fourteen, driving the family vehicle up and down Princess Street – under the approving and cautious eye of his father, of course.

Ra'ad prevailed and told Lina to sit in the front passenger seat next to her brother. Grinning broadly at Mohammed, Lina jumped in and strapped on her seatbelt. Most families find their own natural order and when it came to the family car, Lina's regular seat was on the rear passenger side. This was a novelty. Guzin sat beside her husband on the back seat, chuckling to herself and feeling a bit like a teenager. Ra'ad was silent, and sat with his arms hanging limp and fingers curling into his palms on either side of him.

Mohammed navigated the short journey without incident and with just the right amount of speed and braking finesse. As he turned into Ramadan Street, he spied a parking spot directly outside the Al Shah Ba'a and pulled in with a showy turn. Mohammed couldn't have been more chuffed. Once out of the car, Ra'ad announced that instead of eating inside the restaurant, he wanted to take dinner outside on the bonnet of the car. It was an entirely unconventional way to dine at the Al Shah Ba'a, but Guzin shrugged; if that's what Ra'ad wanted, then that's what Ra'ad would get. She didn't want to disturb the mostly convivial mood that had replaced the melancholia of recent months. Anyway, she reasoned out loud, they had eaten in more unorthodox restaurants on their many travels around the world during Ra'ad's diplomatic heyday. And they were adequately dressed for the crisp night air.

Ra'ad went inside and told the maitre d' their plan. Looking slightly amused, he gave Ra'ad no argument and was probably thinking that if this particular customer was willing to pay the hefty prices for dinner for his family, then he could eat wherever he liked. In the years after the war, food prices in Baghdad had risen by as much as two thousand per cent. Guzin stayed outside with the children, giggling as they looked through the glass windows at the diners inside, who were looking back at them with bemusement.

Waiters brought a tablecloth and laid it over the bonnet before elaborately setting down a selection of Arabic bread, barbecued meat kebabs, lamb chops, chicken and pickles. While no one would have taken any notice if the family had been on a weekend picnic in the mountains, it was a bizarre sight for Al Mansour, but Ra'ad, Guzin and the children didn't care. They expertly placed the kebabs on the bread first, then the pickles, and rolled them up before tucking in with gusto. When they had finished, Guzin went inside and ordered sweet Iraqi tea, which the waiters dutifully and respectfully presented in small, elegant glasses balanced on pretty saucers.

Despite the atmosphere and the children's glee, Ra'ad seemed contemplative, sad even, but not as mournful and depressed as he had been for the past year. Guzin recognised this new demeanour from the previous week when they had been invited to a dinner party at a friend's house. 'I saw my husband looking at me, drinking and looking at me, and smiling when I caught his eye. He knew something, but I didn't understand,' she explains. That night at the Al Shah Ba'a, Guzin said nothing about Ra'ad's reflective mood, hoping, ultimately in vain, that by avoiding the issue, his sadness might miraculously disappear.

'I felt at that time there was something, because all night I looked at my husband but I didn't say anything. I am always crying about that now,' Guzin says. 'He tried to pretend in front of me and the children that nothing was wrong. He would say, "It's nothing, I'm just tired". He always tried to keep us happy. But something must have happened.

'After that night, we didn't go out together again and now I ask myself why he wanted to see his son drive. He said, "I am happy because my son is a man". Maybe he knew something. Why was he very sad? It was the first and last time he sat in the back of the car with his son in the front. I will never forget that night. He was very sad, and all night I looked at his face, but I did nothing.'

Chapter Sixteen

The seven-hundred-year-old university on Palestine Street in Al Mustansiriya is forty-five minutes away from Al Mansour, give or take. Five days a week Ra'ad Said drove Lina through the bustling streets of Baghdad to her classes at the university, where she was studying for a degree in English literature. There were no buses from Al Mansour and Ra'ad, being a protective father, didn't think it was safe for Lina to travel on her own in a taxi. Depending on the route, which in turn depended on the traffic in the congested metropolis of five million people, they would cross the Tigris over one of Baghdad's twelve bridges, most of which led in the general direction of Al Mustansiriya University. The campus was located in the northeast of the city, just a short distance away from the sprawling slums of Saddam City, home to between two and three million Shiah Muslims who were largely resentful of Saddam's regime.

Usually Ra'ad took the Al Ahraf Bridge, which crosses the Tigris at its mid-point and is the most direct route from

Al Mansour, taking them past the national parliament and the state-owned television and radio stations. Whatever route they took, there was always something interesting to look at in the huge city.

Lina enjoyed the morning commutes with her father because it gave them precious time together. Ra'ad often reminisced with Lina about his own days studying for a law degree at Al Mustansiriya. It held fond memories for him because it was there, in the students' union hallway in 1973, that he met her mother, whom he described as an intellectually feisty young beauty. The combined academic and romantic roles that the university had played in her family history were the reasons Lina chose to study at Al Mustansiriya, giving up a coveted position at magnificent Baghdad University, which sat at the end of a peninsula in a bend of the Tigris. It was closer to home and the more prestigious of the two, but it did not have the same sentimental pull as the family's alma mater.

On the morning of 8 December 1995, Lina and Ra'ad spent most of the journey to Al Mustansiriya talking about her impending mid-year exams, which were only days away. Lina had turned twenty the previous April and was in the third year of her degree, so the exams were crucial. When they arrived, Ra'ad gave Lina a kiss on each cheek and bid her farewell, saying he would be back to collect her in the afternoon. He turned the car around and retraced the route to his office in downtown Baghdad. It was a routine trip. In fact, the morning was like any other. Mohammed had left for school at the Alhseiyn Secondary School for Boys, which was closer to Al Mansour, and Guzin took her usual cup of tea in her bedroom while Bessma, the housekeeper, busied herself cleaning downstairs.

Around ten o'clock Lina telephoned her mother with the news that her afternoon lectures had been cancelled and she wanted her father to come and pick her up earlier than usual. Guzin said she would ring Ra'ad in his office to make arrangements and told Lina to wait in the library or the cafeteria and call her back in half an hour, by which time she was sure she would have organised her husband's schedule. Lina did as instructed.

Guzin picked up the telephone in the downstairs salon and called her husband's number at the ministry of foreign affairs, but it was diverted to his secretary. After exchanging social niceties, Guzin, affecting a more formal tone, asked to speak with Mr Ra'ad Said, but the secretary said he was not in the office. Ra'ad hadn't mentioned any outside appointments to Guzin, and it struck her as unusual. The secretary responded that Guzin needn't worry because two men from the prime minister's office had arrived and Ra'ad left with them. She believed they had taken him to the *Mujamma Dijla* – the Tigris compound – a walled-off section that stretched for three kilometres on the western banks of the Tigris and contained the main leadership of the Revolutionary Command Council and two presidential palaces.

Questioned further by Guzin, the secretary said she hadn't been told who Ra'ad was meeting with, nor when he was likely to return. The men hadn't given her any details. In Iraq, meetings were conducted at Saddam's pleasure. Many people are known not to have survived them. Guzin was even more concerned but the secretary assured her that Ra'ad had left with the men willingly and everything appeared fine. The only extra detail she offered was that they wore suits.

Guzin's instincts told her to worry but she wasn't sure what about. Her more rational side told her it was nothing – just a routine meeting. She told herself that she would just have to wait until she heard from Ra'ad later that day. She was also distracted by a contractor who was at the Princess Street home working on a wall that needed repairs. Around eleven Lina telephoned wanting to know when to expect her father and Guzin, who still hadn't heard from Ra'ad, told Lina to catch a taxi home because her father wasn't in the office.

Not long after the phone call, Guzin looked out a window and saw a shiny black four-door sedan pull up at the front of the house. It was ominous. The only people who drove black cars in Iraq were members of Saddam's regime. In the back seat she saw her husband and Guzin instantly sensed that something was wrong. He didn't look well. Her heart was racing. Within seconds, two hulking men sporting thick, black Saddam-style moustaches got out of the car and trotted around to the back passenger door. Ra'ad tried to get up but couldn't lift himself so the men pulled him out. He was slumped over and looked to be in pain. They slung Ra'ad's arms over their shoulders and half dragged, half carried him into the entrance lobby at the front of the house.

As they got closer, Guzin noticed that Ra'ad's eyes were bloodshot and his face was bright red, as if it had been seriously sunburned. The two men dropped Ra'ad in a seat in the lobby near an antique telephone table. They turned on their heels and left without saying a word, leaving a panicked Guzin to make sense of the situation. Guzin grabbed Ra'ad's hand, which was burning up, 'like fire', she says now, and asked him what happened.

Ra'ad could barely speak. His limp body was slumped over to one side, his arms hanging down listlessly, his legs splayed. He didn't have the strength to straighten himself in the chair. His hair was dishevelled and his glasses were crooked. But there were no apparent injuries – no obviously broken bones or lacerations. Guzin was terrified.

'What have they done to you, Ra'ad?' Guzin said, looking at her husband in shock.

He said nothing.

'Ra'ad, what's wrong? Tell me,' Guzin said, her voice rising in frustration and fear, holding his hand, which burned inside hers. She tried to make eye contact with her husband, but he wouldn't look at her, or perhaps he couldn't.

Ra'ad's breathing was ragged, but after a few abortive attempts, he managed to speak. 'Don't waste time,' he said, struggling to get the words out. 'Take my children and leave the country. Take. My. Children. Out. Of. Iraq.' Each word was forced, punctuated by Ra'ad's desperate attempts to breathe.

Guzin fought to remain calm. Her mind was a riot of questions and fears as she tried to think what needed to be done. 'I must call a doctor for you,' she said, her voice breaking as she fought back tears.

Ra'ad told his wife that he didn't want her to leave his side. Tears rolled down his cheeks. Then, gasping for air, he looked directly into her eyes and spoke again.

'Don't waste time, take your children and get out. Do not come back. Promise me, Guzin. Do not come back.'

Ra'ad would not let go of Guzin's hand, gripping more and more tightly, as if demanding an answer. 'Do not waste time. Take my children. Guzin, promise me, promise me.'

Ra'ad was crying. His bloodshot eyes had become swollen and his voice was becoming weaker. Guzin tried to move to the phone to ring for a doctor, but Ra'ad held on.

'Guzin, promise me,' he said desperately, one final time. 'Take my children out of Iraq.'

Guzin looked down at her husband and, with the back of her hand, brushed the tears from his face. Her own had started to splash onto his chest, staining his shirt. Guzin didn't know what to say. She didn't know what had happened to Ra'ad, or where he had been the last few hours or what he had gone through. The possibilities were too barbaric to imagine. Every Iraqi feared Saddam Hussein's death and torture chambers and knew what the regime was capable of. Hardly a single family remained untouched by the suffering. Over the decades of Saddam's rule, tens of thousands of people had simply disappeared without trace, or returned from torture sessions with mangled bodies and shattered hearts and minds.

Guzin's heart ached and felt like it was about to burst. She had watched as her husband suffered through the last year, miserably alone, and she had been powerless to help him. And now, this. Words choked in Guzin's throat. She tried, but couldn't say anything. She looked into Ra'ad's eyes as he stared back, and then, with a simple nod of her head, Guzin silently promised to take Lina and Mohammed and flee Iraq.

Chapter Seventeen

Ra'ad Said died on 12 December 1995, at 3.30 am, the blackest time of night. Mohammed was just fifteen and not quite ready to be a man, but that role was now thrust upon him. He was the eldest and only surviving male in the immediate family, and as is customary in Iraq, he therefore became the head of the household. His dying father had prepared him for the eventuality four days earlier, in the hours after he was unceremoniously delivered home by the two government agents. His voice sounded as if it had been scratched by broken glass.

'Take care of your studies and your family,' Ra'ad told Mohammed as he lay on his bed with a doctor standing to one side in the room. 'Do not leave them – always stand beside your mother and sister.'

The doctor was a family friend whom Guzin called moments after the government agents left the house. He had arrived within the hour but was unable to determine what had happened. Throughout the course of the day, more doctors came to the house and were similarly confounded by Ra'ad's condition. When Mohammed arrived from school, he was shocked by what he saw. The house was in chaos. Guzin was hysterical, shouting at the doctors to do something for her husband. Anything. Lina returned from university and, upon seeing her helpless father, began to cry. She had never seen him sick a single day in his life and his listless form scared her.

As the afternoon wore on, Ra'ad's condition deteriorated. He was losing the ability to speak and his body was slowly becoming paralysed, limb by limb. With no evident injuries, the doctors concluded that Ra'ad's symptoms were consistent with poisoning and took him to the Al Sha Fa'a hospital in Al Mansour. Once there, one of his lungs collapsed and he was immediately placed on a ventilator in the intensive care unit.

It is now almost eight years since that day in 1995, and Mohammed Said is a self-contained, watchful young man of twenty-three who carries the burden of the loss of his father and the responsibilities he inherited with his death. Mohammed is sitting at the dining room table in the rented flat he shares with his mother in Sydney. Guzin is pottering around in the kitchen a few feet away, making herself busy. Mohammed keeps his voice deliberately low, not wanting his mother to overhear the conversation, knowing how much the details of that day traumatise her still.

'That night when we went to visit him in the hospital, he couldn't talk because he was on a ventilator,' Mohammed says. 'He had to take off the face mask. The last thing he told me was, "Take care of your family", and then he said "Goodnight". I think he knew he was going to die because he didn't tell us anything. He never told us anything about his work – he would just say it was okay. He didn't say what happened or what he did.'

Mohammed falls silent, collecting his thoughts and staring at his clasped hands resting on the table. 'I promised I would take care of my studies and family and never leave them alone. My father seemed to relax because I promised him what he asked me to promise.'

Ra'ad spoke to Lina next and tried to reassure her that he was fine. He wanted to protect her from the horror of what had happened.

'When I looked at him I felt he knew he would die. His smile was not the same,' Lina says, recalling that day. 'When he said, "Don't worry, I will be fine", he said it strangely. He looked sad. He tried not to show it but I could actually see it from his face.'

The next three days were hellish. A series of doctors were unable to make an accurate diagnosis, and because Ra'ad could not talk, he could not help them. Their efforts were further hampered by the imposition of United Nations sanctions against Saddam Hussein's dictatorship, which meant that the medical system was hopelessly inadequate. Corrupt Iraqi officials and profiteers diverted legitimate medical supplies onto the black market, where they were sold for inflated prices. Subsequently, hospitals did not have adequate or appropriate medicines and equipment.

Guzin resumes the story where Mohammed left off: 'Nobody knew what had happened to him. He was paralysed and he had lost his voice and I was shouting. I was very afraid. I didn't want to see him ill or sick and I said, "Nothing has happened to you, you will be okay". Lina said, "My father is very sick", and I told her nothing happened to him. I didn't want to believe that he was very sick, so I told her it was just the flu, he had a cold. And from Ra'ad there was nothing, just tears.'

The next day Guzin called the department of foreign affairs and told them Ra'ad was unwell and would not be coming to the office. No one protested, nor did they offer any assistance. But one of Ra'ad's colleagues told Guzin that her husband had been taken to the office of Deputy Prime Minister Tariq Aziz, who was fresh from boasting on the Iraqi news service that Iraq was moving from 'revolutionary to constitutional legitimacy'. The so-called shift was occurring in the wake of the 99.96 per cent favourable reponse to the October referendum in which Iraqis were asked, farcically, 'Are you in favour of Saddam Hussein assuming the post of president of the Republic of Iraq?' Ra'ad's colleague was not sure how long Ra'ad was at the deputy prime minister's office, but he told Guzin that Ra'ad was subsequently taken to the general intelligence service office in Al Mansour. He knew nothing more than that.

Ra'ad's condition worsened. He was falling in and out of consciousness but nobody could tell Guzin what was wrong with him. When he was awake, Guzin stood by his bed holding his limp hand, and Ra'ad cried, unable to communicate any other way. 'I never slept,' she remembers. 'I didn't trust anybody enough to sleep. I didn't know what to do.'

In desperation Guzin rang her neighbour, Niran, whose husband worked as an engineer on a project for the Ba'ath government and had some well placed contacts. Niran told Guzin that Ra'ad had been taken to the intelligence service headquarters the previous day. 'They killed him,' Niran told Guzin. 'My husband was told that an officer gave him something to drink.' It was confirmation of a terrible suspicion.

During the next six months, various international humanitarian organisations would accumulate information about poisoning as a means of assassination in Saddam Hussein's regime. Amnesty International's 1996 annual report contains a chilling account of how, as early as 1980, Saddam's agents of death executed his opponents and critics, by poisoning them with heavy metal toxins, particularly thallium, which is used to kill rats. Odourless, colourless and tasteless, thallium was one of Saddam's favourite poisons, possibly because death is agonisingly slow. They diluted the thallium in beverages, which were then offered to unsuspecting victims during routine interrogations. Death occured after several days. The descriptions of those deaths are frighteningly similar to what happened to Ra'ad. The symptoms include the rapid onset of abdominal pain, nausea and vomiting, weakness, ataxia (the loss of full control of bodily movements), confusion, hallucinations and coma. Amnesty specifically noted, some by name, ten individual cases of thallium poisoning in the northern and southern regions. The victims had all been active in opposition to Saddam's Revolutionary Command Council. Each was poisoned and, according to the report, 'died several days later'.

The Amnesty report and another by the United Nations special rapporteur on the Commission on Human Rights also noted other methods used by Saddam's secret police to deal with dissenters. Its methods for keeping its people in line were among the most evil in the world. Critics of the government had their tongues cut out; supposed dissenters have had their limbs cut or burnt off in order to force confessions; people were executed by being dropped slowly into vats of acid or were hanged in public; in order to eke out information from them, nursing mothers had their newborn babies taken away and held just out of reach in front of them while the infant starved to death. Thieves had their hands cut off by doctors under orders from Saddam. Several hundred army deserters and defaulters were subjected to the amputation of one ear for a first offence, and the other for further offences. They were also branded with an X symbol on their foreheads during the same operation, most of which were performed in public hospitals. Doctors were routinely threatened with reprisals if they refused to carry out the operations. And victims of these atrocities were prevented from obtaining follow-up treatment.

Rape of women and the application of electrical wires to genitals became effective tools to gain confessions. Officially sanctioned rape was endemic – girls, wives, elderly women – all were victims. Videotapes of rapes were sent to the husbands or fathers or brothers of the victims in order to blackmail them into cooperating with the regime. Some Iraqi authorities even carried identity cards listing their official duty as 'violation of women's honour'.

The United Nations' special report, which was delivered to the General Assembly in New York City less than one month before Ra'ad died, also recounted the torture of political opponents, including two cases in which victims were systematically sprayed with sulphuric acid during an interrogation. One was forced to stand in a tub of filthy water up to his nose so he could barely breathe and was at risk of drowning. They were also hung from their hands which were tied behind their backs, destroying their shoulders, or made to sit on glass bottles for varying periods of time thereby damaging their rectums.

Author Kenneth M. Pollack's litany of the regime's viciousness, as described in *The Threatening Storm*, is equally disturbing. 'This is a regime that will force a white-hot metal rod into a person's anus or other orifices . . . This is a regime that will behead a young mother in the street in front of her house and children because her husband was suspected of opposing the regime.'

Ra'ad's death was never officially reported to Amnesty, but years later when Guzin applied for refugee status, it would be heard by the United Nations High Commissioner for Refugees.

◆ ◆ ◆

Mohammed Said woke with a jolt at 3.15 am on 12 December. He had been dreaming of his father, who had spent the past four days in hospital. Ra'ad was dressed in something light, and flying away from his son. In his dream, Mohammed was sitting on the ground as his father looked down and said 'bye'. Then he flew off. 'I couldn't go back to sleep and ten minutes later I got a telephone call from my uncle at the hospital who said he was coming back to the house,' Mohammed says. His sister Lina was with him, and together they waited for their uncle with rising dread.

'He took me and Lina and he hugged us and he said, "Your father was very tired". I knew, and I said, "You must be joking", because that night when I was beside my father, he was alive. He said, "No, your father is tired and he just left life". I couldn't be sure, I wanted to see. We were just shocked because we didn't know what to do. His death happened very fast.'

Guzin had spent every single minute of the past four nights sitting beside Ra'ad's bed in the intensive care unit at the Al Sha Fa'a hospital. She could not bear to leave him.

It is bad enough watching a loved one fade away when their illness is clearly defined and doctors can chart the course of disease, but the medical uncertainty of what was happening to her husband made Guzin's suffering that much more painful. It was harder still when the children came to visit their father. Every time Ra'ad saw Mohammed and Lina, he started to cry. Seeing her husband hooked up to a ventilator brought back memories of her mother's death fifteen years previously. Majida had a heart attack after a short illness and died in a hospital room, also while on a ventilator.

'It was raining that Thursday,' Guzin says, remembering the last day of Ra'ad's life. 'It was the first day of rain in Baghdad in a long time. I was very sad. It was raining the day my mother died and I said then that it was as if the sky was weeping. And now the same thing was happening – I was scared my husband would die. I felt a choke in my throat, I felt I was drowning. I sat down in front of the monitors and I remembered it was the same situation with my mother. And every minute and every second I felt it in my heart.'

Guzin was watching over her husband at 3.30 am when an alarm sounded a monotonous flat note on the life support machine and a straight line appeared on the monitor. Panic roared through her and she screamed for help. The hospital room instantly turned into an emergency room. A doctor who had taken Ra'ad's blood pressure just minutes earlier raced back in and applied defibrillators to Ra'ad's chest, but they failed to restart his heart.

'I was just crazy. I was shouting at the doctor, "You killed my mother, now you've killed my husband. You could do nothing. You didn't have the knowledge to save him",' Guzin says, taking herself back to that night.

Guzin's brother-in-law Mohammed told her to leave, but she protested and watched as her husband's lifeless body failed to respond to further treatment. A doctor pronounced Ra'ad dead. Guzin walked out the door of the intensive care unit, a soul-destroying picture of anguish and desperation. 'I never saw him again after the line went flat. I didn't see anything at all because I was out of my mind with shock,' Guzin remembers.

Guzin went back to Princess Street with her brother-in-law. She kept her eyes squeezed shut as she entered the house, not wanting to see it without Ra'ad and not wanting to see her children's faces, knowing she would break down if she saw them suffering. She covered all the windows and mirrors with sheets, and took to her bed, torn apart by grief. She spent the next two weeks under constant sedation. Guzin believed that with Ra'ad's death she had lost the best part of herself. She was numb with sorrow and felt stranded without him. Her pain was indescribable – not only had she lost her husband, but she had lost him violently to a barbarian who was destroying her country.

As the new man of the household, it was Mohammed's job to organise his father's funeral. As is customary in the Islamic faith, the body must be prepared for a rapid burial. Mohammed, with the family driver Fathy, brought Ra'ad's body home where, in a traditional ceremony, they cleansed it for burial. Mohammed dressed his father in white shrouds, as is customary, and sprinkled him with a traditional perfume. Mohammed read from the Koran. The all-male funeral cortege travelled to a nearby mosque for a short ceremony, after which Ra'ad was buried in a cemetery more than an hour's drive north of Baghdad.

Later that day, scores of people came to the house to pay

their respects. Guzin was too distraught to leave her room and had to be sedated. Lina, who was twenty, stood in her mother's place and received the lines of well-wishers, offering them strong black Iraqi coffee and finding some measure of solace in their kind words. Lina's best friend Furat was by her side, helping her through the ordeal.

'It was a very hard time because everything was new. I didn't even know how to welcome the people. I didn't know what to do. I didn't know how because it was the first time, and I really didn't want people coming to the house, because why were they coming? My father had died and I refused to believe it. I didn't want to know, I didn't want this to happen,' Lina says now. The passage of eight years has done nothing to ease her sorrow.

'What I feel now is what I felt that very first moment – I feel as if I am in two parts, and one of them has died with my father. I feel he is my soul and when I heard that my father had died, I said to him, "Why didn't you take my soul with you so I won't feel the pain after you have left me?".

'We shared the same things, we shared our music, we loved the same songs. My father and I ate seafood together and my mother and brother didn't. We liked mostly the same things. He was my friend and I was his friend. Once he told me he loved me so much that it was with tears. He was like a candle, he gave a lovely light to us, he gave me a lovely light that shined in my life and protected me from the darkness of life. He protected me from the hard things and hard times.'

For two weeks Guzin stayed in her room, grieving for her lost husband and the loss of innocence of her children. The death certificate said Ra'ad had died from a heart attack, but she didn't believe it, nor did many of the mourners at the funeral who cried of the regime, 'they killed him, they killed him'. One of her friends, a doctor who attended Ra'ad, told her: 'We don't know what happened to him, but he went with his secrets.'

Buthaina could not come to Iraq to be with her sister because she had just had an operation on her back, but Buthaina's husband Mohammed came from Jordan and every night for two weeks he watched over his sister-in-law to ensure she was safe from harm. Her beloved father Shawket couldn't come because he could not step inside Iraq, having left the country in 1978. It was heartbreaking. Guzin couldn't even look her children in the eye because she saw their father in them and she felt for them the sharp pain of his absence.

'Sometimes at night I would see Ra'ad,' Guzin says. 'I'd hold his pyjamas and breathe the scent of him. Every day I opened the cupboard and I smelled his clothes. He was just forty-eight years old. Why did they kill him? I didn't want him to die. I want him here in my heart and my arms. I saw him die in front of my own eyes. They destroyed my life.'

Right then, in the aftermath of Ra'ad's death, Guzin could never have imagined that her life could be worse than it already was without Ra'ad there to protect and love her and their children. But it was about to get worse. Much worse.

Chapter Eighteen

The Mukhabarat did not need invitations. Members of Saddam Hussein's secret police arrived unannounced and at whatever hour suited them best to unleash their special brand of terror. Late at night or in the early morning, they came armed with no explanations, only the reflected arrogance of a tyrant's orders, or an unofficial death warrant written on a piece of paper that could never be found.

Three thugs from the Mukhabarat smashed their fists on the front door of Guzin's Princess Street home sixteen days after Ra'ad's death. Their timing was malevolent. Their pattern was to wait for the moment when they could strike the greatest amount of fear into a victim, and they had planned the visit to Guzin with strategic timing. Her brother-in-law Mohammed Al Tell had flown home to Jordan the day before, after spending two weeks with Guzin and his niece and nephew, Lina and Mohammed. The Mukhabarat had been watching the house. They knew that Guzin and the children would be alone for the first time since Ra'ad's death.

Guzin was in the lounge room when the banging on the door shocked her out of her silent despair. Lina and Mohammed were busy elsewhere in the house. Guzin answered the door to three large men staring in at her. They weren't smiling. Her heart somersaulted in horror. She instantly recognised one but, in her shock, couldn't place him. He was tall and lean but his handsome face was contorted into an expression of pure aggression. He was the first to speak.

'Let us in,' he said, trying to push past Guzin. He spoke in a thick peasant accent.

'No,' said Guzin. She surprised herself with her defiance, and stood directly in his path. 'Who are you? Why are you here? Show me your licences.'

Guzin had been around the Ba'ath government long enough to know precisely who they were but she played dumb and began to act as if she was maybe a little crazy, throwing her arms around and acting out of control.

The men began to laugh at her, a cruel taunt, thinking she was demented with grief at the loss of her husband. They were not strangers to the behaviour caused by sorrow, for they had inflicted it many times.

'It's better if we go inside,' the familiar one replied in an almost conciliatory tone.

Guzin knew better than to say no a second time and stood back as the three men stomped through the entrance lobby and into the main lounge room. She was desperately trying to remember who the agent was when the second officer, who had a shock of dyed blond hair, informed Guzin that henceforth she and her two children were under house arrest on orders from the president of the Republic of Iraq, the great leader Saddam Hussein.

Guzin was stunned. She stood stone-still in silence as he continued barking out his orders.

'You are to have no relationships with people. You are to contact no one. You are not to go out. From this day forward, your son will not go to school and your daughter will not go to university. There will be nothing. You will stay at home and go on as usual. You will make no changes to your other arrangements,' he spat.

He demanded that Guzin turn over Ra'ad's diplomatic passport and official credentials. In a cunningly pre-emptive move, Guzin had hidden the valuable documents when Ra'ad told her to flee the country. Fully comprehending Ra'ad's dying request but not sure if it would ever be necessary, she had the good sense, at least, to protect her family's identity papers. She put them in a plastic bag and hid them in the garbage. Thinking quickly, Guzin handed the secret police her husband's briefcase but said he had always kept the documents at the foreign affairs headquarters for safekeeping, and it sounded perfectly plausible to Saddam's henchmen.

The agents carried out a desultory check of Ra'ad's briefcase and then quickly searched the house. They examined Guzin's own diplomatic passport but found nothing else in the house of interest to them. The blond Mukhabarat agent told Guzin they were only allowed out of the house to visit a doctor, whom the Mukhabarat had approved. Bessma and Fathy could run errands and buy food for the family. They could also receive visits from three friends whose names the agents had written on a list.

Guzin was astonished that the secret police knew and had vetted their friends, but they didn't say why they had chosen these three. Perhaps, Guzin thought to herself, it was because the secret police wanted Guzin to pretend that nothing had changed in their lives, that they weren't under house arrest. The Mukhabarat had clearly done their homework – a chilling thought for Guzin. It was a frightening and yet bizarre situation. Guzin and her children were under house arrest and yet they were permitted to have three visitors and still employ their housekeeper and driver, who could come and go at will.

Before leaving, the blond agent told Guzin that she must not tell a soul about the visit. She nodded her head in agreement, knowing that to argue could prove fatal. Then the blond played his trump card. 'If you tell anybody about this meeting, we don't know what will happen to your son.'

Guzin froze with fear. The words were almost identical to those that Ra'ad had first uttered four years earlier on the eve of the first Gulf war in 1991 when he explained why he had to return to Iraq. Guzin remembered the look of sheer horror on Ra'ad's face when he put down the telephone after being told that if he didn't return to Baghdad, his son would be killed – it was indelibly etched in her mind. The three agents stared at Guzin as the words sunk in. Beads of sweat formed on her brow and upper lip. It was December, the beginning of winter in Baghdad. The one with the familiar face smiled a knowing half-smile, and the Mukhabarat were gone.

Guzin stared blankly after them. She felt as if the wind had been knocked out of her. She closed the front door softly, and then collapsed in the chair in the lobby where Ra'ad had slumped that day he returned home with poison raging through his body. An antique mirror with an elaborate gilt frame and an ornate clock were side by side on the wall opposite her. Guzin noticed it was just after nine in the morning. She sat perfectly still and stared at the wall, the words that threatened her son repeating themselves over and over in her mind. The children came downstairs and asked what was wrong. Guzin told them nothing and sent them about their business. They saw Guzin's distress and did as she asked.

In its own macabre way, the pernicious threat against Mohammed brought a wave of clarity to the revelations of the previous weeks, all of which had been shrouded in Guzin's grief and therefore never fully explored. 'I just began to feel that what the people said at the funeral – that they killed him, they killed my husband – was right,' Guzin says.

She sat in the chair as if suspended in time. She couldn't move. Mohammed was in danger. It was exactly how the Mukhabarat operated – ensure parental compliance by threatening children. The blond thug hadn't actually said they would kill Mohammed, but the threat was there. The hands on the clock moved around the face hour by hour. Nine. Now ten. An hour had passed, and still Guzin couldn't move. By mid-afternoon she felt as if she had been turned to stone. Physically she was catatonic but her mind was a riot of thoughts.

For the past sixteen days Guzin's despair had been as pre-dictable as the daylight that delivered it. Ever since Ra'ad died, she had been living a half-life bathed in misery and washed bare of any chance of a future. The wretchedness of her grief was consuming and isolating. The well-intended condolences that came from those who knew and loved Ra'ad struck her as barbed platitudes, long lines of cruel words strung together on a hollow promise for a better tomorrow. In her heart she knew they meant well, she truly did, and she knew they hated to see her suffer. But how could she – Guzin – *move on*? Did they think her husband had meant so little to her? That she could forget him, forget what happened to him, and how he was stripped of his dignity in death? She wondered to herself exactly how long it would take for the wounds to heal as everyone said they must. Another week? A month, a year? She knew the answer: never.

Guzin felt Ra'ad's death pressing down like a rock on her heart, constricting her. She felt the hopelessness of being dismissed as a woman alone with no man to support her in a society where a woman without a man is sometimes considered less than nothing. But the Mukhabarat's intimidatory tactics had, incredibly, the opposite effect on her than intended. She had no doubt they meant business and was not about to disobey their orders, but Guzin was a mother and her natural instinct was to protect her children. At any cost.

'At that moment, I felt very strong,' she says of the instant she came to her senses and decided what must be done. The arrival of the Mukhabarat and the threat against Mohammed formed the mantle on which their future now hung. The imminent danger was like a compass pointing true north, giving Guzin the direction she needed. Guzin was going to keep the promise she had made to Ra'ad.

Lina and Mohammed were worried about their mother and told her she needed to eat. Guzin had Bessma prepare a snack and she herded the children to the kitchen table. 'Something has happened to us,' Guzin started, struggling to find words that would not terrify her children, particularly Lina, who had been hit so hard by Ra'ad's death that she had been unable to return to university and spent hour after hour each day crying for her father.

Guzin told her children that the men who had been at the house earlier were from the Mukhabarat, the secret police, and that effectively, from that point on, they were all under house arrest. The Princess Street house was their prison and they couldn't stray beyond the fences that contained it. Each of them was to obey the order, Guzin stressed, and they needed to be aware that everything they did was being watched, either by the secret police themselves or by any number of the regime's sly army of informers. And, she said, she didn't know how long it would last.

Guzin's heart thundered in her chest, but she was determined to keep her voice calm for the children's sake. She knew it would be hard, she said soothingly, but they had no choice. They would not be allowed to take their three little dogs, Chico, Cindy and Susie, for walks beyond the fenced-in villa. There would be no school, no university, no friends. Mohammed was horrified – he was a teenager, it was impossible: *how could he not see his friends*? Guzin understood his anguish but, she said, the Mukhabarat are capable of anything.

Barely three weeks earlier their lives had been turned upside down, and now they were being thrown from side to side. Everything had to change. Guzin told Lina and Mohammed that they would all sleep together in the master bedroom where they could watch over each other at night. They were to be allowed three visitors but when these friends came, they were not to talk about their father under any circumstances. They were not to discuss politics. Ever. If anyone asked them for an opinion they were to feign ignorance. If they wanted to say anything that was remotely sensitive, they had to write it on a piece of scrap paper and then destroy it immediately.

Mohammed was enraged at what he was hearing. 'Some day I will kill whoever killed my father,' he said in anger.

Lina, unable to help herself, cried chest-heaving sobs that nearly doubled her over. Guzin put her finger to her lips, a sign to be silent. She had no idea if the house was under electronic surveillance, but nothing would surprise her. She didn't want either Mohammed or Lina to say something that could get them killed.

Guzin was almost finished. 'I want to tell you something. Your father was very faithful to his country and he was a very innocent and good man. He did nothing wrong. You have to be very proud that he was your father, and I promise I will do everything to make you happy.'

The children nodded. Turning to Lina, Guzin continued. 'You have your father's name and if you love your father you will respect his name. You have to respect our traditions.' Lina understood implicitly what her mother was saying. As a young woman, her virtue was of paramount importance and Lina understood that in protecting herself she was protecting her father's name. If she did anything wrong, Guzin said, people would assume it was because her father was dead and that she and her mother were not of good character. Lina nodded.

Guzin looked at Mohammed. 'You have to behave always and remember that you are now your father. You are a boy but you must be a man and you will protect your father's name. You will be educated. You must behave as he did and respect his name,' Guzin said. Mohammed had already promised his father he would honour the family name and look after his sister and mother, and he fully intended to do so.

That afternoon they moved Lina's and Mohammed's

beds from the upstairs bedrooms to Guzin's master suite, where they were lined up alongside one another, hospital style. Guzin went through the house systematically and locked each window and all the doors – permanently – including the ones that led on to the balconies. They drew all the curtains and kept them shut tight. There wasn't even an uncovered centimetre to look through. The house had been turned into a fortress.

Guzin gathered all their personal documents, every single thing that could confirm their identity and their existence: the children's school records from their earliest days abroad, their certificates of identity, and their diplomatic passports, both the current ones and those that had expired which she had kept as souvenirs. She stuffed them into a huge garbage bin outside. She retrieved documents of property ownership and Ra'ad's business papers and stored them in a plastic bag. She collected photographs and put them together with the journal her father had kept for her all through her childhood. As she looked at the cover, she was overcome by emotions. It had been years since she'd seen it. She opened the book at random. As if by magic, it was an entry Shawket Najim had recorded in 1977, a homily about character and honour. The timing couldn't have been better.

'A person does not have success in life unless he is of good character,' Shawket wrote, his penmanship a series of exquisite fine lines in Arabic. 'He must be of good behaviour and he must have good relationships with other people. His character comes before his family name, and before his education. A person must be of good character and behave well.' Next to his inscription Shawket had affixed an old black and white photograph of himself standing beside his wife Majida, both smiling broadly for the camera. Guzin was overcome by her father's sentimental touch.

Guzin's jewellery and the gold she received for her engagement and wedding more than two decades earlier were stashed in a small box and hidden in the main bedroom. In the back of her mind, she remembered Shawket telling her that during a crisis, valuables and jewellery could be used as currency if needed.

Over the next few weeks Guzin devised a plan to smuggle the documents, passports, jewellery and money out of the house with the help of her Sudanese driver, Fathy. Bit by bit, paper by paper, he took them to two of Guzin's oldest and most trusted friends in Baghdad, Luay and Dhia. Luay's mother, Madiha, had been one of the dearest friends of Guzin's mother, Majida. They came from the same distinguished background and, like the Al Tell family had in Jordan, they made their own significant purchase on Iraqi society during the royal heyday before the Ba'ath Party's ascent. Madiha and Majida had maintained their friendship all their lives. After Majida's death, Madiha became an ersatz mother-figure to Guzin, and Luay and Dhia, her sons, became like brothers. Guzin knew she could trust them one hundred per cent. By the end of the month, the most important documents would be spirited to the relative safety of Luay and Madiha's home.

Within the space of several hours that afternoon, Guzin and her children had made the house as secure as they possibly could. That night they slept in the same room, together with their three dogs. Guzin barricaded the bedroom door with the French provincial dresser. They piled furniture up against the window, blocking any entry or exit. A makeshift fortress. In any other circumstance the novelty of the situation would have been entertaining, but any levity was lost amid the state of perpetual fear they had been thrown into.

Once the children were sleeping, Guzin lay on the floor near the door so she could see any shadows moving under the door in the room outside the bedroom. She was also closer to the three beloved family dogs, Chico, Cindy and Susie, a Chihuahua, a Maltese terrier and a tiny bitzer who was a variety of breeds. The dogs were acutely aware of distant sounds and their ears immediately pricked up at the first hint of noise, alerting Guzin to danger or intruders. She was too terrified to sleep and stayed awake until daylight crept through a tiny crack that appeared in the curtain. Paranoid about being spied on, she leapt to her feet and pulled the curtain shut even more tightly. When the children woke, they did a quick check of the house and found everything exactly as they had left it. They had survived their first night under house arrest, but the persecution had only just begun. It would last another three years.

'Lina had many problems after her father's death,' Guzin says, sitting in her dining room in Sydney a week before what would have been Ra'ad's 56th birthday. 'She was always breaking down, saying that her father was travelling outside of Iraq and would be back soon. When we told her he wasn't coming back, she broke everything in the house – she was heartbroken. For four months she was like this. Eventually we had to take her to her father's grave so that she could understand that he was dead. Mohammed took her and he brought her home and we gave her tablets to let her sleep. Slowly, step by step, she is getting better. But even now, every day, every night, she cries.'

Guzin sits with her hands stretched out in front of her,

unconsciously holding the corners of the table, her shoulders hunched forward. She looks as if she is physically bracing herself against the agony of her children's heartache. 'Even now, Mohammed can't sleep with the curtains open. For three years we were afraid to open the curtains in case they were standing on the other side or they could see in. They were always threatening us, starting off slowly, affecting us psychologically. We became tired. Sometimes at night they put so much pressure on us that we couldn't sleep and we sat between the beds with our heads down.

'I began to worry that they might kill my son with a bullet and I tried to protect him by sitting in front of him, covering him. I was afraid that my daughter would be raped – what will happen to her after that? In this society, I can't explain it. At the same time I had to pretend I was strong if I wanted my son and daughter to be strong.

'But even now, Mohammed has lost his smile. It's hurting me – you don't see him smile, and even when he smiles you feel that he is sad, very sad. He says nothing. He won't tell me how he feels, how he is thinking. In Arab society they say the men must not cry but I don't believe in this. I always say you are a human being, you have emotions, so if you feel you need to cry, you can. It doesn't mean you are weak, no, because you are strong to feel those emotions.

'Every night, every day I spent time with the dogs, speaking to them. They were with me, they understood me, they understood these things inside me, this pain. I couldn't talk to my children because I didn't want to burden them and frighten them. Sometimes when I wanted to be alone, I went outside into the garden and sat on the swing. Sometimes I went to the cupboard and held my husband's clothes, just to smell him, and I'd walk around the house looking for him, saying, "Ra'ad, where are you, Ra'ad?" I thought he would answer me, but of course he wasn't there.

'The regime of Saddam Hussein broke our hearts and stole everything in our lives.'

◆ ◆ ◆

The identity of the Mukhabarat agent with the familiar face had been niggling away in the back of Guzin's mind for days when, all of a sudden, the same three agents were on her doorstep again. This time they didn't bother to knock, they just pushed through the front door. Lina and Mohammed were in the downstairs lounge room listening to music with their mother when the thugs stormed in. Bessma was in the kitchen. Even though Guzin was under house arrest, she hadn't relinquished her hired help. After all, the agents had told her to continue life 'as normal'. Her driver Fathy was still employed even though his duties had been drastically curtailed as a consequence of the house arrest order, but Guzin felt obligated to him and Bessma. After all, they were poor people and relied on Guzin for an income, and Guzin, even in these more straitened times, still had her family money, not to mention her pride. It was against her character to let them down.

As soon as she saw that face again, she recognised it. It was Ali Al Delamy, the Mukhabarat secret policeman who had worked with Ra'ad at the embassy in Yemen in 1980–82 when Iraq was about to embark on the war with neighbouring Iran. Thirteen years had passed since then, but Ali had lost none of his good looks or his athletic physique. The corners of his dark eyes were a little more lined with age but, other than that, he was the same. He was tall and had a prominent cleft in his chiselled chin. He had a thick head of dark brown hair which he wore swept to one side, and skin the colour of lightly roasted almonds.

In Yemen, Ali had been a friend. He even lived with Ra'ad for a short time in the official diplomatic residence. He had loved the children, Lina and Mohammed, who were in the room now but whom he studiously ignored. Guzin felt a rush of relief in the pit of her stomach but before she could say anything, Ali charged over to her and slapped her to the ground with such force that it twisted her wrist out of place. She was shocked. The children screamed and started to go to her aid but were ordered to be silent and stay put. The Mukhabarat would brook no disobedience and their powerful presence warned them off.

Guzin sat crumpled in a heap on the floor, in shock and holding her injured arm. Ali Al Delamy gave no indication that he had recognised her or the children, or even that the name 'Ra'ad Said' rang a bell. Guzin was certain he knew who they were, but she didn't dare say anything. Ali then led the other two agents in a search of the house. They began to pull the bookcases down, and Guzin begged, 'Please, just the books'. They pushed her aside and slammed her into the wall. Ali slapped her across the face. As they rampaged through the house, they took papers that Guzin had deliberately left in the drawers after their first sweep of the house weeks earlier, just in case they returned. They were not important – everything Saddam's hoodlums might have considered of value had been hidden since their last visit. They found Ra'ad's briefcase, and this time took it with them. They tipped up garbage bags but not the one Guzin had hidden the documents in. They were so close that

Guzin breathed a sigh of relief when the secret police went past it.

Finally they were ready to leave, but Ali Al Delamy went back to Guzin. He paused for a split second and looked her in the eye and in that instance she was sure she detected a momentary flicker of recognition. If so, it didn't matter.

'If you say anything about this, we will kill your son,' Ali Al Delamy said.

With that, they stalked out of the house.

The first threatening phone calls came later that night. At around three o'clock, a ringing pierced the stillness and Guzin, Mohammed and Lina awoke to instant terror. Guzin picked up the telephone and heard a string of epithets from a man threatening to kill her son if she or either of her children ever spoke of the Mukhabarat's visits or the house arrest. She listened in silence and didn't respond.

The speaker's accent was rich with Tikriti colloquialisms, identifying it as one of Saddam's henchmen. Then the phone went dead as the person on the other end of the line cut the connection.

Five minutes later, it rang again, and it continued ringing all night, but after picking it up a third time, Guzin told the children not to answer it. The pattern would be repeated for days in a vicious yet unpredictable cycle. Sometimes there would be five, ten, even fifteen telephone calls in a row for several nights running, then nothing for weeks. And as suddenly as it stopped, it would start again, but at different times during the day. Guzin and the children felt a quickening pulse every time the telephone rang and they feared picking it up but they had to, otherwise people would become suspicious, especially Guzin's father and sister, who knew her so well. They couldn't forget that the Mukhabarat had ordered Guzin to tell no one they were under house arrest. It was a savage twist, and made them feel complicit in their punishment.

The psychological horror was almost as bad as the violence and the threats of murder, and it was just as debilitating. 'They wouldn't let us sleep,' Guzin recalls. Each phone threat was more menacing, more vile, and they didn't care who was on the receiving end. 'They said that my father had some papers that they needed and if we didn't give these papers to them, they would never leave me alone. They would keep making my life hard,' Lina recalls. 'They said I should tell my mother to bring the papers. But we didn't know what papers they were talking about.'

Over the weeks and months they developed a routine to survive. Guzin took her regular morning tea in her bedroom at eight-thirty, proffered on a tray by Bessma, and the children went to their own rooms upstairs to prepare for the day, which they spent variously using the computer, reading and trying to keep up with their studies. But they became increasingly bored in their confinement. Guzin spent an enormous amount of time reading and chatting with her dogs in the garden. Mealtimes broke the monotony, and occasionally they received a visitor. At five-thirty each afternoon, they gathered in the dining room for the traditional Iraqi tea and spent half an hour together, making conversation or sometimes in total silence depending on their mood. The greatest amount of energy was spent on being prepared for, and then surviving, the Mukhabarat's menace.

The harassment continued and the pressure inside the Princess Street house was escalating. Twice Guzin took an overdose of tablets hoping to go to sleep to escape the provocation, and twice she was rushed to hospital to recuperate. The psychological and emotional toll was enormous, the stress unbearable.

Guzin did not tell her children how she was feeling, nor did Lina or Mohammed confide their own personal terrors to their mother. No one wanted to add to the burden they all knew the others shared. They were afraid that if they spoke about their fears, the talk would make it more real, and the more real it seemed, the bigger their living nightmare would be. Somehow, each thought that their own private territory of hell could be better managed as an isolated island. It was excruciating for Guzin to see her children suffering but they refused to talk to her about it.

Similarly protective, she didn't mention to the children that she knew one of the secret police, Ali Al Delamy. Because it was so long ago, she was sure Lina would have forgotten him and Mohammed was not even two when they left Yemen and wouldn't remember his time there. Besides, at that point she wasn't sure if Ali Al Delamy was still the trustworthy young man she had known in Yemen, especially after he slapped her to the floor, injuring her arm. Guzin also knew the Mukhabarat would be back again. She knew they wanted answers from her but she could tell them nothing, and even if she could have, she wouldn't. Guzin decided to bide her time before taking a risk with Ali Al Delamy.

Meanwhile, Lina was being wound tighter and tighter by the persistent terror. She was a volatile cocktail of nerves, fear and anger. Physically exhausted and after weeks of sleeping in the same bedroom as her mother and brother, she snapped. A young woman of twenty, she needed her privacy – she wanted to be able to sleep alone and cry alone. She stormed out of Guzin's makeshift panic-room downstairs and ran up to her second-floor bedroom, which opened onto a balcony.

Weeks earlier Guzin had drawn all the curtains, and each day she walked through the house making sure they were fully closed. Lina, in a fit of pique, drew the curtain halfway open, if only because her mother was so insistent that they remain closed. Her anger was making her do irrational things. Dressed in her pyjamas, she went to sit in her favourite chair. It was almost midnight when she heard a gentle knocking on the window. Lina ignored it, thinking it was the wind rattling the two French doors, or maybe a cat walking along the balcony and scratching on the fly-screen. She went to her wardrobe and opened it, and as soon as she turned her back towards the balcony, she heard a man calling out, 'Lina, Lina.'

Lina spun around and saw a man staring through the window at her. It was dark outside and she couldn't be sure who it was but she thought it might have been one of the Mukhabarat agents. 'It was a nightmare. It was really terrible. I thought he was holding a gun because I didn't do what he told me,' Lina says now, referring to the telephone threat to deliver her father's papers.

Terrified for her life, she dropped to the floor and crawled as fast as she could into her en suite, where she stayed curled in a foetal position in the corner for fifteen minutes before bravely sneaking out another door and down the stairs to the locked door of Guzin's bedroom. 'Mama, mama,' she cried. Guzin heard her daughter and opened the door to see Lina curled up on the floor, sobbing.

'I was afraid he would kill me,' Lina said.

Guzin knew there would be no respite.

Chapter Nineteen

The terror had been building, and then it was on. It was March 1996, three months after Ra'ad's murder. Guzin was ordered to the intelligence service headquarters by three of Saddam's handpicked thugs, who disgorged themselves from the telltale black car of the Mukhabarat and marched to her front door.

'You have to come with us,' they demanded. The blond monster was present but Ali Al Delamy was not.

For months now Guzin had been at sea with her emotions. One moment she was flattened by grief, another haunted by despair, then drowning in depression. Now she was angered into defiance, the young girl whose father had taught her to be strong and told her she could do anything. 'You can kill me right now, right here in my house,' she said, standing up to the Mukhabarat, drawing on a ferocity she hadn't felt in the months since her husband had been killed.

The special police assured Guzin they were not going to kill her, not there and then, nor later at the intelligence headquarters which was located a few streets away in Al Mansour. They just wanted some information. Guzin was not giving in easily. She didn't want them to see her as a vulnerable woman whom they could manipulate, a victim. She wanted to be the Guzin of old.

'I am not going with you in your car. What will the neighbours say? You are three men, I have no husband,' she said.

Ironically, considering the occasion, a sense of Arab custom prevailed and the men allowed Guzin to follow them in her own car but warned her that if she deviated just one inch, she would pay. They were waiting for her as she stepped out of her car at the Mukhabarat headquarters; Guzin was flanked by two agents and one followed behind as they guided her into the evil building into which hundreds of people went but never returned.

Guzin was led into a large room painted a dirty white and told to take a seat. She heard the door being locked behind her and realised she was alone. None of the agents had come in with her. She looked around the room and was relieved to see that it was not one of Saddam Hussein's notorious torture chambers equipped with instruments of pain and death. The room had high ceilings and windows were cut into the top of the wall and draped with short, industrial-grey curtains that looked as though they had never been washed. The windows were too high to see out of and Guzin wondered if they looked to an outside court-yard or a hallway, or some other kind of hell. A large rectangular table sat in the middle of the room surrounded by a scattering of blue plastic chairs with black metal legs. In one corner she saw a television set and a videotape player. Nearby was a tape-recorder with a radio tuner. The floors were covered with scuffed linoleum, and the table was chipped and cracked. The whole room was lit by a bare bulb hanging on a wire from the ceiling.

Guzin waited in trepidation for what seemed like an eternity but was really only an hour. For the life of her she couldn't imagine what they wanted. Ra'ad had never revealed in detail the scope of his work as a diplomat in the foreign ministry. He merely painted it with broad brush-strokes, and Guzin had been busy raising a family so didn't pay too much attention anyway. Part of the Mukhabarat's duties were to run the regime's slippery network of inform-ers and the activities of foreign embassies in Iraq and, conversely, Iraqi embassies abroad. Surely they would already know everything there was to know, if indeed there was anything to know. And yes, Guzin thought to herself, she and Ra'ad had always opposed Saddam Hussein's dictatorial rule, at least privately. But to survive life either under or within his regime, one gave an outward appear-ance of compliance, which is what they had done. There was no other way.

Guzin was smart enough to know that the long wait was part of the Mukhabarat's web of psychological terrorism. Knowing it gave her no end of self-satisfaction. She kept reminding herself of her promise to Ra'ad, and how she had to be strong so she could take their children and flee Iraq. After an hour, a man casually sauntered in and put a video-tape in the machine. He hit the play button, looked at Guzin with a smug sneer, and walked out without saying a word. Guzin was alone once more and she turned to the television.

A static hiss filled the room and electronic snow appeared on the screen before it dissolved into a picture of graphic torture. The videotape was a catalogue of the Muk-habarat's crimes. A warning of what might happen to her.

Guzin sat stock still, aware of every muscle in her body as she watched the systematic violence on the screen in front of her. Her blood roared and echoed through her ears, and her palms began to sweat. It was impossible to remain unaffected by what she saw. Victims with their faces twisted in agony. A large tank of water in which people were forced to stand for days. If they fell asleep, they drowned. Victims' soundless screams. A man with his hands nailed to a post to keep him standing in place. Monsters in full flight.

She had watched an hour of this testament to torture and could stand no more. The wanton brutality was evidence of man's capacity for evil. Suddenly, four men burst into the room, a tidal wave of testosterone and terror. Ali Al Delamy looked directly at Guzin and held her stare long enough to convey that he knew who she was. She had to trust her instincts, she just knew. She returned the look. He nodded ever so slightly, and she was sure.

'What do you think of what you saw, Mrs Najim?' the interrogation began.

Guzin was prepared. She was sitting up at the table, her back ramrod straight, her head high, not a skerrick of fear to be seen.

'I can't see anything from here because I don't have my glasses,' was her bold retort.

With lightning speed, Ali Al Delamy leant across the table and slapped Guzin hard across the face, twice, knocking her head to one side and then back across the other. Guzin was mortified but she refused to give in. She didn't cry. Breathing deeply, poised, she simply turned back to face him, her eyes as cold as any executioner's. She didn't even lift her hand to her face to ease the pain.

'I don't want you to speak back,' he shouted at her.

Guzin nodded.

Relying on every ounce of female intuition and gut instinct, she sensed that he was protecting her. He had seen her in a diplomatic setting in a foreign country and knew how independent she could be. In Yemen, Ali had witnessed a woman who was self-confident and a social equal to any man, no matter if he were a politician or diplomat, or a member of the military or secret police. They had been good friends.

Guzin remembered laughing with Ali about Saddam Hussein's peasant behaviour, his ridiculous penchant for dressing as a Shi'ite, then a Kurd and then a soldier, or as a respectable businessman with his sharp suits and Kevlar-lined pork-pie hats – all to build his cult of personality. They had mocked the large number of Saddam's uneducated cousins and half-brothers who lined the upper ranks of the Ba'ath Party. Ali had been in awe of Guzin's privileged background compared to his own, and she and Ra'ad gave him an entrée to a world he had never seen before.

At that moment in the interrogation room, with the stinging, red palm prints of Ali's hands burning on her cheeks, Guzin believed she could still trust him. Ali's violence and warning not to talk, Guzin suspected, were to protect her from herself and to conceal from his fellow Mukhabarat agents that he knew her. Later, she would learn her instincts were right.

The interrogation continued with the blond agent doing the talking, playing the 'good cop' to Ali's 'bad cop'.

'Why did you show her this film? We don't need these films with Mrs Najim,' he said, a crocodile smile spreading across his face. 'Your husband was our friend.'

'I have nothing to say,' Guzin replied, earning herself another slap across the face.

'There are documents we need and you are going to give them to us. I want you to behave and obey,' he said.

'I have nothing. You can come and search my house.' Guzin was confident they would find nothing because her driver Fathy had already smuggled most of their personal documents out of the house.

The interrogation lasted six hours, during which Guzin was taunted and repeatedly slapped across the face. The agents said they knew she was politically active at university. They also knew all about her family's history, how her father Shawket had left the country in 1978 and never returned. She refused to cry and never broke down. At the end of the tortuous day, the blond agent told Guzin that if she didn't comply and furnish the documents they demanded, her son or daughter would be killed. Then they sent her home.

'Many times they hit me because I was defiant. I didn't want them to see me weak. They told me they wanted to break me because I was too strong-willed, but I think I broke them,' Guzin says now, recalling the three years of persecution she suffered in Iraq. 'These people, I know them; if they find you weak they will destroy you. They are sick, and if they find you strong, they will think sometimes before they hit you. They hit me many times and I hated myself because I couldn't kill them or do something against them at that time. I think that's why I became ill – I wanted to punish myself. Why couldn't I do anything to them?

'I told myself I would leave Iraq because they wanted me there, and in that way I would break them. But first my son had to go because they began to threaten him. I wanted to leave Iraq but I knew that if I wanted to leave safely, I would have to obey them and pretend that everything was okay. So I began to plan how to leave.'

Guzin Najim had lived on the periphery of politics all her life and she knew how it worked. To survive the house arrest and to plan her escape, she had to play the Mukhabarat at their own game. Internally, every minute of her life was a slow death, but she had to put on a brave face. Her health deteriorated, she refused to eat, and she suffered an ulcer and depression. There were times when she was so lonely and despairing that she wanted the ground to open up and swallow her. But she knew she had to honour her promise to Ra'ad. Even in her darkest hour, the promise pulled her towards the light. To get there, Guzin had to convince the most powerful of all of Saddam Hussein's intelligence agencies that she was complying with their orders.

The Mukhabarat never gave up. Over the months the same three men ran a relentless campaign of harassment directed at Guzin, Lina and Mohammed. One night Ali Al Delamy, the peroxided blond and a third secret police-man whose name they never knew arrived at the Princess Street house at eight o'clock. They tore the house apart looking for Ra'ad's papers: they wanted Guzin to hand over the documents she didn't have and it seemed as if they would do anything to get them. But again they found nothing. The cruel blond took their failure out on Guzin, pushing her headfirst into a wall, busting her lips and cutting her forehead. He slapped her and pushed her to the ground in front of her children. She rarely fought back because to do so would only enrage Saddam's henchmen even more. To them, Guzin was just another victim they could torment.

SANDRA LEE

As part of the ongoing harassment, the Mukhabarat arrived at the house most Fridays, and at various other times during the week. Sometimes Ali would be alone, at other times he would be accompanied by the blond agent and the nameless third man. Sometimes they would storm through the house causing mayhem, breaking things and making a mess. At other times they merely made their presence felt, verbally abusing Guzin. They also continued their barrage of late-night telephone calls. 'Are you awake? Why are you awake? We want the documents. Give us the documents or else we will kill your son and daughter.' They burned Mohammed's car, an American-made Chevrolet, in the garage as Mohammed and Fathy looked on, helpless to do anything. They strolled with an insouciant nonchalance on the footpath outside the house, menacingly present and accounted for.

Ali Al Delamy, she had noticed, was no longer violent during the visits. He never spoke to Guzin in front of the other two officers unless he absolutely had to and then he was as aggressive as the blond. But Ali and Guzin were making contact – slowly developing a system of communication using subtle movements which no one else could detect. For instance, if Guzin responded to the Mukhabarat's questions favourably or if he wanted to warn her, Ali would give her a certain look, not quite a nod and a wink, but something like it only much more subtle. It started slowly and grew over time as she learned to trust him. Trusting anyone in Iraq, regardless of instincts, was a hazardous game and potentially lethal.

But if it was hard for Guzin, it was especially hard for her children. 'Life was terrible under house arrest. We were not allowed to see most of the people we had known and there

214

was so much pressure on us, too much pressure on us. I didn't know what to do. I was very confused,' Lina says now. 'People came from time to time but most of our friends stayed away after my father's death. I was heartbroken. My father wasn't there to listen to the music with me anymore. I lost a friend and a father.'

When Ali arrived alone at Princess Street, he and Guzin spoke, hesitantly at first, reacquainting themselves in the most generic of ways, letting little comments about Saddam Hussein or shared moments in Yemen slip into the conversation. On one such visit towards the end of 1996, after almost a year of nonstop harassment, Ali told Guzin, 'Don't worry, everything will be as you want.' It was Ali's sign to Guzin that she could follow her instincts and trust him.

Guzin and her children never gave in. Despite the stress and the constant threat of death, they refused to let Saddam Hussein and the Mukhabarat break their spirit. It helped that Guzin felt she had an ally in Ali. Somehow, she thought, he would help her escape, but she still wasn't ready to confide in him. It helped too that Shawket Najim secretly sent five hundred American dollars to his daughter each month so she could survive. But when things got tight, she was forced to ask Fathy to sell some belongings. He wasn't under house arrest and in Baghdad, which was still under United Nations sanctions, household commodities were coveted items. Through her driver Guzin sold a television set, a radio and other electrical appliances.

Towards the end of the year, Ali Al Delamy and his vicious blond partner arrived for what Guzin expected would be their usual round of Friday morning Mukhabarat mayhem. Instead, they told Guzin that the conditions of the house arrest had been eased – they could now go out to shop and visit friends every two to three weeks. She couldn't quite believe what she was hearing. It was as if someone was playing an awful trick. The blond had delivered the news with as much pathos as he could muster – which is to say, none. Guzin wasn't sure she should trust her own ears. Guzin almost collapsed with joy, but, Ali warned her sternly, she was still under suspicion and they should be wary because the intelligence police would be watching them as closely as ever. Guzin didn't care. She said she had nothing to hide. Nor, for that matter, had Ra'ad.

But, more importantly, she asked, exactly what does it mean? Could Mohammed return to school? Could Lina start attending classes at the Al Mustansiriya University again? Ali said yes, to all of it. Guzin was elated. It meant that their lives would be closer to normal and she would have the freedom to plot her escape. But it did not end the reign of terror.

Guzin and the children were happy to put the living hell of 1996 behind them. They began visiting the same three friends who had been included on the Mukhabarat's list, all of whom said they were happy to see Guzin and the children out of the house once more. Whenever a friend had arrived at the house to pay a visit that past year, Guzin sent Lina or Mohammed to tell them that she didn't want to see anybody. Everyone put Guzin's self-imposed isolation down to her grief over Ra'ad's traumatic death, and they probably assumed that a year was a reasonable mourning period. Thankfully, no one had suspected the truth: that they were under house arrest.

In January 1997, Mohammed was back at school, this time at the Al Mansour Secondary School. He had missed a year but he was so bright he made up his academic shortfall in no time and had moved to the top of the class in his chosen subjects of Islamic education, Arabic, English, solid and analytical geometry and calculus, biology, chemistry and physics. He began playing soccer and tennis with his friends and spent time hanging out like a regular teenager, at least as much as possible. Lina returned to university, where she picked up her studies in English literature and resumed her friendship with Furat. She could get lost in the world of literature and it gave her something to focus on to take her mind off her father's death.

Their hopes for a normal life were short-lived. They were still under siege even though the imprisonment had been relaxed. Three weeks later, Mohammed was walking along the footpath in Al Mansour when a familiar black car prowled alongside him. The window was slowly wound down and a secret policeman pointed his pistol at Mohammed's head and pretended to fire. Another warning.

'They said don't go out alone and don't go far from home. Don't go to clubs and don't meet friends if they are far from where you live, don't think that you are free,' Mohammed remembers. 'I was only sixteen, seventeen, and I played some games with them. I would go out a little distance down the road and then turn around and come back. If they followed me, I would know it was them. It was frightening, yes, of course, because they would walk past the house on the footpath just to let us know they were there. They were always ringing and hanging up, to see if I was home or if my mother was home and to let us know that they were watching us. Sometimes when we were out of the house, they would come and leave something inside as a sign that they had been there. They would put a pen or a piece of paper on the table or on the floor.'

One afternoon Guzin walked in to the house to find it completely ransacked. She wondered if the intelligence agents had hidden a listening device somewhere, because nothing was stolen. Guzin and Mohammed frequently left a matchstick stuck between the front door and doorframe, or a sprinkle of talcum powder on the door handle. If either was disturbed when they returned home, they knew that the Mukhabarat had paid a visit. Each intrusion simply cautioned Guzin and her children to maintain their vigilance.

As soon as Mohammed turned eighteen, he got his driver's licence so he could drive to the cemetery where his father was buried and attend to his grave. It was more than one hundred kilometres from Al Mansour and beyond the geographical limits prescribed by the Mukhabarat, who had ordered him not to stray far from home. But Mohammed refused to abandon his responsibilities to his father and insisted on going. His mother couldn't stop him. One day Mohammed had spent several hours at the cemetery, talking to his father, praying and cleaning the grave. He was cruising back home towards Baghdad on one of its famous six-lane highways when a four-wheel drive vehicle pulled out in front of him and crashed straight into Mohammed's car. It was the Mukhabarat, unleashing yet another weapon in their terror arsenal.

'I was very shaken up about the accident. I was afraid the car would catch fire. I left the car and everything in it, and rang a friend who came and got me. They watched me, they knew where I was going to be driving,' Mohammed says.

Lina did not escape unscathed even though she could melt, with relative anonymity, into the huge student body at Al Mustansiriya University. She often spent her free hours between lectures at the café or in the library. Before long, two agents were towering over her. 'We are here, Lina, don't feel that you are free. We are always watching you,' they said.

Lina was petrified but she said nothing to anyone, too fearful of the possible repercussions. Every ten to fourteen days, the same two agents would show up, their sinister presence another method of harassment. They varied the timing of their appearances, turning up as if at random and always demanding the elusive documents she knew nothing about. Lina was sure she was under constant surveillance – how else would they know her schedule and when best to confront her without making a scene? The menace was all too perfectly timed to be pure luck. It wasn't how the Mukhabarat worked. Their intimidation was crippling.

'I never told my mother because she was already having a hard time and was sad. It was hopeless – I couldn't put more pressure on her. I wanted to talk to someone but I couldn't. I was frightened. The only thing they ever said was that they needed some papers that were important,' Lina recalls. 'I kept it all inside. It was very hard. I wanted to speak to someone about it but I couldn't because maybe I would hurt everyone by talking. I would have liked to talk to my father's friends, both psychiatrists, Sari and Tariq, because I knew they would help me, but I was afraid that if I told them the Mukhabarat might hurt them. I couldn't even tell my best friend Furat. She doesn't know how my father died, and I don't know what happened, even today, I don't know. I just want to know why.'

With her children gone during the daytime, Guzin began cultivating her dear friends Luay Al Douri and his mother Madiha. The two families had been friends for decades. Their house in neighbouring Al Yarmouk felt like a safe haven to Guzin. She never had to worry about being invaded by the Mukhabarat and knew she could speak freely. Madiha was related to a top-ranking member of Saddam Hussein's cabinet and the proximity to power provided a certain protective coating. When it came to Saddam Hussein, they both thought alike.

Luay had been educated in the United States and received a degree at one of the more prestigious engineering universities on the east coast. He spoke fluent English and spent four years studying and working in America, during which time he developed a global political outlook that reflected that of Ra'ad and Guzin.

In early 1997 Guzin gave Luay power of attorney over her financial affairs. Because Guzin was a widow and had no brothers or other male relatives in Iraq, it was entirely appropriate from a societal point of view. But for Guzin, it was purely pragmatic. She told Luay that if anything ever happened to her, he was to divide her estate evenly between her two children and ensure they were adequately provided for and taken to safety. Luay was a friend and considered it an honour.

That same month, Mohammed was again harassed by an agent in the Mukhabarat uniform who pointed a gun at him as he was walking in Princess Street. Guzin had had enough. She decided to reveal her escape plan to the children. Too frightened to speak in the house, Guzin took Lina and Mohammed for a walk around the picturesque streets of Al Mansour. She told them that she wanted to leave Iraq, that it was becoming too dangerous for them to stay any longer.

Guzin was worried that the children, particularly Lina, who had always been so timorous, would be too frightened to take the risk. But their responses surprised and pleased her. They both wanted to leave Iraq as soon as possible. 'I had to leave Iraq and my family had to leave Iraq because if we stayed, I think what happened to my father would have happened to us,' Mohammed says, sitting in his mother's flat on a clear blue winter's day in Sydney before getting up to close the curtains – a hangover from his days in Baghdad under house arrest. 'In 1996 they took away my studies and freedom. So my family and I had to leave because if I stayed I would have had many problems with them. I would always have been visited by the intelligence service.'

Guzin made them promise to tell no one. The plot had to be a secret and she alone would decide when to go and who to turn to for help. Guzin also told Luay and Madiha, who offered to help. They both agreed the risk was enormous, but the benefits would be priceless. After all, what price freedom?

Under the aegis of finessing her legal situation as a widow, Guzin began visiting Luay and Madiha more and more frequently. Each time, she brought a bag of personal clothing or valuable household items which Luay would spirit out of Iraq to Jordan, where Guzin's father and sister still lived. Luay frequently travelled to Jordan on business and so had a ready-made excuse for the trip. He could easily take Guzin's property in the car with him. Luay would take amounts so small that, if detected, they wouldn't raise an eyebrow because he could claim they belonged to him or his mother. It was a slow and meticulous process, but step by step, bit by bit, Guzin was liquidating her Princess Street home.

Her Sudanese driver Fathy also helped. Previously he thought he was taking Guzin's documents to Luay's house for safekeeping, but now he understood why Guzin had asked him to do it: secretly, she had been planning her escape. Fathy's best friend was the driver for a Sudanese diplomat in Iraq and, as such, had access to an official car and, crucially, diplomatic immunity. Fathy occasionally accompanied his friend on trips to Jordan, and began taking with him little stockpiles of Guzin's belongings. He refused to accept Guzin's offer of payment, saying he was happy to help her after all she had done for him in the post-war years in Iraq. Ironically, as Guzin's family driver he ranked among the best paid workers in the entire country – after Saddam's fellow Tikritis in the Ba'ath Party, that is. Saddam Hussein had destroyed the middle class and degraded the professional ranks so that teachers and doctors and the like earned less than the blue collar workers who were fortunate enough to find work.

Meanwhile, amid all the chaos, another ray of hope emerged and it was exactly the distraction Guzin needed. Lina was falling in love.

Ahmed Al Douri is a true romantic; a modern, educated man, tall, lean and handsome. Born in Baghdad on 1 January 1970, he has thick black hair that stands up straight if cut short enough, smiling almond eyes, elegant long fingers and a voice as smooth as honey. His coup de grâce: kindness and intelligence. 'Lina and I were neighbours in Al Mansour and our families knew each other. One day, I saw her and our eyes met. We felt, both of us, that we are right as husband and wife. Just from one look,' he says.

Ahmed's family lived on Princess Street just a few minutes walk away from Guzin and Ra'ad. Ahmed had watched Lina growing up, but she was five years younger than him and still in high school when he went to Baghdad

University to study for a degree in graphic design. Being older, he didn't pay her any attention, but Lina's brother, Mohammed, played soccer with Ahmed's younger brother and they hung out together. Their parents were also friends and, before Ra'ad's death, were frequent visitors to each other's homes. It was in 1997 at one such family visit that Lina and Ahmed realised their mutual attraction. They began talking and getting to know each other, but she was worried that her family's circumstances would repel him. So too was Guzin. Ahmed instantly knew he wanted Lina, but there was a hurdle. Two, in fact. Big ones. Namely, the Mukhabarat and Guzin's secret plan to flee Iraq.

Guzin wasn't sure how much Ahmed knew about her husband's death but living on Princess Street, as both families did, she was sure he would have heard the gossip. After all, Ra'ad was a diplomat and Al Mansour was top-heavy with diplomatic residences, and Baghdad was a city where gossip and information were traded like gold. Ahmed knew that Ra'ad had died very quickly and in 'mysterious circumstances' and he had even heard some neighbours say 'they killed him, they poisoned him', they being the Mukhabarat. However, because he was working long hours as a jewellery designer in a local store, he didn't socialise much with the neighbours and his knowledge was limited to the local grapevine, which didn't interest him.

Guzin knew Lina was falling in love with Ahmed, so before the customary visit of Ahmed's mother and aunt to say Ahmed wished to marry Lina, she decided she would have to tell Ahmed the truth of their future. Ahmed was the eldest of five children – he had three sisters and a brother – and like all eldest siblings, he had a familial duty to them and his parents, Hana and Jamil Al Douri. Guzin wasn't sure how he would take the news, but she knew she could trust him. The families had known each other a long time and considered each other respectable and honourable people.

Guzin invited Ahmed to her house and sat him down in the lounge room. There, with photographs of Ra'ad lining the bookcases and coffee tables, Guzin told Ahmed that she planned to flee Iraq with her son and daughter. Their future, she said, would not, could not, be in Iraq. It was too dangerous. They lived under the constant threat of murder from the Mukhabarat. Guzin said that if Ahmed refused to join them or, more importantly, refused to let Lina leave with her and Mohammed, then she would refuse to give her permission for Lina to marry him, as was her maternal right in the absence of Lina's father. It was that simple. Guzin was brutally honest with Ahmed. She had to know where he stood and she made him promise her that he would tell no one of the plan.

Ahmed was equally frank and sincere. He was in love with Lina; he could not see a future without her. Ahmed said he supported Guzin and would go with them. He knew the risks were enormous. Indeed, they would be enough to stop a lesser man in his tracks. Ahmed would be leaving his beloved parents and his brother and sisters and going to a country where he would not be guaranteed a job. Under Jordanian laws, Iraqi citizens must get government approval to work, and it's not always easy to do so. He was also placing himself in great personal danger. Ahmed had never been on the Mukhabarat's radar, and by escaping Baghdad – assuming they succeeded – he would become a marked man. The journey itself would be arduous and fraught with danger, the gravest being detection followed by execution in the dust bowl desert off the side of the Baghdad–Jordan Road. Saddam Hussein did not like defectors or deserters and dealt with them accordingly.

But Ahmed was in love and he saw his future with Lina even beyond the borders of Iraq. 'Before our engagement I was not satisfied about my life in Iraq, especially after 1990 when the situation changed,' Ahmed says, referring to the Iraqi invasion of Kuwait and subsequent Gulf war. He is sitting in his Sydney unit in the middle of winter in 2003, exactly six years after he first realised that Lina was the one. 'The good, well-known people lost their jobs, they lost their properties. The government would not let you work, even if you had a good company, an established workplace, they would come to you and take forty per cent of your income. Like the Mafia. If you said you didn't want to share, they would destroy your life and your job.

'I supported Guzin's decision because I was dissatisfied, because there was no future in Iraq for myself or my wife. And after that, what if you have a family and you have a son – how will you raise him? If you want to teach him good things you have to face the community and society, and you cannot trust the society. Before the 1980s, I saw Baghdad as a lovely place to live but anyone older than that used to say that before the seventies, it was much more beautiful.'

Days after Guzin confided to Ahmed her plan of escape, his mother, Hana, and aunt arrived at her house, with Ahmed in tow. They had come seeking Lina's hand in marriage to Ahmed. They told Guzin that Ahmed wanted to be engaged to Lina, who was wearing jeans and sitting nervously beside her mother. Guzin thanked Hana for the honour and said they needed time to think about it. As Lina says now, 'It's not an easy thing to say. It's marriage.

It's your whole life. And I asked my uncle about Ahmed's family, and he told me they were good people, and finally I said, "Yes".'

For two days Ahmed was a bundle of nerves, waiting to hear what Lina's answer would be. When his mother returned to Guzin's home to receive the news, Ahmed stayed at home. He told his mother to ring as soon as Guzin gave her word – either yes or no. They lived only a few minutes away but he couldn't wait another excruciating second for Hana to return by foot.

'They called me from Guzin's house and said, "Yes. Come now, they want to see you",' Ahmed grins as he remembers the telephone call. He raced to Guzin's and they celebrated.

On 5 October 1997, Guzin's and Ahmed's families took two suites at the Babylon Hotel overlooking the River Tigris and Lina and Ahmed officially celebrated their engagement with a pool party for their family and friends. Their courting had begun. Their journey hadn't even started.

Chapter Twenty

Guzin Najim had a made a promise and she had a plan. Come hell or high water, she was going to escape Saddam Hussein's savagery in Iraq and take her children to freedom. There was just one problem – she didn't know how to put her plan into place, particularly while under the constant surveillance of the Mukhabarat. While her friend Luay Al Douri and her driver Fathy had been helping her by secreting documents and possessions and gradually transferring them to Jordan, neither Luay nor Fathy had the wherewithal to facilitate the next, most dangerous step – the actual escape from Iraq.

There was only one way out of Baghdad alive and that was by road, and all roads out of the capital were manned at checkpoints by Saddam's armed guards and soldiers who demanded certificates of identification and officially stamped exit visas before granting passage. Iraqi women under forty-five could not leave the country alone without the written permission of their husband, father or brother, which posed a particular problem for Guzin. She had no husband and no brother, and her father was in Jordan, and in any case was persona non grata in Iraq. She could possibly get around that by falsely stating her age, raising it by four years, but it was another risk.

Flying was not an option. Commercial flights into and out of Baghdad had ceased at the end of the first Gulf war when the United Nations imposed no-fly zones in northern and southern Iraq, which were patrolled by American fighter jets. Commercial airlines were in danger of being mistaken as enemy aircraft and shot down. Skirmishes between the US fighter pilots and the depleted Iraqi air force were frequent. Whenever a belligerent Saddam Hussein wanted to flaunt his authority, he sent his helpless warriors on virtual suicide missions to breach the north and south no-fly parallels, which earned them hostile artillery fire from the United States forces there to enforce the sanctions. The airspace over the Iraqi capital was under Saddam's personal control, and the only people who flew there were the Iraqi air force or those game enough to board helicopters with their leader. Helicopters were easy assassination targets in the coup-happy country.

Guzin was running out of options and she had few people whom she could turn to. Enter Ali Al Delamy. Guzin's secret friend in the secret police was the most obvious solution to her problem and, in reality, her only hope. Ali had the connections Guzin needed and knew his way around the maze-like corridors of the corrupt Iraqi bureaucracy. He had access to people in power and knew how susceptible they were to a handsome kickback for an illegal favour. Bribery and politics made for easy bed fellows, particularly in Iraq.

Guzin's instincts told her that she could trust Ali, and Guzin was a woman who always trusted her instincts. Ever since he and his Mukhabarat comrades had arrived at her home sixteen days after Ra'ad was murdered, Ali and Guzin had slowly been reconstructing a friendship of sorts built on an intricate system of eye contact and covert conversation. It was inherently dangerous. She was a suspect – for what she's still not sure, even now in 2003 – and Ali, at any moment, could have turned Guzin over to whatever hell Saddam's soldiers could conjure. But she had persisted and Ali had responded in his own way. Had he been caught fraternising, as it were, with an Iraqi dissenter, he would have been imprisoned for his betrayal of the Mukhabarat, and possibly tortured or executed in one of the torture chambers with which he was so familiar. The next time Ali arrived alone at Guzin's home, she would test the waters to see if he was as faithful and loyal as she suspected. All she had to do was wait. A perfect opportunity presented itself towards the end of November 1997.

It was a routine Mukhabarat visit, like so many others over the previous two years. Guzin took Ali into the garden where she felt safe to talk. She conducted only the most banal conversations inside the house in case the intelligence service had planted electronic listening devices. And if she did speak about anything important with the children or guests inside the house, she always masked the conversation by turning up the volume on the television, radio or CD player. There were times when the Princess Street house sounded like party central.

Guzin was about to take an enormous leap of faith, one that could end up costing lives – hers and her children's. The only real indication she had ever had that Ali was sympathetic to her plight had come approximately a year earlier when he said, 'Don't worry, everything will be as you want.' Since then, there had been no overt sign from Ali that he actually would help. Still, Guzin had to take the risk. He was her only hope.

They had been dancing around their conversation for a while when Guzin adroitly steered the discussion to the future. Using her charm and not a little self-deprecation, she took a deep breath and, affecting the most casual and joking manner possible, began to speak. Considering her stomach was awash with nerves, it was an admirable achievement. 'You know, Ali, if I do it, they will find me and kill me,' Guzin said with a laugh that, to her, rang hollow and false because it was. She had deliberately avoided the words 'escape' or 'flee', or even the more innocuous 'leave', because she wanted to be imprecise in case her ploy backfired.

Ali stood by, watching her. He was intelligent and had always understood Guzin's double-talk. He certainly didn't seem shocked. To Guzin, Ali had the look of a man who was expecting something more.

She pressed on, this time taking a more direct approach, reading his face, testing his reactions to her words. 'If I escaped,' she started, trying to sound light-hearted, 'they would get me.'

Ali appeared inscrutable, with the face of a poker player, or a man used to snuffing out his emotions.

'But they will not win. Even if I manage to flee and they kill me, it will be a victory because I will not be living like this anymore,' Guzin said.

Ali took his time to respond, but when he answered Guzin, it was with an Arabic proverb. 'Enti wuledty qabl Al-shaytan bi shahrain,' he said quietly. Roughly translated, he told Guzin she had been born two months before Satan, and it meant that she was ahead of him, cleverer than him, and would outsmart him – Satan being Saddam Hussein.

Arabic people often talk in riddles and rely on ancient proverbs or colloquialisms to convey a message, and Ali's reply was a good sign. Without actually saying it, Ali had offered his support and shown her respect. It gave Guzin the confidence she needed. That night Guzin told Lina and Mohammed that everything would be all right. But she didn't go into details. She was yet to reveal Ali Al Delamy's identity to them, believing they were safer not knowing.

Two days later, Ali returned to the house. It was mid-afternoon and, being winter, the sun had already begun its slow descent on the horizon beyond the western banks of the Euphrates. Guzin had risen from her afternoon nap and was about to take tea with her children. Lina and Mohammed were startled when they saw Ali.

Guzin rushed him into the garden, wrapping her arms around her chest against the winter chill. This time, he was more forthcoming. 'I will help you, Guzin,' Ali said anxiously, looking over his shoulders to make sure no one was within earshot. 'You must trust me and rely on me because I promise to be loyal to you and your husband's memory. Don't worry, I will help you leave Iraq.'

Guzin's instincts had been right. And Ali had begun to play a dangerous double-game.

Chapter Twenty-One

Nineteen ninety-eight was a year of living dangerously for Guzin and a year of living romance for Lina. While one was caught up in the stealthy planning of an escape from Baghdad, the other was enveloped in planning a big wedding right in the very heart of it. The two events couldn't have been more opposite, and yet, in their very essence, one presented a perfect cover for the other.

Lina chose 1 September for her wedding breakfast. But as is the Iraqi tradition, the marriage and the wedding celebrations were actually divided into three separate parts throughout the year leading up to the grand wedding day. The first important date was 16 April when, under Sharia law, Ahmed Jamil Al Douri and Lina Ra'ad Said invited the Sunni Muslim registrar to Lina's home on Princess Street to witness the young couple sign the official marriage contract. They set the time for four in the afternoon and invited only close family and friends of the bride and groom for the ceremony in which Lina and Mohammed both accepted each other as future husband and wife. Afterwards, they continued courting just as any other engaged couple did.

Most of Ahmed's friends were already married and they acted as chaperones for the young lovers. They dined occasionally at the al-Alwiya club, which opened in 1920 soon after the British defeated the Ottoman empire and established the first constitutional monarchy of Iraq. Ahmed's other favourite was the Hindiya club on the banks of the Tigris, which enjoyed a large Christian clientele. The couple rarely went to the nearby Hunting Club, even though it was perfectly located around the corner in Al Mansour. It was the unofficial social headquarters of Saddam Hussein and his ruling elite. The irony, of course, was that the Hunting Club was the place where the anti-American president liked to indulge his penchant for American food and whiskey or cheap rosé. The Hunting Club also had tennis courts, a swimming pool and an equestrian centre. But because of the habitual patrons, Ahmed and Lina gave it a wide berth.

On 20 April, Ahmed, a traditionalist, hosted the second pre-wedding party for two hundred and fifty friends. It was a male-only affair and the men gathered at the Alsyed club in Al Mansour to drink thick Iraqi coffee and sweet tea and nibble on delicious hand-made chocolates. The guests wished Ahmed a happy future with Lina and hoped they would be blessed with many children. Ahmed, meanwhile, was busy designing and making his and Lina's matching wedding bands – a mix of yellow and white gold. For her part, Lina was in the throes of organising the September wedding celebration at the Al Melia Mansour hotel on the Tigris, to which almost four hundred people would be invited. She had to decide on a wedding dress, a veil, the food, flowers and the theme of the party. The hubbub of the impending wedding celebration was a perfect foil for the other plan being developed at the Princess Street household. The escape.

The visits from the Mukhabarat had taken on a new meaning for Guzin since Ali Al Delamy became her accomplice. However, they were no less menacing. In fact, if anything, they had become more dangerous. The stakes were now incredibly high, particularly for Ali, who would be considered a traitor to the regime, the most venal sin of all.

At the end of winter in early 1998, the stakes were raised even higher. Under the auspices of another official Mukhabarat visit, Ali told Guzin that he would smuggle her family out of Iraq and across the border into Jordan, but it would cost her. Ten thousand American dollars. It was an extravagant fee, roughly twenty million Iraqi dinars, which is enough to buy a decent house in Baghdad, where the average monthly wage for those lucky enough to find work is five American dollars. It was a staggering amount of money considering the economic fortunes of most Iraqis.

Ali told Guzin that without the money, the escape was impossible. The cash was vital to grease the palms of the myriad of corrupt Iraqi officials who would have to be paid off along the way, from the bureaucrat who would forge exit visas and seal them with the official government stamp to the guards at the checkpoints they passed through. He had to pay drivers and people who ran safe houses, border patrol guards and political apparatchiks who might accidentally come across paperwork they otherwise wouldn't have seen. As well, there were bound to be informers seeking payola for information on who was corruptible and who was not. Their assistance, silence and compliance all came with a fee. This was Iraq.

Money was not an object for Guzin, and she gave Ali the go-ahead. Guzin's assets were tied up in property in Iraq and Jordan, as well as coming from her father, Shawket, in Jordan. Now seventy-four years old and in declining health, he had been sending his daughter five hundred American dollars each month for the last few years and she had been stockpiling what she could for a rainy day. Her mother-in-law, Fakhira Nouri, also sent money disguised as gifts to her grandchildren. Guzin already had part of the money in safekeeping with Luay and could easily accrue the remaining cash in stages. She enlisted two other friends to help, a dear neighbour named Khalida um Hussam, and Sari, the psychiatrist friend of Guzin and her late husband, Ra'ad. Guzin protected the cash by dividing it between the three of them. No Iraqi in their right mind kept their money in the banks in Baghdad. It was too vulnerable and could be misused by Saddam Hussein to prop up his regime.

Ali told Guzin it would take several weeks, and maybe months, to devise an escape plan, but just the same, he advised her to start preparing for what would be a lightning fast departure which could come at any time of the day or night. Her preparations, he warned, should be subtle so as not to alert the authorities. An escape of this enormity required the utmost strategic planning. Ali was taking nothing for himself except the honour of helping Guzin and her children. As well, he told Guzin that once he had safely escorted them as far as he could, he was going to continue the journey and flee Iraq himself. If everything went according to plan, Ali would cross the border into Syria about the same time Guzin would cross into Jordan. She was stunned.

Effectively, Ali had just announced he was going to desert the dreaded Mukhabarat. Guzin could hardly begin to imagine what they would do to Ali if he was caught. Not only was he a deserter, but he had helped her and her family escape. It was the only time Guzin was happy that Ali had never married. He had told her all those years ago in Yemen that he dreamed of having a wife and children, but the cards hadn't fallen his way and he had remained a bachelor. His parents had died within two months of each other the year before, so he was, ostensibly, a free man. His actions would not put anyone else at risk.

Guzin was eternally grateful and thanked him. Slowly, over several months, Ali had earned their trust. He told Lina that one day she would know what had happened to her father. He confided in her and Mohammed that Ra'ad had been 'forced to drink something' the day he was interrogated. Ali said he was not at the headquarters during the interrogation, but other Mukhabarat officers had confirmed it with him. In her heart of hearts, Guzin trusted him and the risks he had taken, but still, silently, at that very moment she was praying that Ali Al Delamy was not about to rob her blind or blackmail her. She prayed to God that this was not a set-up.

Meanwhile, the harassment never ceased. In January 1998 Guzin decided to celebrate the end of Ramadan at the Al Rasheed hotel as she had done so many times before with Ra'ad when the children were younger. For the past two years, she hadn't been able to bring herself to go, but for once she was feeling buoyant. The overall mood in the household had been lifted by the impending wedding and escape. And Mohammed was about to complete his final year at high school and sit for his international

Baccalaureate exam. Everyone could see light at the end of the tunnel.

Guzin reserved a suite at the Al Rasheed and a table in the National Restaurant in the lobby. The hotel was a shadow of its former self, but was still as glamorous as it was possible to be in post-war Iraq. Lina brought Ahmed along. It was the first time they had celebrated the festival together. Everyone was excited because they hoped it would be the last time they ever spent Eid el fitr at the Al Rasheed.

The evening went well. They had a slap-up traditional Iraqi meal and listened to the band. Guzin and Mohammed got to know a little more about Ahmed, and the young men instantly bonded. Mohammed had never had a brother, and they found they had a lot in common. Lina was delighted that her younger brother was getting along so well with the man she would soon marry.

Guzin was thrilled too. Watching Lina and Ahmed, who were so obviously in love, gave her a sense of security. Guzin felt that Lina would be safer once she was married to Ahmed. Ostensibly, she would no longer be a single young woman at risk of being raped by the fearsome Mukhabarat, who would go to any lengths to get what they wanted from Guzin. It had been two years since Ra'ad's death, and still they hadn't given up their vile campaign of terror. One of Guzin's greatest fears had been that Lina would be raped. As Ahmed's wife, Lina became his responsibility which, effectively, gave her another level of protection from the endless harassment.

After dinner they went back to the suite. As soon as they walked in, they realised that the Mukhabarat had paid them a visit while they were downstairs in the restaurant. Guzin had left a box of matches in an overnight bag on the bed; the entire contents of the matchbox had been lined up, head to toe, in the middle of the floor. Nothing had been stolen, but there was no doubt the secret police had gone through everything. How else could they have found the box of matches tucked at the bottom of the bag? The display of matches was a message to Guzin that she and her children were forever being watched. It was a cruel form of mental torture. Lina became hysterical and wanted to go home where she felt safer, so they immediately checked out of the Al Rasheed.

As the months moved on, Guzin began to withdraw from her limited social life. She wanted nothing to go wrong with the escape plans. Ali Al Delamy and his two fellow Mukhabarat goons continued their harassment, and whenever he could, Ali assured Guzin that he was making progress. She told him she had the money and that when he was ready, she could get it immediately. Whenever Guzin said she was upset, he'd reply: 'Yes, of course you are', or 'Okay, it won't be long now'. To anybody who might have overheard, Ali's comments would have meant nothing, but to Guzin they were confirmation that he was on their side. Meanwhile, with Lina about to be off her hands, Guzin started to concentrate on Mohammed. He was included in Ali Al Delamy's escape plan, but she wanted to get her son out of Iraq before then, if possible, and she had been assiduously pursuing every available option.

The only way for Mohammed to leave Iraq with the regime's imprimatur was as part of an official international university program. The school year had come to a close and Mohammed had graduated from high school with straight As. Each time Guzin tried to get official approval for Mohammed to go to Jordan, she was rebuffed. The regime was so suspicious that Mohammed would not return to Iraq that they refused to release to him his high school certificate. He needed the certificate so the Jordanian Embassy would accept him as a student. Guzin went directly to the Jordanian Embassy with Mohammed's school reports and copies of his diplomatic passport but, infuriatingly, they claimed to be bound by bureaucracy. She asked them to contact the Iraqi education ministry directly and they did, but were told that the Iraqi ministry did not have a Mohammed Ra'ad Said registered in any of their schools. It was a lie, but Guzin was stuck.

She went back to the education department and found a sympathetic official who, for a fee of US$2300, said he would provide the required high school certificate. It was a bribe. Guzin paid. But even with the required certificate, the government would still not approve Mohammed's exit unless Guzin guaranteed that her son would return to Iraq within six months. Saddam's regime liked guarantees, which, in this case, meant Guzin had to sign over a house she and Ra'ad had built in Baghdad. The guarantee, of course, was another straight-out bribe. This was, after all, Saddam Hussein's Iraq. Guzin had no choice. She paid.

And so Mohammed was ready to leave. It was the second week of July and summer was melting the asphalt streets around the central bus station in downtown Baghdad. Guzin had purchased two bus tickets for Mohammed so he wouldn't have to sit next to anyone on the ten-hour journey to Jordan. She knew he would be upset and wanted to make the trip as comfortable as possible, given the circumstances.

Guzin, Lina and Ahmed accompanied Mohammed to the station for their final farewells. To anyone who happened to see them, they looked like a typical family sending their son on a summer holiday or off to university across the border. But for Mohammed, it was a poignant and heartbreaking moment. It was the last time he would ever be in Baghdad. Though no one said it, they were all gripped by the same terrible knowledge that if things didn't go right with the escape, it could be the last time they saw each other alive.

Mohammed put on a brave face as his mother spoke. Fighting back tears, Guzin addressed Mohammed not as her son, but as a man. 'You are now, instead of your father, the head of the family,' she said, her voice cracking. 'You have to be very strong. Maybe I will not come, maybe I will have to stay in Iraq – I don't know what will happen.'

'If you don't come, I will come back to Iraq and get you,' he replied.

'I want you to be strong. You must call me as soon as you cross into Jordan.'

The emotions were overwhelming and as Mohammed boarded the bus, he began to cry. Even though he tried to hide his face, his mother, Lina and Ahmed all saw the tears as he waved goodbye when the bus pulled out.

The next ten hours were excruciating. Guzin had no way of knowing whether Mohammed was safe. She worried about the secret police. She worried that they had followed her son and arrested him. She worried about crashes on the six-lane highway to Jordan. She sat on the floor in the entrance lobby hovering over the telephone, waiting for Mohammed to ring. At ten o'clock, the phone rang. It was Mohammed.

'Everything's okay,' he told his mother as Bessma, the housekeeper, sat on the floor beside her.

On hearing Mohammed's voice, Guzin broke down and cried oceans of tears. One of her children had made it to safety. She had fulfilled half of her promise to Ra'ad. She only had Lina to go.

◆ ◆ ◆

Ahmed Jamil Al Douri and Lina Ra'ad Said were officially married on 1 September 1998. She was twenty-three, he was twenty-eight. Lina was radiant in a stunning sleeveless full-length gown in traditional bridal white. It had a full skirt and an intricately embroidered lace bodice. A diamond tiara held the veil in place, its two metre-long train trimmed in lace. She wore her hair loose down to her shoulders but swept back from the forehead in a modest Jackie O style. Accenting her décolletage was an exquisite gold necklace, a gift from her new husband's family. She also wore a matching bracelet. Ahmed wore a dark navy suit and a subtly patterned tie, not to mention a smile that never faded all day. From the moment he saw his bride being escorted towards him by her uncle, Ahmed looked for all the world to be the happiest man alive.

The wedding ceremony was held at Lina's home. Only family and the closest friends were invited, which is the traditional Iraqi way. It was an emotional day, particularly because Lina's father, Ra'ad, wasn't there to walk her down the makeshift aisle and hand her to Ahmed, who stood waiting for her with an open pink rose clasped in his hand. Lina had cried tears of sadness for her absent father, and also for her brother in Amman. Guzin didn't feel it was safe enough for Mohammed to return from Jordan, where he was planning to start university. At least there he was out of the clutches of the Mukhabarat.

After the service, the wedding party proceeded to the Al Melia Mansour hotel, where four hundred invited guests celebrated from eight that night until one o'clock the next morning. They dined on an array of traditional Iraqi and international food, and drank imported wine if they so desired. Lina wanted her wedding to be different, and chose Zorba the Greek for her bridal dance. She and Ahmed performed the difficult dance to perfection. 'I felt just like a bird – it didn't feel like I was wearing a long and heavy dress,' Lina says, smiling as the memories of that day wash over her. 'And all of our relatives joined in. It was beautiful. I will always remember that day.' Ahmed, ever the romantic, simply says: 'It was marvellous.' The newlyweds enjoyed a two-week honeymoon at the hotel, living in luxury and getting to know each other as husband and wife. Before long, Lina was pregnant.

With the wedding over and Mohammed safely ensconced in Amman, Guzin rattled around the commodious Princess Street property on her own. The Mukhabarat made the most of the opportunity, harassing her at every chance. The abusive phone calls resumed almost immediately, and the frequency of their visits increased. Once again Guzin felt as if she were under total house arrest. She rarely ventured out and was waiting and praying for any news about the escape.

Finally, in early October, one month after Lina's wedding to Ahmed, Ali Al Delamy paid a solo visit to Guzin. He was driving one of the menacing cars used by the secret police and, as usual, was wearing his side-arm. Ali looked sterner than usual, and he had no time for small talk. Guzin's heart froze. He looked different but, as she soon found out, there was no need for panic.

Once they were in the back garden, Ali told Guzin that the plan was in place and she should be prepared to go at any time within the next few weeks. He couldn't say exactly when. To do so was too risky. The fewer people who knew about the precise timing the better, and the operation would be executed only when all the conditions were perfect. But Ali assured Guzin that everything was set up. All the right people were in place to facilitate a smooth journey from Baghdad to Jordan. He had official exit visas and passports, and safe houses already arranged. And, he said somewhat triumphantly, no one would dare question a member of the Mukhabarat.

Guzin was stunned. Finally, after all this time, it was about to happen.

Ali Al Delamy told Guzin to sort out her affairs and pack up whatever valuables she could without drawing attention to herself. The house should not look as though it was about to be vacated. Guzin told Ali that she would be leaving with her daughter Lina and son-in-law Ahmed, as previously agreed. They had returned from their honeymoon and were living with Guzin. He told her to ensure they were prepared with their own bag, already packed. There would be no time to waste. They would all have to go when he said, ready or not.

Finally, Ali raised the issue of the money. Ten thousand American dollars. 'Make sure you have it ready,' he said.

Without it, the best-laid plan could collapse in a heap and, he warned Guzin, she would only have thirty minutes notice, maybe an hour at the outside, to get it when they were ready to go. For the escape to succeed, everyone had to be prepared to within an inch of their lives.

Ali didn't need to say it, but they would only get one chance.

Chapter Twenty-Two

When the Mukhabarat called on Guzin Najim at night, it was usually by telephone. But at nine-thirty on Friday 30 October 1998, Ali Al Delamy stood on the front step at the Princess Street house. He rapped softly on the door and waited for Guzin to answer. A look of surprise swept across her face as she opened the door. Ali put his forefinger to his lips and shook his head vehemently – a signal to be quiet. Guzin nodded, understanding. She had been waiting anxiously for this moment for the past three weeks, the anticipation eating away at her like acid. Each time she heard a knock at the door or a car pull up outside the house, she leapt to her feet, wondering if it was Ali. This time, it was.

Ali was a furious whirlwind of energy. He pushed past Guzin and went straight into the lounge room to the television. He turned the volume up as loud as it could go, which made Guzin think that the house had indeed been bugged, as she suspected. Ever so quietly, Guzin told Ali that Lina and Ahmed were with her. They had been drinking coffee when he arrived. He nodded his acknowledgement, just once, then did a quick circuit of the downstairs section of the house to make sure the house was in order and there would be no telltale signs that they had escaped.

After the ritualised harassment of the past three years, Ali knew Guzin Najim's house like the back of his hand. He had been there when Guzin was told, just sixteen days after her husband had died in 1995, that she was under house arrest. Almost three years later, he was helping her escape from it. The irony was absurd.

Guzin was a few steps behind Ali, shadowing his every move, waiting for his next instructions. He was wearing a pale grey suit, a white shirt and a tie, and she could see a pistol holstered on his hip, its hard shape protruding through his jacket. He thrust a crushed piece of paper into Guzin's hand and she quickly read it. She thought her heart was going to rip a giant hole in her chest. The note, scrawled in Ali's urgent handwriting, confirmed what she had been waiting for all that October. They were about to embark on the most dangerous journey of their lives.

Ali towered over Guzin, but leaned down so he was almost level with her. He was alert. He had the eyes of a fox and they darted around the room, constantly alert, checking. 'You have thirty minutes. I'll be back at ten o'clock to pick you up. Be ready when I return. Make sure you have all your money,' Ali said in his throaty Arabic. As he walked out the door, he told Guzin to pack clothes, papers, anything of value that she hadn't smuggled out during the past year. Guzin panicked. She wondered if she was doing the right thing. With the TV roaring in the background, she prayed out loud to God that she hoped she wasn't going to get them all killed. But she reminded herself that she had been living a slow death for the past three years and, even worse, so had her children. To maintain the status quo would surely kill them.

'It was either death, or death living in Baghdad. We were alive in Baghdad but nobody knew that inside we were dying,' Guzin says now. 'I chose to escape from Baghdad regardless of what happened because we were not living like human beings. We were dying every hour in other ways. I thought, I have to go. Maybe I will die, maybe I will live, but I have to save the future of my children.'

With Ali gone, Guzin took Fathy into the garden and told him they were about to escape from Baghdad. He had been expecting it and tears welled in his eyes, but there was no time for emotions.

'Go to Luay and Khalida,' Guzin told Fathy, an urgency in her voice that he'd never heard before. 'Ask them for the money. Be careful, Fathy. Make sure you are not being followed.'

Fathy did as he was asked. Guzin had less than thirty minutes before Ali was due back so he took the car. Guzin had spoken to Sari, the third friend to whom she had entrusted her money, during the week and he brought the cash he had been keeping on her behalf when he dropped by for what was, supposedly, a casual visit. All she needed was the remaining six thousand dollars that Luay and Khalida had been minding for her.

Luay lived less than a ten-minute walk away and Khalida was just two doors down on Princess Street but Guzin could never have gone by herself in case the house was being watched by someone other than Ali. Nor could she have walked to Khalida's home. Women do not walk alone in

Baghdad, and to do so at night would be dangerous and, in Guzin's case, extremely suspicious. Guzin went back inside to her bedroom and collected the bag she had packed weeks earlier, as Ali instructed.

The clock was ticking. She had twenty-five minutes. She rushed around the house trying to choose what else she needed. She picked things up and hurriedly put them back, not sure if she should be practical or sentimental. Her mind was on fire with anxiety. Guzin rifled through Ra'ad's most cherished possessions, which she had kept in place as if he were still alive, almost as a shrine to his memory. She picked up a Cross pen set which included two beautiful silver fountain and ballpoint pens, and laid the box on top of her clothes. She grabbed his gold pencil, his favourite gold cufflinks, a pipe and his old square-framed spectacles. In they went. She spotted the elegant black Mont Blanc pen that Ra'ad used for special occasions and remembered how he signed his name with such a flourish. She took it too. She also managed to fit Ra'ad's black overcoat as well as his favourite scarf and gloves in the bag. They were sentimental reminders of the only man she had ever loved and even now, in Sydney, she still brings out his coat to feel him close.

Guzin looked at the clock. Fifteen minutes. She saw Ahmed in the lounge room looking out at the garden. It had become his favourite room in the house, a place where he and Lina spent their quiet moments together. Ahmed was deep in thought. He looked at Guzin and smiled at the inevitability of what lay ahead, and then gestured towards the door where he had put his and Lina's bag. During the week, he had told his parents that he would be going away for a second honeymoon with his wife, but he gave them few details, not wanting to endanger them. His stomach was churning. He was tense, but he held himself together. He had to, for his wife's sake.

Lina was as scared as she had ever been and was crying. Ahmed tried to calm her, but it was no use. She was sure they would be caught while escaping and summarily executed, their bodies dumped off the highway and left to rot in the desert. It was as if she could already see it in her mind. Ahmed wrapped his arm around her and hugged her close. It was all he could do.

Carrying her bag, Guzin went to the bookcase and took down the Arabic–English dictionary which she had bought in 1986 before she and Ra'ad left for his posting to Kabul. She doesn't know why she wanted to take it – it was a huge, two-volume tome covered in red leather and as heavy as two telephone books, but it meant something to her. She couldn't know then how good a choice it would prove.

Guzin looked around the house which was still decorated with magnificent furniture and artwork that she and Ra'ad had collected around the world during their days in the diplomatic corps. The delicate Persian rugs would be left behind, as would imported furniture from China, the paintings by Ra'ad's mother, Fakhira, and the French provincial dressers. It broke her heart, but she had no choice. Besides, now she had much more important things on her mind. And time was running out.

Guzin was agitated. It had been twenty minutes since she sent Fathy to retrieve the money from Luay and Khalida. They lived so close, and it was late. There would be little traffic around Al Mansour. It shouldn't take this long. Where was he? The anticipation was agonising. The two little dogs, Cindy and Susie, were in the lounge room, sensing Guzin's fear and cowering from her frantic pacing.

Dogs have a sixth sense and Guzin suspected they knew she was about to leave them. She cried at the thought, but Bessma and Fathy would remain in the house, at least for the time being. Chico had died the day before and they buried him in the front garden in a rainfall of tears.

Guzin didn't know what to do. She raced outside looking for Fathy and lit a cigarette to calm her nerves. She looked into the darkened garden and walked over to the gardenia she and Ra'ad had planted years earlier. She began to cry as the memories of the good times they had shared at Princess Street came flooding back. But her mind kept flashing to her last image of Ra'ad in the house, the one that tormented her – of him slumped in the antique chair in the entrance lobby the day he was delivered home, his body poisoned. It was awful. That was the day that had delivered them this fate. 'Waste no time,' Ra'ad had told her. 'Take my children and leave my country. Take my children out of Iraq.'

'I said, "I have to leave, I have to leave. I want to die, I am so lonely, but I have to protect my children, I have to protect Lina and Mohammed",' Guzin says now, clutching her chest and sobbing as tears stain her cheeks, the memories overwhelming her.

'I looked into the sky and I said, "I have my promise, Ra'ad. I have to keep my promise".' In the three years since, she had done all she could to do that. Mohammed was safely in Jordan, and by ten o'clock, if all went according to Ali's plan, she would be on the road to join him, together with Lina and Ahmed. *Insh'Allah*, God willing.

Guzin looked at her watch, counting the minutes. Fathy had been gone too long. She was petrified thinking that something had gone wrong. Suddenly she heard the car in the driveway and then Fathy's familiar voice: 'Miss Guzin, here are the envelopes'.

She hugged him with relief. She had minutes to spare. She opened the envelopes and did a quick count, and added the remaining cash. The total came to $10,000. All in green American notes. Minutes later, another car. Guzin's heart skipped a beat. Ali Al Delamy was on time.

He walked in and checked that Guzin was prepared. She handed him the envelopes stuffed with cash. He took Ahmed's passport and together the men put the bags in the trunk of the car, a light blue-grey Toyota Super Saloon. Ahmed was surprised to see boxes of cigarettes and Pepsi Cola. Ali, who had barely uttered a word to Ahmed, said simply, 'For the guards', and Ahmed understood. Bribes. Together with some cash, these little items – true luxuries in Baghdad – would buy them their freedom.

Guzin stood staring at the house, Cindy and Susie at her ankles, not wanting to leave but not wanting to stay either. Ali, seeing her trepidation, walked over to Guzin and put his arm around her shoulder and gently prompted her. 'Yullah,' he said, a tenderness smoothing the hard edge of his uncultured accent. 'We have to go.'

Guzin could not close the front door, it was too final, and she took one last long look at Fathy and Bessma and smiled a goodbye. Guzin had paid them both for the next six months and she told them to stay in the house as if it were their own. Bessma said she would remain in the maid's quarters and bring her mother to live with her. Fathy said he would return to the Sudan. He couldn't bear living in Iraq without Guzin and her children.

Guzin let Ali Al Delamy lead her to the car, where Ahmed and Lina were waiting. Tears spilled from her eyes.

Ahmed took a deep breath before getting in the car. He sat in the front passenger seat while Lina and Guzin sat in the back. Ali, naturally, was in the driver's seat. Systematically, he looked at his passengers, one by one, eye to eye. 'Be calm. Behave as normal,' he said. 'You must not show fear on your face. Everything will be fine. We just have to get through the checkpoints.' It was easier said than done.

Ali steered the blue Toyota slowly down Princess Street and turned onto Al Mansour Street, driving directly past the Mukhabarat's headquarters. He wound his way through the exclusive streets of the district, not for a final sentimental sightseeing tour, but to make sure they weren't being followed. The Mukhabarat was the mother of all of Saddam Hussein's police and intelligence services, and it was known for spying on its own. Ali knew the techniques. At thirty-seven years of age and with nearly two decades in Saddam's intelligence service, he had done it himself thousands of times.

Ali also used the drive as an opportunity for Lina to calm down. The poor girl had been living with a siege mentality for three years now and had been constantly terrorised. The thought of being caught mid-flight had made her physically sick. The last thing he needed was to have her crying hysterically the entire journey, especially at the checkpoints.

Under normal circumstances, the trip from Baghdad to Amman takes ten to twelve hours, but Ali estimated this trip might take up to twenty-four, possibly even more. He factored in checkpoints, time out for bribery, plus necessary stops at safe houses. But anything could go wrong. The escape could be over at any checkpoint, and there would be several of those.

Ali seemed to be in no hurry to exit central Baghdad. He drove southwest, down Al Kindi Street past the Arabian Knight Monument and the historic clock tower, heading towards the Tigris. He told Guzin they needed to look casual, like a group of friends heading for a meal. Their first stop, he told her, should be at one of her favourite restaurants, so she chose the Al Sirawan restaurant in the exclusive al Karradah district, on the eastern banks of the Tigris looking back across the water to the Republican Palace. They crossed the river at the Arbataash Tamuz bridge. They looked like any of the hundreds of their fellow Baghdadis enjoying a Friday night out, not four desperate people escaping from Saddam Hussein's regime.

Ali was alert and agile, looking every which way to ensure they had not been noticed. He barely spoke as they took their seats in the Al Sirawan. Guzin and Lina had already eaten so they ordered Iraqi tea and sweets. Ahmed ordered kebabs but he was so stressed that he couldn't taste them. They left half an hour later. Ali drove to Gréaat, a crowded club and restaurant area. On any other night they might have enjoyed dinner at one of the restaurants which serve masgouf and kebabs on their tessellated terraces stepping down the banks of the Tigris. But this was not any other night. Ali Al Delamy was doing what he had been trained to do, except in the reverse order. He was watching to see if they had been followed. If they had been, the crowded streets of Gréaat were an excellent place to lose the tail.

Guzin was tense and Lina's nerves were shot to pieces. But they went along with Ali – they had to, they had put their faith in him. After he was sure the coast was clear, they got back in the Toyota and drove through the city, criss-crossing the Tigris using different bridges, backtracking over streets they had been through. They passed Saddam Hussein's own monument to ego, the Victory Arch: two swords that crossed 140 metres above the highway held up by giant hands modelled on the dictator's. Part of the arch had been built in Sheffield, England, to commemorate Saddam's 'victory' in the Iran–Iraq war. He commissioned the structure two years before the war was over.

They went northeast through the Iraqi capital and, after about thirty minutes of driving, turned onto the Jordan–Baghdad Road, heading due west. It was about 11.30 pm. Guzin looked at Lina, who was sobbing uncontrollably. She looked out the back window, catching Ali's eye in the rear-view mirror as she turned back to face the front. They smiled at each other with relief. They had not been followed. Everything was going to plan. They had escaped the city limits.

Ali hit the first checkpoint fifteen minutes out of Baghdad. The name of the Jordan–Baghdad Road does it no justice. It is actually a massive six-lane highway with double shoulders, wide enough to accommodate combat tanks as it famously did in April 2003 when American and British tanks rolled into Baghdad to liberate Iraq from Saddam Hussein's iron-fisted grip in Operation Iraqi Freedom. Ali slowed the car as they approached the checkpoint and an armed soldier waved him to a stop. Guzin looked at Ali and he said to remain silent. It felt as if the oxygen had been sucked out of the car and they were in a vacuum. The car was totally silent. They could all hear themselves breathing, including Lina who had, miraculously, calmed down. Ahmed feared they had been betrayed, and that this was the begining of their end.

Ali Al Delamy offered the guard his Mukhabarat identity card, which immediately had the desired effect. 'I thought you were a family,' the guard said by way of apology.

'Business,' Ali scoffed. The business of the Mukhabarat was deadly; the guard could only imagine what the women in the back of the car were going through.

Ali grinned at his passengers as he drove off and they responded to his triumph with nervous smiles. They hadn't even been out of Baghdad for more than fifteen minutes and already they had been stopped. How many more times would it happen? The Jordan–Baghdad Road is 544 kilo-metres long, starting on the western outskirts of the city and running almost in a straight line due west across the desert to Jordan. Five hundred and forty-four kilometres, several checkpoints, armed guards, and Saddam Hussein's secret police. It was going to be a hellish trip. No wonder Lina could barely cope.

As Guzin remembers it now, every second was a torture for them all. 'Every minute in the car I thought about my husband and my life and my son in Jordan. And if we died on this trip, what would happen to my son? I was just thinking, thinking what to do. Sometimes I thought, if they catch us I will say to them, "Leave my daughter and kill me, it's my fault, not her fault. I forced her". I felt very hot and then I told the driver to stop and I vomited blood. I had an ulcer. There were too many hours to go. I didn't care about myself, I just wanted to leave for my daughter's sake, because my son was already in Jordan.

'I thought about how, when my children went back to school, I went to the cupboard to look at my husband's clothes. For three years I left the toothbrush where it was, and his shaving equipment and his colognes. One day I saw my son playing with Cindy, the dog, and I looked at his face and thought, he does not have a father to teach him how to shave. That hurt me so much, especially when he started to shave for the first time. And I was thinking about the most painful thing, how when I saw my friends, I had to pretend everything was good and I was happy,' Guzin says, dissolving into tears. 'Sometimes they'd look at me very strangely, maybe thinking, she doesn't care about her husband, but of course I do.'

Ali had been driving for hours by the time they made their first destination at Ar Ramadi, a lush green oasis-type city on the Euphrates. Ar Ramadi is a departure point for the trade routes across the desert to Damascus and Amman, and is surrounded by farms and factories. They had been stopped at several checkpoints along the way. They were waved through one, but at another, Ali's stash of cigarettes and Pepsi Cola was used to smooth things over. And probably some cash. Guzin is not sure if any money changed hands, but anything was possible. This was Iraq. At a third checkpoint, Ali's Mukhabarat identity card worked yet again to their advantage.

Ali drove to a safe house and took the passports and other documents he had acquired for the purpose of the escape, as well as the $10,000 cash. A man came out and spoke with Ali before they went off into a room. No one asked why. It was better that they didn't know. They changed cars, trading the Toyota Super Saloon for an older sedan. He stocked the car with water and they were back on the road.

Ali told his passengers that he gave the man their passports and the $10,000 and they would be returned to him at Ar Rutba, their next destination. It was a four-hour trip and would put them about 100 kilometres from the Jordanian border. There was no radio in the car and Lina tried to sleep, but she kept waking up at every bump in the road. Guzin was quiet, unable to sleep. She kept thinking of her promise to Ra'ad and praying that they would make it alive.

Guzin tried not to think about what she had left behind, but it was impossible. In her haste, she had forgotten her wedding photographs, the videotape of Lina's engagement and birthday, and 'the small things that make me Guzin'. She thought of seeing Mohammed again, and her father, whose health had declined in recent months. Her mind was working overtime imagining a future without fear and she prayed that the passports would be at Ar Rutba by the time they arrived.

Looking back towards the east from where they'd just come, Guzin saw the first hint of sun blossoming on the horizon. It was a new day. They arrived at Ar Rutba around eight o'clock. Even though the Ba'ath Party had headquarters on the main street, Ar Rutba had largely been ignored by Saddam Hussein since the end of the first Gulf war in 1991, when it was overrun by coalition forces on their way to Baghdad. As such, the scrappy desert town was an eyesore on the highway. Just as Ar Ramadi was a starting point for traders, Ar Rutba had developed a reputation as a base for thieves and smugglers.

Ali drove to one safe house and was met by yet another nameless man who ignored the passengers. Within minutes, Ali was back in the car, driving to another safe house in another part of town. 'Security reasons,' was all he said before assuring them they would be safe. His passengers were beyond terror.

They arrived at a second house and an old lady offered

them breakfast as they were hustled inside. Despite the long night behind them, nobody was hungry and Guzin, Lina and Ahmed kept to themselves, speaking softly to each other. The strangers disturbed Lina and she broke down yet again. Guzin slapped her to try to get her to calm down. 'I don't know what to do with her,' she said to Ahmed. He held his wife of eight weeks. He was just as scared of being caught as Lina but he had to remain calm for her sake. They had come so far, but they still had several hours to go. Ali was deep in negotiations with some men, out of earshot. Guzin saw a little child but she didn't come near them.

Guzin, Lina and Ahmed waited in the house for several hours. Finally, Ali returned and said they were moving to yet another house and they changed cars a second time. By mid afternoon they were back at the house they first stopped at when they arrived hours earlier that morning. Guzin was exhausted and scared. She didn't know if she could trust these people who were so unlike her and yet so obviously a part of the cobweb of corruption that was spiriting them to freedom. Soon, God willing, they would be at the Jordanian border, the final point to freedom. While they waited at a ramshackle old hut in the desert, a man arrived and began to talk with Ali. He confirmed the arrangements and said everything was in place. He handed the passports to Ali, who inspected the 'official' exit visas which Guzin's $10,000 had paid for.

Ali turned to Guzin and told her that he was leaving them. He planned to travel north through the desert and cross the border into Syria. Hopefully, he said, he would eventually make his way to the United States – to Saddam Hussein's regime he would be a traitor, performing the ultimate betrayal. Lina, Ahmed and Guzin were to remain at the house until they were collected by a taxi which would take them across the border. The driver had been paid and was part of the escape plan, Ali said. He gave the passports to the head of the household for safekeeping. Everything would be fine, he assured Guzin. She said she hoped he was right.

Before Ali left, he told Guzin that he had always intended to help her escape from the first moment she mentioned it to him in the garden at the back of the house on Princess Street. 'I respect you and your husband,' Ali said to Guzin. 'I wanted to honour that. I wanted to help you escape.'

Guzin was in tears. She had trusted him to take her this far and she hated to see him go. She was terrified that, without him, the escape would fall apart, but Ali promised her that the next phase of the trip would go exactly as the rest had. He must go, he explained, because it was too dangerous for them to continue as a group. The powerful influence of his Mukhabarat identity card might not work at the approved border patrol point where she and her family were crossing with legal documents, however illegally obtained. Ali was going to slip quietly across the border somewhere in the desert and disappear – another ghost of the regime. She wished him luck, and he was gone.

Guzin, Lina and Ahmed waited a few more hours before they were collected. It had been a long day and twenty-four hours since they left Baghdad when, finally, a taxi arrived driven by a weathered man who looked to be in his mid-fifties but could easily have been at least ten years younger. It was pitch black outside. He collected the passports and passengers, put their bags in the boot of the car, and made a few jokes to try to lighten the mood. He had done this many times before and the anxiety on the faces of his passengers was nothing new.

Turaybil, the official crossing between Jordan and Iraq, is located almost at the midpoint of the 181-kilometre stretch of border shared by the two countries. The six-lane highway feeds into a chicane which leads to the patrol checkpoint, an imposing brick and concrete structure sur-rounded by razor-wire topped fences which were lit by fierce spotlights.

The taxi stopped. They got out of the car. Guzin was sure the Iraqi guards could hear her heart pounding in her chest. This was it. They were, for all practical purposes, on their own. Ali Al Delamy had disappeared into the desert long ago. If they didn't get through here, Guzin, Lina and Ahmed would be arrested. To say they were terrified is an under-statement. The taxi driver was relaxed and joked with one of the Iraqi soldiers, who seemed indifferent as he checked the passports he had been handed.

Guzin put on her best airs and graces. 'Good evening, officer, how are you?' she said, trying to sound casual.

He continued to flip through the pages, searching for the exit visa and the official Iraqi government stamp. He checked the names and photographs against the faces before him.

They waited, barely breathing, but Guzin forced a smile. They couldn't have come this far to get nowhere. Guzin prayed, and held Lina's hand tight to make sure she didn't break down once more. Ahmed did his level best to remain cool. Suddenly, the border guard looked at Guzin. She froze under his unforgiving gaze. He looked at Lina and Ahmed, the newlyweds. Then, without a word, he stamped their passports with the official Republic of Iraq seal.

Guzin felt her stomach turn. She couldn't believe it. Ali was right. They were almost free. They walked past the soldiers armed with automatic weapons, got back in the taxi and drove out of the Republic of Iraq into the no-man's land that led to Jordan.

For Ahmed, that short two-kilometre stretch was the longest part of the journey. It was after two o'clock in the morning, and every second of the five-minute ride felt like an hour. 'I was like someone who was carrying a heavy rock and he just throws it away,' Ahmed says now of the moment they passed from no-man's land through the Jordanian checkpoint.

The taxi driver stopped and Guzin got out of the car. She was free. Her daughter was free. Within three hours, they would be with Mohammed. She fell to the ground of the Hashemite Kingdom and kissed it, crying with joy and relief.

'Ra'ad, Ra'ad. We are free. Your children are free. I have kept the promise.'

Chapter Twenty-Three

November is a beautiful time to arrive in Amman and for Guzin, the month turned into a festival of emotional homecomings. The first was with her son, Mohammed, whom she hadn't seen since his bus pulled out from the central bus station in Baghdad three months earlier. Before her papers had even been processed at the Jordanian border patrol, she asked a guard for a telephone. She wanted to hear Mohammed's voice and tell him they had survived the tortuous journey through the Iraqi desert, and that very soon they would be a family once more.

Slowly, nervously, she dialled the number for her sister's house in the upmarket district of Al Rabyah, just a little north of central Amman. Mohammed had been living with his aunt and uncle, Buthaina and Mohammed, as well as his two cousins, Ramez and Omar, ever since he arrived in Jordan in July. It was around 2.30 am and Guzin knew her son would be awake, waiting for her telephone call. She had spoken to Mohammed just minutes before she began her escape from Baghdad with Ali Al Delamy. Then, using the special code that they developed in the months while Mohammed was away, Guzin told him that 'maybe, one day I will come'. It was the signal. He knew they were about to escape.

That was nearly thirty hours earlier and Mohammed had been to hell and back fretting about his mother and sister. He knew he would only hear when they arrived safely in Jordan. If, God forbid, something went wrong, he might never hear from them again. He remembered how frightened he was at the Iraqi border when he crossed three months earlier. It had taken him one and a half gut-wrenching hours to have his passport stamped. When the phone rang, he rushed at it, almost tackling it to the ground.

'Mohammed?' Guzin said, her body trembling.

'Mama,' he replied.

They both burst into tears.

'Mohammed, we are safe. We will be safe. We are waiting for you,' Guzin said.

Mohammed told his mother that he would leave Amman immediately and be at the border as fast as he could get there. It is 350 kilometres from the Jordanian capital to its eastern border but at that time of night the trip would be plain sailing. Mohammed took the Motorway 15 north until it connected with Highway 10 just past Mafraq. Then it was due east to the border on the same stretch of road through the eastern desert of Jordan. He drove through the night and headed directly into the sun as it rose on the horizon, arriving at the border just after six.

As soon as he saw his sister and mother, he wrapped his arms around their shoulders and hugged them together, a family once more. They could barely speak. Looking to

Ahmed, Mohammed reached out and shook his hand, welcoming his new brother-in-law to the family. He had sorely missed being at his sister's wedding and as the head of the family, it had left a deep scar.

Buthaina and her husband Mohammed Al Tell had prepared a celebratory lunch to welcome Guzin and Lina to Jordan, and also to meet Ahmed. When Guzin arrived, she was overcome with joy. Her father Shawket was standing in the front door waiting for her. With his erect military posture, he stood like a sentinel as Guzin climbed out of the car and ran over to him. Shawket had never been as proud of his eldest daughter as he was at that moment. She had survived the murder of her husband, and she had honoured her promise to him to escape from Iraq. There was nothing more important, he said, than what she had done – she had given their children a better future. And, she had done it on her own in the most trying of circumstances.

'You are the one who raised me to be strong,' Guzin told her father. 'You are the one who helped me escape.'

The reunion went on for hours until the travellers almost collapsed from exhaustion. Buthaina and her husband generously turned the master bedroom over to the newlyweds, Lina and Ahmed, and took the spare bedroom for themselves. Guzin and Mohammed moved into the self-contained flat above the house, where Guzin slept for twelve hours straight before getting out of bed and joining the family for yet another celebratory meal which went on well into the early hours of the next morning.

Over the following month, Guzin and her children were feted at a series of homecoming parties thrown by a string of relatives on her late mother's side, from Irbid in the north to Amman. Guzin had dozens of cousins and uncles, nieces and nephews, and it seemed that each and every single one wanted to throw a party to celebrate their escape from Baghdad and hear about the brave journey. She happily returned several times to Irbid. It was a place dear to her heart and each time she went she reminisced about yet another of her happy childhood memories.

Except for her father's failing health, Guzin couldn't have been happier. Mohammed was a typical teenager and, with his family reunited, he began to relax and enjoy life a bit more. He had been accepted to study pharmacology at Al-Isra University and would begin his studies the following February, 1999. He bought himself a car and had already made several friends. Ahmed found work as a graphic designer with a Canadian company, and Lina soon announced she was pregnant, with a baby due the following August. At forty-three, Guzin would be a grandmother. Lina's announcement explained why she had been so emotional during the escape – hormones and fear. To top off their happiness, Guzin and her children were granted permanent residency in Jordan, the native country of her late mother, Majida Al Tell.

Had Ra'ad been there it would have been perfect, for it was everything that he wanted for his wife and children. Safety, and the promise of a good future.

◆ ◆ ◆

It is impossible to know who the Mukhabarat discovered missing first: Guzin and her daughter or Ali Al Delamy. And it is difficult to know who they missed more – their fully trained henchman or their terrorised and prized victims. But whomever it was, they were not about to let

Guzin go. The Mukhabarat were persistent like that. They were always hunting for signs of anti-Saddam sentiment and tracking down and assassinating dissenters and deserters, particularly those who sought sanctuary in Arabic countries close by.

Ever since its formation, the Mukhabarat had exercised its torturous practices with impunity, not only within Iraq but beyond its borders. It has assassinated its victims in London, Jordan, Dubai, Italy, Pakistan and Thailand, just to name a few. It was the Mukhabarat that, at Saddam Hussein's behest, launched a failed assassination attempt on the first President Bush while he was on a business trip in neighbouring Kuwait in 1993. Five years earlier, the British government expelled a number of Iraqi diplomats, claiming their primary function was to spy on and intimidate exiled opponents of Saddam Hussein in London – people like Guzin's old university lecturer and former Iraqi Ambassador to Britain, Dr Hisham Al-Shawi, who defected and joined an Iraqi opposition group. 'Assassinations are only the most visible part of the foreign operations of the Iraqi secret police. Harassment is also common,' international non-government group Human Rights Watch wrote in a 1990 report called *Institutions of Repression*. 'Iraqi dissidents who have managed to flee have found themselves hounded from one country to the next.'

Guzin was 900 kilometres away from Baghdad, but before long she realised it wasn't far enough away from harm. The first phone calls came within weeks of Guzin arriving at Buthaina's house. Initially they were straight-forward, if overly officious, and came from the Iraqi Embassy in central Amman. Guzin was surprised that she had been found, but part of the Mukhabarat's widespread duties included monitoring embassies at home and abroad. An official demanded that Guzin hand in her passport to the embassy, as well as those of her children. She refused. They rang for four consecutive days and the tone became more threatening with each call.

'Whatever you do, you will not see me again,' Guzin snapped at one official who told her to present herself at the Iraqi Embassy at ten o'clock the following morning.

The calls kept coming and Guzin gave them the same response. Her residency, which had been granted by the minister of the interior, Mr Nayif Saud al-Qady, meant she could live safely in Jordan and had the same protection as any Jordanian citizen. She would not go anywhere near the Iraqi Embassy. Guzin didn't know what would happen if she did, but she assumed that once within the embassy, which was immune from Jordanian laws and prosecution, she could be detained. She would not take that risk.

With her continued defiance, the Mukhabarat upped the ante. One day while she was out walking around the neighbourhood, a man sidled up to her. 'It will be better for you to go back to Iraq,' he said.

Guzin was shocked. She had never seen the man before and never expected to be tracked down and subjected to further harassment. The Mukhabarat had found her, the menace was back, but she was not about to be beaten. 'If you are a man, do what you can but you will not get me again,' she said defiantly. But the reign of fear was about to explode into violence.

Weeks later, Guzin was attacked by a man while returning from doing the weekly shopping at the local Safeway supermarket. She was hit across the face and pushed to the ground just a few metres from the front of Buthaina's home.

'We are going to kill your son if you don't give us the papers,' the man hissed.

The attack, so close to home in the middle of the afternoon, was brazen. Guzin was hysterical. How could this have happened? She was supposed to be safe in Jordan. Her family called the police, who immediately went to the university to ensure Mohammed was safe. A policeman was stationed at the house and Guzin and her children were placed under guard for two weeks, during which time the harassment and intimidation ceased. Clearly, the Mukhabarat had the family under surveillance – a horrifying thought. Everyone in the household was at risk.

Soon after the police guard was lifted, they struck again. This time, Mohammed was attacked while leaving the same supermarket where his mother had been the day she was attacked. He was walking to his car when two men strode up behind him in the carpark. They pulled him around, forcing him to drop the grocery bags. They roughed him up, ripped his shirt open in the skirmish and threw him to the ground, towering over him. Mohammed, who was then eighteen and of average height and slight build, feared for his life. The men were aged in their mid-thirties, stocky and dark-skinned. Their luxuriant black moustaches were a dead giveaway as to their identity.

'They came to me and said, "Go back to Iraq, you have to go back soon". And they grabbed me by the arm and they pulled my clothes and I said, "Okay, okay". And they left me,' Mohammed recalls. 'But after a few weeks, they came to the university and they sat beside me on the bus and told me, "Don't look at us, just look straight ahead". One sat in front of me and one beside me. "You have to go back to Iraq". They were speaking in low voices so no one else could hear. I wanted to get off at the next bus stop but they got off the bus instead. They had to be coming a lot to know my lecture timetables. They had to have been watching me. Another time, I finished at the lab at three o'clock in the afternoon and was about to go home. One of the men came on the bus after I boarded and sat with me. So he knows what time I am there.'

The bus driver reported the first incident to the university's security department, who, in turn, called the Jordanian police. Mohammed resumes the story. He has just pulled the curtains closed in his mother's apartment in Sydney. 'My teacher called me and took me from the lecture and he told me that they knew that the Mukhabarat came to the university and told me to go back to Iraq. The police came to the university. Three cars. The dean of the university said, "Don't worry, you are safe. They will come and take you home, you are safe".'

But they weren't safe at all. The intimidation and harassment continued. Guzin was the victim of a blackmail attempt by an Iraqi informer who discovered where she was living. He had been spying on the house. Her nephew Ramez was walking along the footpath outside his home when the man asked him if he knew someone from Iraq who lived there. Ramez was only a teenager and thought it was an innocent inquiry from a fellow Iraqi and said yes, he did, his aunt Guzin. Soon after, the man knocked on the door and confronted Guzin, demanding money for his silence on her whereabouts. He said he knew exactly who she was and knew things about her and Ra'ad. Guzin demanded to see his identity, accusing him of being with the Mukhabarat, but the man refused to show it to her. He became angry and began to abuse her, and she slammed the door in his face.

Jordan was not the sanctuary she had hoped it would be. Guzin never felt safe. Neither did Lina or Mohammed, especially after Lina gave birth to a son, whom she and Ahmed named Abdullah. With a newborn in the family, they had even more reason to be worried. Mohammed became so afraid for their safety that he eventually quit university. 'Whenever we went outside the house, we felt like somebody was chasing us,' Guzin remembers. 'I lost my nerve. I was free, but not free from the memory and the pain. They reached us in Jordan. I didn't feel safe.'

◆ ◆ ◆

Ellen Dorfling is a straight-shooter. She joined the Australian Department of Immigration when she was just seventeen and straight out of a Sydney high school. Now forty-one and the second secretary at the Australian Embassy in Lebanon, she has spent the past few years interviewing thousands of refugees who seek safe haven in Australia. It's a tough job – emotional, achingly sad, and yet sometimes, even through the misery, inspirational and uplifting.

In the middle of 2001, a ten-page file landed on her desk with the official seal of the United Nations High Commissioner for Refugees (UNHCR). It recommended that the applicants named within should be considered for resettlement in Australia. The file was stamped in accordance with the criteria set out in the UN's Convention on Refugees. Ellen read the documents and came to the conclusion that the applicants – Guzin Shawket Najim, Lina Ra'ad Said, Mohammed Ra'ad Said and Ahmed Jamil Al Douri – did indeed qualify for resettlement in Australia as mandated by the UNHCR because they had suffered extreme persecution in their native country of Iraq. The story was laid out in all its grisly detail.

Guzin did not feel safe after the monsters of the Mukhabarat followed her to Jordan and continued their campaign of terror against her. She feared they would kill her for the piece of paper that didn't exist.

Guzin was lost. She was under attack and felt humiliated. She couldn't protect her children, a mother's most important task. She had to get out of Jordan but wanted to stay within the greater Arab community. She was rejected by Egypt, Lebanon, Saudi Arabia and the United Arab Emirates, who refused her even the opportunity of a meeting. The rejections stung, particularly since she was an Arab Muslim and they were Arabic Muslim countries. Her own people had refused to help her family. Instead, she was told that her best chance at finding a safe haven anywhere in the world lay with the United Nations.

She was given an appointment at the United Nations' headquarters in Amman on Thursday 5 April 2001. She went in forlorn, thinking it was her last chance, but they said they would accept her case for investigation. If they thought Guzin's case was valid, her family would be called in for interviews, and in the meantime, the United Nations would conduct its own preliminary investigations.

Three months later, at the height of a steamy summer, Guzin and her family were interviewed in Amman. At exactly the same time in three separate rooms, Guzin, Lina and Mohammed were questioned by three UNHCR caseworkers whose names they were never told for security reasons. For two hours, each was grilled about the events in the six years since Ra'ad Said's agonising death.

The interview tactics were standard operating procedure for authorities and organisations who seek the truth, or the closest version of it. Police interview suspects at the same time to see if the stories stand up. Ditto multiple victims. That way, the interviewees can't tailor their answers to suit their own purposes. The story has to remain credible and consistent. It is known as a scale of credibility, and at the end of the interviews, Guzin's story was considered entirely credible. There was no question that she had been through hell, as had Lina and Mohammed. The United Nations staff then investigated Guzin's documentation and bona fides. She was lucky because she had the paperwork with her, having spent two years smuggling it out of Iraq under the noses of the Mukhabarat.

Finally, on 25 September 2001, the UNHCR mandated Guzin and her children on the grounds that they had suffered extreme persecution at the hands of their own government. The United Nations took their passports and, in exchange, gave them official UN identification cards. Status: refugees. Guzin was given the option of resettlement in the three countries which take the greatest number of refugees who qualify in accordance with the program: the United States, Canada and Australia.

America, Guzin reasoned, was too dangerous. It was just after the terrorist attacks on September 11 when nineteen terrorists hijacked four American aircraft and flew them into the twin towers of the World Trade Centre in New York City, the Pentagon in Washington DC and an empty field in Pennsylvania, murdering more than 3000 innocent civilians in a two-hour reign of terror.

Canada was too cold.

And Australia, well, she said with a huge smile,

Australia was just perfect. Ra'ad had always dreamed about visiting Australia, having fallen in love with a picture of Sydney's magnificent harbour and the soaring sails of the Opera House. Timidly, almost girlishly, Guzin told the United Nations' resettlement officer that if she could, her family would take Australia. That is, of course, if Australia would take them. Guzin was told she would have to wait and see, and her case would be processed through the appropriate channels.

Each year under its Humanitarian Program, Australia accepts 12,000 people who have suffered unimaginable horrors in crisis spots around the world. Those in most need – that is, those who have suffered the worst persecution, torture or trauma – are given priority. But before they are granted refugee status, they have to be found to be of good character, robust health and have no criminal record. It was Ellen Dorfling's job, then, to determine whether Guzin, her children Mohammed and Lina, Lina's husband Ahmed and their son Abdullah should be accepted by the Australian government on behalf of the Australian people as part of its Humanitarian Program. Which is how she came to interview Guzin and her family in the UN's Amman office in February 2002. Two-year-old Abdullah played in the background.

Ellen had to confirm the story and evaluate its credibility. The interview lasted an hour and Guzin broke down several times, recalling how they lived with the constant fear of death, harassment and intimidation. Ellen Dorfling had scrutinised the UNHCR report and, with the added weight of her own investigations and the interview with Guzin and her family, had no doubt that they were at risk. 'It rang true, it easily rang true and the family were interviewed and you could see how much they had been through,' Ellen said from Beirut, where she has been posted since April 2001. 'It was a harrowing journey to get out. I thought, this family has been through so much. It was absolutely horrific. It really, really touched me.'

Ellen told Guzin that she had little doubt she would be accepted by the Australian government, but the case had to be processed and they still needed to pass the character and medical tests before they could be granted residency in Australia. It was the closest thing she had ever had to a guarantee, and Guzin was delighted, though she knew she still had to wait. But Guzin and her family's situation was considered to be one of high risk, so the case was processed quickly. Six months later, at the end of August, she received the news that she had passed all the requirements and, if she so chose, she and her family could resettle in Australia with the full backing of the United Nations and the Australian government. She would be granted a visa, the United Nations and Australian Government's special Humanitarian Program would pay for her family's relocation, and in Australia she would have the same rights as any permanent resident, except the privilege of voting. That right belonged to Australian citizens, and in a democracy like Australia it was taken very seriously.

Guzin was ecstatic. She couldn't believe that after so much grief and torture, it was about to be all over. Yes please. Guzin spent the last three months in Irbid on her family's property where her father Shawket had built a house during his years in exile after the royal family was ousted in a bloody coup in 1958. It was an emotional time for the family. Guzin packed up the house, sold her belongings and said her farewells. She spent hours at the cemetery visiting the graves of her parents, Majida and Shawket. Tragically, her father had died from a heart attack on Guzin's birthday in 1999, seven months after she arrived in Jordan. He was seventy-five.

Finally, on 7 September 2002, Guzin took a bus to Amman and collected the three visas from the United Nations office. There was one each for herself and Mohammed, and one for Lina and Ahmed and their son, Abdullah. Guzin couldn't stop smiling as she looked at the sequence of twelve numbers and letters which were, in effect, at least to her, code for 'home'.

In ten days Guzin Najim would be in Sydney, Australia.

Chapter Twenty-four

The Malaysian Airlines 747 began its descent over Sydney around 6 am on 17 September 2002, coming in from the north. It had been eight hours since the plane took off from Kuala Lumpur, with Guzin and her family taking up an entire row in the economy cabin. They had left Amman eighteen hours before that, on a Jordanian Airlines airbus. After a refuelling stopover in Calcutta and a change of aircraft in Malaysia, they were thrilled that their thirty-hour journey was almost at an end.

As the plane flew over the Wollemi National Park to the north of Sydney, Guzin looked out the window and marvelled at the sea of green beneath her, thinking how different it was to the dust bowl surrounds of Sana'a in Yemen. The pilot announced they would be landing at Sydney's Kingsford Smith International Airport in ten minutes and those sitting on the left-hand side of the aircraft would have spectacular views of Sydney Harbour and the Opera House. Guzin looked at her son and daughter and grinned. More than anything, she was dying to see the harbour that Ra'ad had fallen in love with, and the building that enchanted him. When they came into view, Guzin let out a small squeal of delight. The plane banked left, taking in sweeping views of Botany Bay, and touched down at Mascot. Guzin had done it. After a brutal seven years, Lina and Mohammed were safe. She made a promise to her husband, and she had kept it.

Upon disembarkation, Guzin saw a woman approaching her. 'She said in Arabic, "I am Iraqi and I have come to translate for you". When I heard her say "Iraqi", I got upset. I said, "I don't want you to come – go away from me, I can speak English",' Guzin says now. After all she had been through, Guzin was deeply suspicious of her fellow Iraqis and found it near to impossible to trust them, regardless of how far she was from Iraq. The Mukhabarat had gotten to her in Jordan, she thought to herself, why not here?

The woman then spoke to Guzin in English and she immediately relaxed. They went through customs. As a refugee, she did not have a passport, only a single A4 sheet of paper entitled 'Document for Travel to Australia'. The immigration official looked at the paper and the visa attached to the bottom left-hand corner. It was good for single travel to Australia only. Guzin's marital status was marked 'widowed'. He noted that the visa had been granted on 28 August 2002 on the proviso that its holder enter Australia by 22 September and had not married before first entry. With a cheeky grin, he congratulated Guzin on getting in five days before the deadline and then, tongue stuck firmly in his cheek, asked her if she had happened to marry in the days since the visa had been granted. She laughed and said, 'No.'

Already, Guzin liked Australia. 'We went through everything and Salida from the Migrant Resource Centre came to me and she said, "Welcome to Australia",' Guzin says, smiling broadly.

Salida helped Guzin, her children, her son-in-law and her grandson, and together with their 178 kilograms of luggage they were taken to a house in an inner Sydney suburb which had been fully stocked with enough food to last them two weeks. They were given a stipend and told they could stay at the house for six months, but after two weeks they found their own accommodation.

'Australia accepted us and helped us. They helped us without receiving anything from us – I didn't pay anybody to treat me so good and because of this, we respect Australia and Australians and their beliefs, because they respect our beliefs. This is Australia, it doesn't matter the religion or the region you are from. If you are a Jew, Christian or Arab, that's not anyone's business. This is between you and your God,' Guzin says.

Three days later, Guzin boarded a train with Lina and Mohammed and went to Circular Quay. They could have been any other tourists, but Guzin was on a personal pilgrimage for her husband. She needed to see the Sydney Opera House, the building that Ra'ad had fallen in love with. For Guzin, it was a symbol of her enduring love for her husband, the reason she came to Australia.

She emerged from the station to the tooting traffic of the ferries and walked towards the Opera House. It was a brilliant spring day, typical of Sydney. Guzin climbed the front steps of the Opera House, imagining that Ra'ad was with her. 'I feel sometimes that I am holding his hand. He is very warm. And I speak to him sometimes,' she says.

She walked down the left side of the Opera House, taking in the view. To the west were the steel arches of the Harbour Bridge, and just beyond it on the other side of the harbour, the toothy-faced entrance to Luna Park. It made Guzin laugh because it was so different to what she was used to in Baghdad – statues and portraits of Saddam Hussein at every turn. The harbour was picture-book blue, although much smaller than Guzin expected. Flying overhead at 5000 feet, it had looked so vast. At the water's edge, she felt as if she could reach out and almost touch Kirribilli House.

Guzin found a quiet spot and looked up at the white-tiled peaks of the Opera House. She thought of Ra'ad, and her eyes filled with tears.

'I said to him, "I hope you will see me. We are here. Your children are safe and I will be faithful to you. And for your children, I did my best. We will always love you".'

Epilogue

Guzin Najim is sitting in the lounge room of her Sydney flat with the television muted in the background, tuned to the BBC as it so often is. Guzin frequently leaves the television on all day, a habit she developed when the American-led coalition forces rolled into her country at the start of Operation Iraqi Freedom on 20 March 2003. She was glued to the television right until 9 April, when the giant bronze statue of Saddam Hussein in Firdos Square in central Baghdad was destroyed as his regime disintegrated around him.

Guzin does not know what happened to her house on Princess Street in Al Mansour, but the area was bombed during the war. Saddam's general intelligence department – a strategic target – was located just around the corner from her home. Guzin and her family lived through the first Gulf war with bombs going off all around them. She watched the second Gulf war on television from her new home in Australia, praying that Saddam Hussein's regime would be torn apart once and for all, and offering prayers of thanks for the brave men and women of the Australian defence forces who, with their brothers and sisters in arms from the United States, Britain and Poland, went to war to liberate her country.

Guzin still marvels at how much her family's life has changed. Lina is a full-time mother, and Mohammed has his sights set on a medical degree from the University of Sydney. They both want to know what happened to their father but, like the families of the hundreds of thousands of other victims of Saddam's regime, they may never know. Saddam's vicious henchmen did not keep full and accurate records of their crimes.

Lina's husband, Ahmed, is pursuing his career as a graphic designer and speaks to his family in Baghdad as often as possible. They are happy he is in Australia and has made a new life for his son and wife. Abdullah is growing up and by the time he is old enough to start school in 2005, the Jordanian-born son of Iraqi immigrants will be a typical Aussie kid. He has already started to develop an Australian accent.

Guzin's sister, Buthaina, and her family remain in Jordan.

Ali Al Delamy has not been heard of since he helped Guzin and her family flee Baghdad at great personal risk. She hopes he escaped to Syria or the United States, but has no way of knowing. Maybe now that Saddam Hussein's regime is in ruins, Ali will come out of hiding – assuming, of course, that he survived and was not caught by the Mukhabarat.

Bessma, the housekeeper, stayed at the Princess Street home for six months. She was there when the secret police came looking for Guzin shortly after she escaped, but Bessma could tell them nothing. The secret police interrogated

Guzin's neighbours and they too could shed no light on where she had gone. It was a mystery to them. Eventually the secret police told the neighbours that Guzin and her children were on holidays in Mosul, in the north of Iraq. They lied, even in such small defeats, eager to maintain their psychological torment of the Iraqi people.

Fathy, Guzin's family driver, returned to his native Sudan, as he told Guzin he would.

Furat, Lina's best friend who stood by her side during the traumatic days of Ra'ad's death, also fled from Baghdad and lives in Canada with her family.

Guzin's two little dogs, Cindy and Susie, were given to her neighbours by Bessma. The last Guzin heard, they were still alive.

The dreaded Mukhabarat headquarters were destroyed during the second Gulf War in 2003. According to reports in *The Observer* newspaper in London, documents found at another bombed Mukhabarat surveillance centre, located in an unmarked private residence on the Tigris, revealed orders to plant electronic listening devices at homes, hotel rooms and embassies.

Now that Saddam is gone, and with him the vicious Mukhabarat who made her life a living hell, Guzin plans to visit Iraq and see what has become of her country. But she could never contemplate returning for good. These days, she calls Australia home.

'I lost my peace of mind, and my children lost their sense of security in Iraq. My husband was killed. But this rock which is here,' she says, resting her hand in the middle of her chest above her heart, 'I feel it is now lifting. I came to Australia because I want to point my children's feet in the right direction, in this free country, for their future.'

In September 2004, exactly two years after she first arrived in Australia, Guzin Najim applied for citizenship. Ever since arriving in Sydney, she has wanted to be able to call herself an Australian.

It is another promise. This one, for herself. As ever, Guzin will keep it.

A Note from Guzin Najim

For years I have watched in horror as Iraqi people embraced Saddam Hussein and carried his photographs high, chanting their loyalty to him. And as I watched, I waited, hoping instead to see photographs of Iraqi children who were massacred by him, or the Iraqi spiritual leaders, scientists and scholars who were indiscriminately humiliated and butchered by him. Saddam Hussein mercilessly pillaged homes and cities and reduced them to dust. He plundered Iraq's oil for his own empire. When the brave Australian soldiers joined with those of the United States, Britain, and Poland to fight to free my country from Saddam Hussein, I offered a prayer of thanks. I prayed they would succeed and return to their homes safely in the knowledge that they saved us from a tyrant. I would like to offer them my most heartfelt thanks.

My hope now is for people to live peacefully together in

love. Without love we can do nothing. And we must stop the killing.

There are several other people I would like to thank.

My late mother Majida Al Tell was a summit of love and compassion, with an honest-to-goodness ability to nurture and nourish her children and grandchildren. She is deeply missed. My late father Shawket Najim, the man who planted in my soul the seeds of trust, self-esteem and courage. He liberated me from a woman's conventional concepts and ideas, and taught me to believe in myself – for which I thank him.

I can never forget the deep bond and immense love I shared with my wonderful husband, Ra'ad Said, and will miss him every day of my life. His wish brought us to Australia – and for that, I can never thank him enough.

My children, Lina and Mohammed, suffered oppression and torture at the hands of Saddam Hussein's government. They have suffered, but they have persevered. I hope my children's experiences will teach them to be prudent and wise, to rely on God and depend on themselves to build a worthy future. They have always shown strength and good judgement, and I hope that somewhere in their sad hearts, they will find compassion and a willingness to forgive. I am confident that a bright and prosperous future is ahead of them both in Australia.

Many thanks to Sandra Lee, who wrote this book and cried with me as I relived the pain. She supported me and gave me the strength to recall those terrible years. I felt as if there were knives in my heart, killing me day by day, but now I feel that you removed them all. You made me feel that I have done something for my husband's memory and for my children's futures.

Thanks also to Selwa Anthony, who helped make my dream come true, Bronwyn Reid, who helped and supported me, and Atef Hamie, who tried so very hard to make me happy and helped me accept and love my new life in Australia.

A Note from the Author

I would like to thank Guzin Najim for trusting me with her extraordinary story. Having spent hundreds of hours with her, I know what hell she and her children went through. Guzin's bravery in reliving the traumatic past is surpassed only by her bravery in taking the enormous, and potentially fatal, risk to escape from Iraq and fulfill the promise she made to her dying husband, Ra'ad.

As well, I owe a debt of gratitude to Lina Ra'ad Said and Mohammed Ra'ad Said, who, through their pain, shared their memories of their father with me and recounted the terror of life under house arrest. Their courage and spirit is inspirational. Thanks also to Lina's husband Ahmed Al Douri, a true gentleman, who shared his thoughts and knowledge of Iraqi society and culture.

I am deeply indebted, as always, to my wonderful agent Selwa Anthony for her encouragement and for making it all come together, as well as for providing the title. A huge thank you to first reader, über-editor and my very dear friend, Linda Smith, whose suggestions and humour never missed the mark.

Thanks to the dream team assembled once more by Random House: my publisher Elana McCauley and my two incredibly supportive – not to mention cool, calm and creative – editors, Jo Jarrah and Zoe Walton. Kylie Field, what can I say? You make it easy and fun. Thanks.

Gratitude also to Ellen Dorfling, Jackie Frank, Helen Jackson, Anita Jacoby, Pete Pedersen, Bronwyn Reid, the United Nations High Commissioner for Refugees and the Australian Department of Foreign Affairs and Trade.

In researching and writing about the historical and political background of Iraq and the Middle East, I drew on the resources listed in the bibliography. Any errors in these areas or any others are inadvertent, but they are mine.

Of course, a blooming bouquet to each of the usual suspects, the friends and family who know how to keep me sane: Tim Blair, David Burgess, Lynne Cossar, Ron Cutler, Miranda Devine, Debbie Hammon, Sharon Krum, my map man J.P., Anna Raine, Nadia Santomaggio, and 'my' boys – Max and Darcy Burgess, and Tom and Frankie Cutler. They continue to make me happy. Finally, thanks of course to my late mother, Valda May Lee, who gave me so much, and my father, Dixie Lee, who never stops believing in me.

Select Bibliography

Books

Saïd K. Aburish, *Saddam Hussein: The politics of revenge*, Bloomsbury Publishing, 2000

BBC News, *The Battle for Iraq*, BBC Worldwide Limited, 2003

Paul Berman, *Terror and Liberalism*, W.W. Norton & Company, 2003

Joseph Braude, *The New Iraq: Rebuilding the country for its people, the Middle East and the world*, Basic Books, 2003

Geraldine Brooks, *Nine Parts of Desire: The hidden world of Islamic women*, Anchor Books, 1995

Andrew Cockburn and Patrick Cockburn, *Out of the Ashes: The resurrection of Saddam Hussein*, Harper-Perennial, 2000

Con Coughlin, *Saddam: The secret life*, MacMillan, 2002

Dilip Hiro, *Iraq: A report from the inside*, Granta Books, 2003

Efraim Karsh and Inari Rautsi, *Saddam Hussein: A political biography*, Grove Press, 1991 (revised edition 2002)

Norma Khouri, *Forbidden Love: A harrowing true story of love and revenge in Jordan*, Bantam Books, 2003

Bernard Lewis, *The Crisis of Islam: Holy war and unholy terror*, The Modern Library, 2003

Bernard Lewis, *What Went Wrong? The clash between Islam and modernity in the Middle East*, Perennial, 2002

Sandra Mackey, *The Reckoning: Iraq and the legacy of Saddam Hussein*, W.W. Norton & Company, 2002

Kanan Makiya, *Republic of Fear: The politics of Modern Iraq*, University of California Press, 1988 (1998 paperback edition)

Paul McGeough, *Manhattan to Baghdad: Despatches from the frontline in the War on Terror*, Allen & Unwin, 2003

Paul McGeough, *In Baghdad: A reporter's war*, Allen & Unwin, 2003

Turi Munthe, *The Saddam Hussein Reader*, Thunder's Mouth Press, 2002

Peggy Noonan, *A Heart, a Cross, and a Flag: America today,* Wall Street Journal Books, 2003

Kenneth M. Pollack, *The Threatening Storm: The case for invading Iraq*, Random House, 2002

Anthony Swofford, *Jarhead: A Marine's chronicle of the Gulf War and other battles*, Scribner, 2003

Select newspaper and magazine articles and websites
Jon Lee Anderson, 'Saddam's Ear', *The New Yorker*, 5 May 2003

Neela Banerjee, 'Rape (and Silence About It) Haunts Baghdad', *The New York Times*, 16 July 2003

Edward Barnes, 'Sanctuary Under Siege', *Time Magazine*, 29 March 1993

Brian Bennett, Michael Weisskopf, Amany Radwan and Adam Zagorin, 'The Sum of Two Evils', *Time Magazine*, 2 June 2003

Daniel Bergner, 'Where the Enemy is Everywhere and Nowhere', *The New York Times*, 20 July 2003

Mark Bowden, 'Tales of the Tyrant', *The Atlantic Monthly*, May 2002, vol 285 no 5:35

Jason Burke, 'Roll Credits', *The Guardian*, 17 April 2003

Faith J. Childress, 'Lessons for Future in Iraq's Tragic History', *National Catholic Reporter*, 2 May 2003

Dexter Filkins, 'Iraqis Confront Grim Memories', *The New York Times*, 21 April 2003

Dean Fischer, 'Iraq: Inside Saddam's brutal regime – a defector breaks his silence', *Time Magazine*, 18 September 1995

Otto Friedrich, Dan Goodgame and William Mader, 'Master of his University: Iraq's dictator seems capable of doing anything to get his way', *Time Magazine*, 13 August 1990

G. Dwayne Fuselier, 'Placing the Stockholm Syndrome in Perspective', *The FBI Law Enforcement Bulletin*, http://www.fbi.gov/publications/leb/1999/jul99.pdf

Jeffrey Goldberg, 'The Unknown', *The New Yorker*, 10 February 2003

Patrick Graham, 'Arms secrets revealed in spies' files', *The Observer*, 13 April 2003

Stephen F. Hayes, 'The Horrors of Peace', *The Weekly Standard*, 10 March 2003

Christopher Hitchens, 'Saddam's Long Goodbye', *Vanity Fair*, June 2003

Christopher Hitchens, 'The Maverick Kingdom', *Vanity Fair*, December 2002

Sebastian Junger, 'Terrorism's New Geography', *Vanity Fair*, December 2002

Efraim Karsh, 'Making Iraq Safe For Democracy', *American Jewish Committee Commentary*, 1 April 2003

Efraim Karsh, 'Saddam and the Palestinians: American foreign policy on Iraq, Arab-Israeli conflict', *American Jewish Committee Commentary*, 1 December 2002

Sir John Keegan, 'The Radical at the Pentagon', *Vanity Fair*, February 2003

Johanna McGeary, Massimo Calabresi, Michael Duffy, Mark Thompson, Helen Gibson, Scott MacLeod and Amany Radwan, 'Looking Beyond Saddam', *Time Magazine*, 10 March 2003

Judith Miller, 'For Brutality, Hussein's Sons Exceeded Even Their Father', *The New York Times*, 23 July 2003

Edward Mortimer, 'The Thief of Baghdad', *New York Review of Books*, 27 September 1990

Andrew Parasiliti and Sinan Antoon, 'Friends In Need, Foes To Heed: The Iraqi military in politics', Middle East Policy Council, 1 October 2000

Robert L. Pollock, 'Great Expectations: Iraqis embrace freedom – even though it starts off messy', *The Wall Street Journal*, 30 May 2003

Reuters Health, 'How Stockholm Syndrome Entered Public Psyche', cited on http://health_info.nmh.org/HealthNews/reuters/newsstory081820038.htm

David Rose, 'Baghdad's Cruel Princes', *Vanity Fair*, May
    2003
Raymond Tanter and Matthew Fogarty, 'Baghdad's
    Resilient Rogue', *Journal of International Affairs*,
    Spring 2001
The Peace Encyclopedia,
    http://www.yahoodi.com/peace/stockholm/html
Patrick E. Tyler, 'An Open Secret is Laid Bare at Mass
    Grave in Iraqi Marsh', *The New York Times*,
    14 May 2003
United Nations Secretary General, 'Situation of Human
    Rights in Iraq', 8 November 1995,
    http://www.fas.org/news/iraq/1995/a-50-734.htm

Permissions

For permission to reprint, acknowledgement is made to the following:

Saïd K. Aburish, *Saddam Hussein: The Politics of Revenge*: copyright © Saïd Aburish 2000 (Bloomsbury)

Mark Bowden, 'Tales of the Tyrant': copyright © 2002 by Mark Bowden; originally published by *The Atlantic Monthly*; reprinted by the permission of Dunham Literary as agents for the author

Con Coughlin, *Saddam: The Secret Life*, Macmillan, London, UK

Dilip Hiro, *Iraq: A Report from the Inside*, Granta Books

Kanan Makiya, *Republic of Fear: The Politics of Modern Iraq*: copyright © 1989, 1998, The Regents of the University of California

Every effort has been made to identify individual copyright holders. The publishers would be pleased to hear from any copyright holders who have not been acknowledged.